# Natural Experiments of History

# Natural Experiments of History

EDITED BY

**Jared Diamond**

**James A. Robinson**

THE BELKNAP PRESS OF HARVARD UNIVERSITY PRESS

Cambridge, Massachusetts • London, England

Copyright © 2010 by the President and Fellows of Harvard College
Printed in the United States of America

First Harvard University Press paperback edition, 2011

Library of Congress Cataloging-in-Publication Data

Natural experiments of history / edited by Jared Diamond
and James A. Robinson.
p. cm.
Includes bibliographical references.
ISBN 978-0-674-03557-7 (cloth: alk. paper)
ISBN 978-0-674-06019-7 (pbk.)
1. History—Comparative method—Case studies.
2. History—Methodology—Case studies.
I. Diamond, Jared M. II. Robinson, James A., 1960–

D16.N335   2010
907.2—dc22   2009012678

# Contents

# Natural Experiments of History

# Prologue

JARED DIAMOND AND
JAMES A. ROBINSON

The controlled and replicated laboratory experiment, in which the experimenter directly manipulates variables, is often considered the hallmark of the scientific method. It is virtually the only method employed in laboratory physical sciences and in molecular biology. Without question, this approach is uniquely powerful in establishing chains of cause and effect. That fact misleads laboratory scientists into looking down on fields of science that cannot employ manipulative experiments.

But the cruel reality is that manipulative experiments are impossible in many fields widely admitted to be sciences. That impossibility holds for any science concerned with the past, such as evolutionary biology, paleontology, epidemiology, historical geology, and astronomy; one cannot manipulate the past.[1] In addition, when one is studying bird communities, dinosaurs, smallpox epidemics, glaciers, or other planets, manipulative experiments that are possible in the present would often be condemned as immoral and illegal; one should not kill birds or melt glaciers. One therefore has to devise other methods of "doing science": that is, of observing, describing, and explaining the real world, and of setting the individual explanations within a larger framework.

A technique that frequently proves fruitful in these historical disciplines is the so-called natural experiment or the comparative method. This approach consists of comparing—preferably quantitatively and aided by statistical analyses—different systems that are similar in many respects but that differ with respect to the factors whose influence one wishes to study. For instance, to study the ecological effect of woodpeckers known as Red-breasted Sapsuckers on related woodpeckers known as Williamson's Sapsuckers, one can compare mountains, all of which support Williamson's Sapsuckers but some of which support Red-breasted Sapsuckers while others do not. The science of epidemiology is virtually the study of such natural experiments on human populations. As one example, we have learned which human blood groups provide resistance to smallpox, not as a result of manipulative experiments in which we inject people carrying different blood groups either with smallpox virus or with a virus-free control solution, but instead as a result of observations of people carrying different blood groups during one of the last natural smallpox epidemics in India several decades ago. Physicians who were present in a remote village at the time of the outbreak determined villagers' blood groups and observed who got sick or died and who did not.[2]

Of course, natural experiments involve many obvious pitfalls. These pitfalls include the risk that the outcome might depend on other factors that the "experimenter" had not thought to measure; and the risk that the true explanatory factors might be ones merely correlated with the measured factors, rather than being the measured factors themselves. These and other such difficulties are real—but so are the difficulties encountered in executing manipulative laboratory experiments or in writing noncomparative narrative accounts. An extensive literature is now available on how best to overcome these pitfalls.[3]

For example, consider a question that is currently of much practical interest: does smoking cause cancer? It is possible to write a moving, nuanced, in-depth biography of one particular smoker who did die of cancer, but that narrative doesn't prove that smoking causes cancer in general or even that it caused that particular cancer. Some smokers don't get cancer, and some nonsmokers do get it. As we have learned, there are many other risk factors for cancer besides smoking.

Hence epidemiologists routinely gather data on thousands or millions of individuals, code them not only for whether they smoke but also for their diet and many other factors, and then carry out a statistical analysis. Such studies yield familiar and now widely accepted conclusions. Yes, smoking is strongly associated with some (though not with other) forms of cancer, but one can also recognize many other causes by means of statistical analyses. Those other causes include dietary fat, dietary fiber, dietary antioxidants, sun exposure, individual air pollutants, specific chemicals in our food and water, numerous hormones, and hundreds of different genes. Hence no epidemiologist would dream of identifying *the* cause of cancer just by telling the story of a single patient, but one can convincingly identify many causes of cancer by comparing and statistically analyzing many people. Similar conclusions and similar pitfalls that need to be addressed apply to multicausal historical phenomena.

On reflection, one might also expect comparisons and quantitative methods and statistics to play an uncontroversial middle role in the study of history. Historians are constantly making statements of the form "This changed (or increased or decreased) with time," or "This was more than that," or "This person did more (or less) than, or behaved differently from, that person." But merely to make such statements, without providing the underlying numbers and doing the associated statistics, is to frame the comparison without carrying it out. Already in 1979, the historian Lawrence Stone made this same point in his discussion of the role of quantification: "Historians can no longer get away with saying 'more', 'less', 'growing', 'declining', all of which logically imply numerical comparisons, without ever stating explicitly the statistical basis for their assertions. It [quantification] has also made argument exclusively by example seem somewhat disreputable. Critics now demand supporting statistical evidence to show that the examples are typical, and not exceptions to the rule."[4]

In reality, the various social sciences concerned with human societies have made uneven use of natural experiments. Although there is widespread acceptance of natural experiments in archaeology, cultural anthropology, developmental psychology, economics, economic history, political science, and sociology, in the field of human history other than economic history their use has been patchy. Some historians merely call for more use of natural experiments; others claim that other historians already do use them a lot; and still others actually do use them, though sometimes not consciously or without making full use of the methodological advantages potentially associated with this approach.[5] But many historians do not use natural experiments at all and are skeptical or hostile to the approach, especially to systematic comparisons involving quantitative data that are analyzed statistically.

Numerous reasons contribute to this skepticism. One reason is that the discipline of history is variously grouped either with the humanities or with the sciences. At one major American university, for instance, the undergraduate college places the history department under the dean of humanities, but the graduate school places it under the dean of social sciences. Many students who choose to train as historians rather than as economists and political scientists do so explicitly to avoid having to learn mathematics and statistics. Historians often devote their careers to studying one country or geographic region within one slice of time. The special expertise required to master that region and period leads its students to doubt that a historian who has not spent his or her life acquiring that expertise could write knowledgeably about that region and period, or that they themselves could knowledgeably compare it with a different region and period. The lengthy training required of graduate students in history involves strong socialization about what history is and is not, and about what methods are or are not proper for historians. Many American historians reacted to the debate initiated by a particular school of quantitative history, termed cliometrics, by becoming less quantitative—as if the weaknesses claimed by critics of this particular approach applied to all quantitative analyses.[6] Historians often believe that human history is fundamentally different from the history of cancers, chimpanzees, or glaciers, on the grounds that it is much more complicated and involves the motives of individual humans, which supposedly cannot be measured or expressed in numbers. However, cancers, chimpanzees, and glaciers are also very complicated, and they pose the added obstacle that they do not leave behind any written archival evidence of their motives. In addition, many scholars, such as psychologists, economists, scholars of government, and some biographers, now are able to measure and analyze the motives of individual humans by means of retrospective analyses of documents of dead people as well as interviews with still-living people.

Our book seeks to showcase the comparative method in history and to examine some techniques for solving its obvious pitfalls by presenting a set of eight studies in seven chapters (Chapter 4 includes two studies). Our target audience is not just those historians receptive to (or at least not implacably opposed to) the comparative method, but also the larger number of scholars in allied social sciences that already widely employ the comparative method. We write for undergraduates as well as for established scholars. We do not assume familiarity with statistics or quantitative analyses. The eight studies (two of them coauthored) are by eleven authors, two of whom are traditional historians based in history departments, while the others are drawn from archaeology, business studies, economics, economic history, geography, and political science. These studies are designed to cover a spectrum of approaches to comparative history, in four respects:

First, the approaches range from a nonquantitative narrative style traditional among historians, in the early chapters, to quantitative studies with statistical analyses familiar in the social sciences outside history departments, in the later chapters.

Second, our comparisons range from a simple two-way comparison (the nations of Haiti and the Dominican Republic sharing the island of Hispaniola) to three-way comparisons in two chapters, through comparisons of dozens of German regions, up to comparisons of 81 Pacific islands and 233 areas of India.

Third, the societies that we study range from contemporary ones, through literate societies of recent centuries for which we have abundant written archival information, to nonliterate past societies for which all our information comes from archaeological excavations.

Finally, our geographic coverage offers something for historians of many different parts of the world. Our case studies encompass the United States, Mexico, a Caribbean island, Brazil, Argentina, Western Europe, tropical Africa, India, Siberia, Australia, New Zealand, and other Pacific islands.

Traditional historians will thus find the approach of the first four studies in this book familiar in that they develop evidence in a narrative style, compare small numbers of societies (three, seven, three, and two, respectively), and do not present statistical comparisons of quantitative data in the text. The approach of the remaining four studies differs from that of most traditional historians but will be familiar to some historians and to scholars in related social sciences, in that they are explicitly based on statistical comparisons of quantitative data and they compare many societies (81, 52, 233, and 29, respectively).

In Chapter 1, Patrick Kirch asks why history unfolded so differently among the dozens of Pacific islands colonized by a single ancestral people, the early Polynesians. Kirch focuses on three islands or archipelagoes spanning the range of sociopolitical and economic complexity in Polynesia: the small island of Mangaia, which developed as a small-scale chiefdom; the medium-sized Marquesas archipelago, which came to support multiple independent warring chiefdoms; and Hawai'i, the largest Polynesian archipelago outside New Zealand, which developed several large-scale competing polities characterized as emerging "archaic states," with each occupying one or more islands. Because all of those Polynesian societies lacked writing, Kirch's study rests on linguistic, archaeological, and ethnographic evidence rather than on the written archival evidence emphasized by historians. Kirch's research is therefore conventionally labeled as archaeology rather than as history, although his questions are ones familiar to traditional historians. Kirch notes that similarities in cultural traits among societies may arise either through parallel retention of the same ancestral trait (so-called shared homologies), independent development (so-called analogies), or borrowing. Hence Kirch sets out a methodologically rigorous approach to comparisons that he terms the phylogenetic model, and he uses multiple lines of evidence (the "triangulation" approach) to reconstruct aspects of past societies and cultures.

James Belich (Chapter 2) adds to the extensive literature on frontier societies, such as those of the American West, by comparing seven such nineteenth-century societies: those in the United States, the "British Wests" (Canada, Australia, New Zealand, and South Africa), Argentina, and Siberia. These societies differed in many obvious respects, such as in their proportion of immigrants who returned to the mother country; in their decade of maximum growth and hence the prevailing stage of the Industrial Revolution; and especially in that five of the societies were Anglophone, one (Argentina) was Spanish-speaking but received even more Italian than Spanish immigrants, and one (Siberia) was Russian. Despite those different "experimental conditions," Belich's most striking conclusion is that all of those frontiers repeatedly traversed similar three-step cycles of an explosive population boom marked by net imports of goods and capital, then a dramatic "bust" decimating growth rates and bankrupting farms and businesses, and finally an export rescue creating a new economy based on mass export of staples to a distant metropolis. Belich documents a total of twenty-six such cycles on his seven frontiers. Their repeated emergence suggests that the underlying similarities of population and economic dynamics of all of those frontiers overrode the influences of their differences in immigrant commitment, decade of growth, stage of industrialization, and mother country. More generally, Belich's results illustrate that students of comparisons must be alert not only to differences but also to similarities in outcomes: *convergent evolution*, to borrow a term from evolutionary biology.

Stephen Haber (Chapter 3) compares the United States, Mexico, and Brazil with respect to the nineteenth-century origins of their banking systems, whose differences had heavy consequences for the subsequent modern histories of those three countries. Haber's case study contributes to a general question that has been much studied by economists, political scientists, and historians: why do some countries have large banking systems that allocate credit broadly, thereby permitting rapid growth, while other countries have scarcely any banks at all, thereby constraining growth and limiting societal mobility? As an example of national differences, in the year 2005 private bank loans equaled 155% of gross domestic product in the United Kingdom, 98% in Japan, 15% in Mexico, and 4% in Sierra Leone. Those national differences in banking systems are obviously related to differences in democratic governance, but that raises the question of the direction of causation: do democratic institutions promote large banking systems, or, conversely, do large banking systems promote democratic institutions? To reduce confounding variables in his natural experiment, Haber selects three large New World countries, all of which obtained their independence within a few decades before or after 1800, and all of which started nationhood with no chartered banks (because their former European colonial rulers had forbidden them). That selection by Haber reduces the complications that would have been encountered by extending the study to European countries, which already had chartered banks (and important differences in their banking systems) as of 1800. Each of the three New World countries chosen provides smaller internal natural experiments embedded within a larger natural experiment: not only did they differ in their political institutions, but also those institutions in each country changed over time during the era studied (from independence until roughly 1914).

In the last and smallest-scale study among our four narrative nonstatistical case studies, Jared Diamond (Chapter 4) compares two societies—Haiti and the Dominican Republic—that divide the Caribbean island of Hispaniola across one of the most dramatic political boundaries in the world. Viewed from an airplane, Hispaniola is bisected by a sharp line: to the west, the brown, treeless expanse of Haiti, heavily eroded and more than 99% deforested; to the east, the green of the Dominican Republic, still nearly one-third covered with forests. The political and economic differences between these two countries are equally stark: densely populated Haiti is the poorest country in the New World, with a weak government unable to provide basic services to most of its citizens, while the Dominican Republic, though still a developing country, has an average per capita income six times that of Haiti, many export industries, and a recent succession of democratically elected governments. A small part of those differences between modern Haiti and the Dominican Republic is due to differing initial environmental conditions: Haiti is somewhat drier and steeper, and has thinner and less fertile soils, than the Dominican Republic. But the largest part of the explanation lies in their colonial histories: western Hispaniola became colonized by France, eastern Hispaniola by Spain. That difference in colonial power initially produced major differences in slave plantations, language, population density, social inequality, colonial wealth, and deforestation, leading first to differences in the struggle for independence; then to differences in receptivity to foreign investment and immigration, and differences in perception by Europeans and Americans; more recently, to differing modern long-lasting dictators; and finally to the different conditions of these two countries today.

The other study of Chapter 4 goes to the opposite extreme: after that small-scale narrative comparison of the two halves of a single island, we consider a large-scale statistical comparison of sixty-nine Pacific islands, and of the wet and dry parts of twelve of those islands. The starting point of this study is the romantic mystery of Easter Island, famous for its hundreds of toppled giant stone statues: why did Easter Island end up as the Pacific's most deforested island, with virtually all of its native tree species extinct, and with heavy consequences for its wood-dependent human society? But Easter Island is just one data point in a larger natural experiment, since deforestation among the Pacific's hundreds of islands ranged from complete (as on Easter) to negligible. Diamond's database includes the islands studied by Kirch in Chapter 1 and settled by Polynesians, as well as islands settled by two related groupings of Pacific peoples (Melanesians and Micronesians). Because tree growth and deforestation depend on many factors, it would have been impossible for a narrative study of just one or two islands to help us understand this range of outcomes. But the large number of islands available for analysis makes it possible to identify significant influences on deforestation from nine separate factors, several of which Diamond and his collaborator Barry Rolett did not even imagine might be important until they carried out their statistical analyses. Of wider interest to historians was the possibility of extracting these conclusions even without measuring deforestation quantitatively: Rolett and Diamond only ranked it crudely on a five-point scale from severe to mild. Historians often seek to understand outcomes that are difficult to measure but that can at least be ranked ("big," "medium," "small"). Those historians can make use of the whole branch of statistics devoted to analyzing such ranked nonnumerical outcomes.

The remaining three studies—by Nathan Nunn (Chapter 5), Abhijit Banerjee and Lakshmi Iyer (Chapter 6), and Daron Acemoglu, Davide Cantoni, Simon Johnson, and James Robinson (Chapter 7)—all describe natural experiments in which the historical consequences of some massive perturbation (respectively, the African slave trade, British colonial rule in India, and institutional changes accompanying French Revolutionary conquests) can be examined because the perturbation operated in a geographically irregular patchwork over a large region. When one compares the perturbed patches with the unperturbed patches, it is thus a plausible hypothesis, worth testing, that average societal differences observed between the two types of patches arose from the operation or nonoperation of the perturbing factor rather than from some other differences between the patches. If, however, the patches with and without the factor had instead been distributed in some geographically regular way (e.g., all the patches with the factor being in the south or at high altitude), it would have been an equally plausible hypothesis that those geographic differences rather than the presence or absence of the factor caused the observed societal differences. Of course, all three studies must also address the question of the direction of cause and effect: did the perturbations really cause the observed differences, or might the instigators of the perturbations (respectively, the slave traders, British administrators, and French conquerors) have instead chosen particular patches in a geographically irregular patchwork because of preexisting differences that should be considered the real causes of the modern differences?

One of those three studies, Nathan Nunn's, explores the longstanding question of the slave trade's legacies for modern Africa, by comparing modern African states whose territories experienced differing impacts in the past from the slave trades across the Atlantic Ocean, the Sahara, the Red Sea, and the Indian Ocean. Many slaves were exported from some parts of Africa, while virtually no slaves were taken from other parts. Today, the former slave-exporting parts tend to be poorer than the former non-slave-exporting parts, and Nunn argues that the slave trades caused the economic differences rather than vice versa. Similarly, Abhijit Banerjee and Lakshmi Iyer address the unresolved question about the impact of British colonial rule on India. They find that areas of India directly administered by the British colonial government in the past tend today to have fewer schools and paved roads, lower literacy, and less use of domestic electricity than areas indirectly administered in the past. Similarly again, Daron Acemoglu, Davide Cantoni, Simon Johnson, and James Robinson explore the debate concerning the effects of the massive institutional changes introduced by French Revolutionary armies and Napoleon into conquered areas of Europe. The authors compare areas of Germany with and without the massive institutional changes, and they describe the historical accidents that caused the changes to be applied in a geographically irregular patchwork over Germany. Those institutional changes led to increased urbanization—but only after a lag of several decades, owing to the lag in arrival of the Industrial Revolution. Whereas areas that had experienced institutional changes embraced the Industrial Revolution, areas that had clung to their old institutions resisted it.

A concluding afterword reflects on methodological issues common to these and other studies of natural experiments of human history by comparative methods. Those issues include natural experiments involving either different perturbations or different initial conditions; the "selection" of sites that were perturbed; time lags for effects of perturbations to emerge; problems in inferring causality from an observed statistical correlation, such as questions of reversed causality, omitted variable bias, and underlying mechanisms; methods for steering between the opposite traps of overly simplistic and overly complex explanations; "operationalizing" fuzzy phenomena (e.g., how to measure and study happiness); the role of quantification and statistics; and the tension between narrow case studies and broader syntheses.

With regard to our book's style and format, we recognize that most multiauthored volumes suffer from having too many chapters and authors, too many pages, too little unity, and too little editing. Both of us have edited at least two multiauthored volumes, and we know painfully well the effort required to achieve a well-integrated result. We calculate that our urgings of the coauthors of those completed volumes cost us on the average, per volume, two friendships for life and several more friendships for at least a decade. Fortunately, all of our current authors have read all of each other's drafts, and in the present case all have remained gracefully cooperative in responding to our endless requests for revision over the two years that we have been working on this project. Each chapter has also been read by a half dozen traditional historians, whose suggestions we have incorporated or taken into account.[7]

## NOTES

It is a pleasure to acknowledge our debts to Robert Schneider and his colleagues, to many others of our own colleagues, and to many anonymous as well as signed reviewers, for their generosity with their time and for their suggestions, which helped shape and improve this book.

1. Ernst Mayr has written thoughtfully about differences between historical and nonhistorical sciences. See, for instance, Ernst Mayr, *This Is Biology: The Science of the Living World* (Cambridge, MA, 1997).
2. F. Vogel and N. Chakravartti, "ABO Blood Groups and Smallpox in a Rural Population of West Bengal and Bihar (India)," *Human Genetics* 3 (1966): 166–180.
3. Discussions of the pitfalls in inferring causes from natural experiments include Jared Diamond, "Overview: Laboratory Experiments, Field Experiments, and Natural Experiments," in Jared Diamond and Ted Case, eds., *Community Ecology* (New York, 1986), pp. 3–22; William Shadish, Thomas Cook, and Donald Campbell, *Experimental and Quasi-experimental Designs for Generalized Causal Inference* (Boston, 2002); James Mahoney and Dietrich Rueschermeyer, eds., *Comparative Historical Analysis in the Social Sciences* (New York, 2003); Joshua Angrist and Jorn-Steffan Pischke, *Mostly Harmless Econometrics: An Empiricist's Companion* (Princeton, NJ, 2008); Guido Imbens and Donald Rubin, *Causal Inference in Statistics, and in the Social and Biomedical Sciences* (Cambridge, 2008); and Thad Dunning, "Improving Causal Inference: Strengths and Limitations of Natural Experiments," *Political Research Quarterly* 61 (2008): 282–293.
4. Lawrence Stone, "The Revival of Narrative: Reflections on a New Old History," *Past and Present*, no. 85 (1979): 3–24, quotation pp. 10–11.
5. An example might be the debate initiated by Robert Brenner's paper "Agrarian Class Structure and Economic Development in Preindustrial Europe," *Past and Present*, no. 70 (1976): 30–75. Papers in the debate were collected by T. H. Aston and C. H. E. Philpin, eds., *Agrarian Class Structure and Economic Development in Pre-industrial Europe* (New York, 1987). The debate concerned why the Black Death had such different consequences in western and eastern Europe. To use the terminology that we shall explain in the afterword of this volume, the debate examined how a common perturbation led to different consequences in different areas as a result of different initial conditions.

6. The debate over cliometrics was explored by Robert William Fogel and G. R. Elton, *Which Road to the Past? Two Views of History* (New Haven, CT, 1983).

7. Some of this discussion is drawn from a chapter by Jared Diamond, "Die Naturwissenschaft, die Geschichte und Rotbrustige Saftsäuger," in James Robinson and Klaus Wiegandt, eds., *Die Ursprünge der Modernen Welt* (Frankfurt am Main, 2008), pp. 45–70.

# 1

# Controlled Comparison and Polynesian Cultural Evolution

PATRICK V. KIRCH

In early January of 1778, Captain James Cook, in command of HMS *Resolution* and *Discovery*, was sailing through uncharted waters in the central North Pacific Ocean, en route to the coast of New Albion, as the Pacific Northwest was then called. The Admiralty had instructed Cook to replenish at Tahiti, an island he already knew well from two previous voyages, then to go northward in search of the fabled "northwest passage." On January 18, the *Resolution*'s lookout spied a high island to the northeast; a second volcanic peak was soon discerned to the north. The following day Cook and his crew made "first contact" with one of the most isolated societies on earth—the Polynesian inhabitants of Kaua'i, one of the Hawaiian Islands.

Cook was no stranger to Polynesia. He had first gone to Tahiti a decade earlier, at the behest of the Royal Society of London, to observe the June 3, 1769, transit of Venus across the sun. That mission accomplished, Cook extended his explorations to other islands of the Society archipelago, followed by an unprecedented circumnavigation of New Zealand. In 1772 the Admiralty dispatched him again to the Pacific, to determine whether or not the long-hypothesized continent of Terra Australis actually existed. In addition to taking his ships farther south than any man had gone before, Cook explored and mapped more of Polynesia, including the Tuamotu Islands, Tonga, the southern Cook Islands, Easter Island, and the Marquesas.

After a decade of sailing throughout the central Pacific, mapping the islands, and observing their inhabitants, Cook had acquired considerable knowledge and insight into the peoples we now group together under the rubric "Polynesian."[1] The first thing to catch his attention when the Kaua'i islanders' canoes came alongside the *Resolution* was that their speech was clearly a variant of the language spoken in Tahiti, more than 2,700 miles to the south. On the eve of his departure from Kaua'i to continue his voyage on to New Albion, Cook penned these words in his log: "How shall we account for this Nation spreading it self so far over this Vast ocean?"[2] He was astounded that people speaking clearly related languages, and by inference sharing a common origin in the not-too-distant past, were distributed from New Zealand to Easter Island and now to his newfound archipelago in the North Pacific. Geographically, Cook calculated, this "Nation" was spread over "an extent of 60° of latitude or twelve hundred leagues north and south and 83° of longitude or sixteen hundred and sixty leagues east and west." Cook, one of the great explorers of the Enlightenment, was confronting a great puzzle of human history. The question of Polynesian origins, and the history of their subsequent dispersal and cultural differentiation, are problems that have ultimately yielded to the methods of controlled comparison.

The perspective I bring to this volume on the use of comparison in historical studies is that of an anthropologist who has spent several decades studying the ancient societies and cultures of Polynesia—those myriad islands and archipelagoes lying within the vast triangle subtended by New Zealand, Hawai'i, and Rapa Nui (Easter Island). As Cook discovered, Polynesia is united by a common linguistic heritage. Archaeology has subsequently shown that Polynesia comprises a historically coherent cultural region because its varied cultures all share many features owing to a common origin in the first millennium B.C. For this reason, Polynesia has more than once been regarded as an ideal region in which to undertake comparative analysis. A number of classic works in anthropology applied such a comparative approach, including Marshall Sahlins's study of the differentiation of Polynesian social structures in relation to environmental differences on islands and Irving Goldman's analysis of "status rivalry" as a key to understanding differences in Polynesian cultures.[3] In the realm of material culture, differences in Polynesian sailing canoes, barkcloth manufacture, and stone adze technology have similarly been subject to comparative study.[4] Douglas Oliver ventured well beyond Polynesia to incorporate Melanesian, Micronesian, and Australian cultures into his magnum opus on Oceania.[5] Historical linguists, for their part, have used their own specialized methods of phonological and lexical comparison to reconstruct much of the Proto Polynesian vocabulary.[6]

My own interest in Polynesia derives from my primary academic specialization of prehistoric archaeology (or "anthropological archaeology" as many label our field, in part to distinguish it from "classical archaeology," which focuses on the Greco-Roman world). But while I have invested much energy excavating the detailed material evidence by which we can date and define the outlines of Polynesian history before the arrival of Europeans and advent of historical documents, I regard such fieldwork as just part of a larger process of historical research and understanding. This is because I firmly believe that the comparative analysis of multiple prehistories can tell us something more profound about human cultures and their long-term development. Over the years I have thus come to regard myself as an "historical anthropologist" and have increasingly drawn on a range of multidisciplinary evidence that includes not only archaeological finds, but historical linguistic data, comparative ethnographic studies, and paleoecological and paleoenvironmental research.

I should disclose another facet of my epistemological foundation, which is that I regard historical anthropology as a "historical science," in the sense that Stephen Jay Gould and Ernst Mayr wrote of historical as opposed to experimental sciences.[7] (Hence I reject a postmodern perspective that regards all constructed "stories" of the past as equally valid.) Indeed, I regard archaeology's role in the science of human history (or "cultural evolution") as analogous to paleontology's role in the science of biological evolution. Both fields uncover the physical evidence of long-term change, cultural on the one hand (artifacts and the detritus of human occupation), biological on the other (bones, exoskeletons, and other fossils). But we can make sense of this evidence only when it is incorporated into a broader paradigm. Much work is now in progress to provide such a paradigm for cultural evolution, a review of which would go well beyond the scope of my essay.[8]

But to return to the concept of *comparison*, it should be noted that this idea is essential to any historical science, including historical anthropology, because we cannot run "experiments" on cultural evolution or long-term change in human cultures and societies. As Mayr astutely points out, the historical (or "observational") sciences discovered an alternative to experimentation by seeking "natural experiments." No natural experiment is more famous than Darwin's finches in the Galapagos Islands, which provided him with crucial evidence for the theory of evolution. As Mayr has stated: "Much progress in the observational sciences is due to the genius of those who have discovered, critically evaluated, and compared such natural experiments in fields where a laboratory experiment is highly impractical, if not impossible."[9] Not surprisingly, perhaps, many of the most famous natural experiments involve islands and archipelagoes.

Polynesia offers just such a set of natural—or in this case cultural— experiments for understanding fundamental processes of historical change on the timescale of one to three millennia. Several factors make the Polynesian islands and their societies a nearly ideal region for comparative historical analysis. First, the islands themselves vary in ways that posed significant adaptive challenges for their human colonizers. They range in size from diminutive (a few square kilometers) to near continental (New Zealand), in form from coral atolls to volcanic high islands of varied geologic ages, and in other aspects of climate and marine and terrestrial resources. Second, all of these islands were discovered and populated by people whose origins can be traced back to the same founding group of Eastern Lapita voyagers who arrived in the Tonga-Samoa region around 900 B.C.[10] Thus the later descendant societies can be compared in terms of those aspects of their cultures that are retentions from the ancestral group, as opposed to aspects that are innovations, or derived traits. And third, the Polynesian societies witnessed by Cook and other Enlightenment explorers at the end of the eighteenth century displayed a remarkable range of variation in their degrees of sociopolitical and economic complexity, from simple chiefdoms in which there was little status differentiation to large polities incorporating tens of thousands into highly structured and hierarchical social formations. Thus Polynesia presents a remarkable opportunity to carry out comparative analysis of social and cultural change within a group of historically related peoples.

To point out that Polynesia presents an ideal region for comparative analysis is one thing; to develop a methodologically rigorous approach to comparison is another. For a start, such an approach must be capable of discriminating between cultural traits that are shared *homologies*, those that are derived or innovated *(analogies)*, and those that were borrowed *(synologies)*.[11] My colleague Roger Green and I have developed such a carefully structured method of comparative historical analysis, which, following an original proposal by anthropologist Evon Vogt, we call the "phylogenetic model." The full exposition of the phylogenetic model, and its essential corollary, the "triangulation approach," is presented elsewhere.[12] Here I briefly summarize the key elements of our approach, which is essential to the comparative analysis presented in the second part of this chapter.

The phylogenetic model is based on the recognition, first made by Kim Romney with respect to the Uto-Aztecan cultures of the New World, that in many parts of the world groups of related cultures (and frequently this relationship is most clearly indicated by the fact that they all belong to a single linguistic family) share a common history or "phylogeny." In other words, the similarities shared by such cultures are homologous. Peter Bellwood has recently argued that rapid population or "demic" expansions of agricultural groups in various regions during the mid- to late Holocene has led to such a pattern of historically related language–culture groups covering significant parts of the world.[13] Examples include the Bantu-speaking peoples of sub-Saharan Africa, the Uto-Aztecan peoples of Mesoamerica and western North America, and the speakers of the extensive Sino-Tibetan, Austro-Asiatic, and Austronesian language families of East and Southeast Asia. Polynesia, which is one branch of the larger Austronesian expansion, is therefore just one of many instances where a phylogenetic model may be fruitfully applied in historical comparative analysis. Because of its discrete island geography, however, with the implication of decreased contact and relative isolation after initial dispersal and settlement, the Polynesian case is ideal for working out methodological principles of a phylogenetic approach to cultural history.

The phylogenetic model uses a sequence of methodological steps to work out the specific history of cultural evolution and differentiation within a group of related cultures (what Romney called a "segment of cultural history"). Beginning with the mapping of the geographical distribution of such a group—for which one has hypothesized such a homologous history—the key first step is to apply the methods of historical linguistic analysis to the set of languages spoken by the members of these cultures, in order to derive a "family tree" or phylogeny of the historical relationships. Although Vogt originally advocated the use of lexicostatistics and glottochronology,[14] such "phenetic" methods are often not capable of revealing the true phylogenetic relationships between the languages in question, and it is thus preferable to apply the traditional "genetic comparative approach" in historical linguistics. This classic comparative method results in a "family tree"-type model of language differentiation.[15] Such a tree or phylogeny provides a model for historical relationships and for the branching or splitting process of linguistic (and related cultural) differentiation over time. The methods of lexical and semantic reconstruction can also be applied once this phylogeny has been developed, in order to reconstruct in some detail the protolanguage and protoculture of the original founding group (in this case, Proto Polynesian language and Ancestral Polynesian culture), as a baseline from which later change and divergence took place.

The phylogenic tree resulting from such historical linguistic analysis should of course be considered a *model* (a complex set of interrelated hypotheses) subject to cross-checking on independent evidence. Such cross-checking can be done by turning to the data provided by archaeology. Does the archaeological record of material culture correspond to the branching pattern suggested by the linguistic record? For example, are sequences of changes in Polynesian pottery, stone adzes, and fishhook styles over time consistent with a model of cultural differentiation such as that depicted in a family tree of the Polynesian languages? In the Polynesian case the correspondence is very good, lending additional confidence in the phylogeny thus proposed. Moreover, archaeology has the capacity to directly date (through radiocarbon and other dating methods) sets of archaeological assemblages that can be correlated with specific branches and protolanguage stages on the linguistic model. Thus archaeology allows us not only to independently test the linguistic model of cultural differentiation within the larger cultural group, but to put this model in a firm chronological framework.

Archaeological research over the past half-century has revealed that the original Polynesian homeland was situated in the Tonga-Samoa region (known as "Western Polynesia"), and that this was first settled by Lapita peoples around 900 B.C.[16] The Tonga-Samoa archipelagoes were the region within which Proto Polynesian language and Ancestral Polynesian culture developed, over a period of at least a millennium. Later differentiation was in part initiated by a mid-to-late first millennium A.D. diaspora of Polynesian speaking peoples out of the Western Polynesian homeland region, eastwards into the central archipelagoes of the Societies, Cooks, Marquesas, Australs, and Tuamotus, and eventually to the margins of the Polynesian world: Hawai'i, Rapa Nui (Easter Island), and Aotearoa (New Zealand).[17]

A further key component of this approach to historical anthropology involves the use of "triangulation," the application of multiple lines of evidence to reconstruct aspects of past societies and cultures.[18] The term is derived by analogy with surveying, in which a point on a landscape can be precisely fixed by taking sight lines from at least three—but preferably even more—points whose coordinates are already known. A very simple example will illustrate the method: triangulation using lexical reconstruction, semantic reconstruction, and archaeological data allows one to reconstruct an essential material feature of ancient Polynesian cuisine: the coconut grater.[19] The procedures of historical linguistics first allow the reconstruction of the Proto Polynesian word, *tuahi, for such a grater. (Note that the appearance of an asterisk at the beginning of a word indicates that this is a reconstruction, as opposed to a word in a modern language.) Applying the data of comparative ethnography, we find that coconut graters throughout Polynesia typically consist of a wooden stool or three-legged base, with a shell or stone (or in modern times, iron) grater head lashed to it. The widespread distribution of this form thus suggests that the ethnographic forms are retentions of an ancestral type. Finally, archaeologically excavated grater heads in basalt from Western Polynesia indicate that this was the original material, with serrated pearlshell heads being a slightly later innovation in Eastern Polynesia. Thus by bringing to bear the evidence from linguistic reconstruction, comparative ethnography, and archaeology, a fairly precise reconstruction of the Ancestral Polynesian coconut grater can be achieved. This example might appear trivial, but the same method may be applied to literally thousands of individual traits, in aggregate building up a robust reconstruction of many domains of Ancestral Polynesian life.

What can comparative analysis of cultural evolution within Polynesian cultures and societies over the period from about 900 B.C. until

European contact in the late eighteenth century tell us about larger problems in human history? For one thing, it can inform us about processes of evolution and transformation of sociopolitical organization within complex, agriculturally based societies. From the phylogenetic model, we have firm evidence that all of the thirty-odd Polynesian societies documented by Captain James Cook and other European explorers at the close of the eighteenth century were descended from a common ancestral culture that flourished in the Tonga-Samoa archipelagoes in the mid-first millennium B.C. Yet these eighteenth-century societies exhibited an amazing range and diversity of social and political structures, all of which clearly emerged following the later diaspora of Polynesian voyagers to the far-flung islands and archipelagoes of the eastern Pacific, each under its own unique set of environmental, demographic, economic, and social challenges and constraints.

In a short essay, I cannot review all of the variation in Polynesian sociopolitical formations; rather, I will focus on three particular cases that encapsulate some of this variation in order to show how the method of controlled comparison helps us to understand how these three societies developed historically from a common ancestor. The cases I have chosen for comparison are Hawai'i, the largest Polynesian archipelago outside of New Zealand,[20] the Marquesas, a midsized archipelago in central eastern Polynesia, and Mangaia, the southernmost of the Cook Islands. All of these societies are part of Eastern Polynesia; thus all were colonized by Polynesians expanding out the core Western Polynesian homeland, both probably late in the first millennium A.D.[21] The founding populations that arrived at Mangaia, the Marquesas, and Hawai'i shared a common set of cultural notions regarding social and political structures, owing to their common origins in Ancestral Polynesian society. And they had approximately the same time frame for their descendant societies to evolve, from initial Polynesian discovery and settlement late in the first millennium A.D. until European contact at the close of the eighteenth century.[22] Yet the societies that had emerged in these islands by the time of Captain Cook's famous voyages at the close of the eighteenth century were remarkably different. Mangaia was politically organized as a relatively small-scale chiefdom in which the exercise of power was overtly militaristic. The Marquesas were divided into multiple independent chiefdoms that frequently raided and skirmished among each other, without achieving any archipelago-wide political hegemony. Hawai'i consisted of several competing, large-scale polities, each occupying one or more islands, and its political organization has been characterized as an emergent, "archaic state." Thus, in less than a thousand years, markedly different sociopolitical formations emerged in these three island settings, out of the same ancestral society.

Before turning to more detailed comparisons between Mangaia, the Marquesas, and Hawai'i, it is essential to briefly review what the phylogenetic model and use of the triangulation approach allow us to reconstruct in terms of the Ancestral Polynesian society and political organization in the period from about 500 B.C. to A.D. 500, prior to the expansion of Polynesians out of the Western Polynesian homeland, into Eastern Polynesia.[23] Ancestral Polynesian societies[24] (henceforth, APS) were fundamentally organized around the kind of "house-based" social groups that anthropologist Claude Lévi-Strauss called *sociétés à maison.*[25] Rather than being based on an abstract notion of "lineage" (as in many African societies), generational descent in house societies is organized around one or more physical dwelling sites and the estate of land associated with that dwelling. Other property both tangible (canoes, trees, etc.) and intangible (names, histories, insignia, privileges) also accrues to houses. People affiliate to one or another named "house" (in Proto Polynesian language, this was called a *kaainga*) by virtue of birth as well as residential choice. A house system of social organization also permits other means of affiliation, such as adoption (a common practice in Oceania), and hence allows for a great deal of flexibility in controlling the size of residential groups in relation to land and resources. The head of a *kaainga* house group was called the *fatu*, an elder, and was most often probably male, in the senior descent line.

A second, and larger, social group was called the *kainanga*, consisting of all the individual house groups (*kaainga*) and their estates within a particular geographic area. Because Polynesian societies had a strong organizing principle of birth order, the individual *kaainga* were ranked with respect to each other, and the leader of the more inclusive *kainanga* group (what some anthropologists have called a "clan"), who held the title of *qariki*, would typically have been a member of one of the more highly ranked *kaainga* houses.[26] This *qariki* was both the secular and ritual leader of the community, responsible along with the collective *fatu* elders not only for making a range of economic and political decisions, but also for leading the community through a year-long sequence of rituals that included yam planting and harvesting, as well as first-fruits.

Ritual or ceremonial life in APS was materially centered on the ancestral dwelling of the *qariki*, typically containing the subfloor burials of his ancestors. The dwelling house itself was called the *fareqatua* ("house of ancestral spirits"), and was situated on a slightly elevated mound called a *qafu*. On the seaward side of this house lay an open, cleared space called the *malaqe*, where important rituals were performed at key times throughout the year, often involving the offering of the psychoactive plant *kava* (*Piper methysticum*) to ancestral spirits. The annual ritual cycle revolved around a lunar calendar of 13 months, with the periodic acronitic and heliacal rising and setting of the star cluster Pleiades (*Matariki*) used to keep the calendar in sync with the solar year. The ritual cycle was closely tied to the horticultural cycle of yam planting and harvesting, which itself was keyed to the distinctive wet and dry seasons of Western Polynesia.[27]

Comparative analysis of Polynesian ethnography and historical linguistics reveals the presence of several other lexically marked social roles and status positions in APS. In particular, there were specific Proto Polynesian words for expert, especially expert craftsperson (*tufunga*), for warrior (*toa*), and for a sea expert, or navigator (*tautahi*). While the *qariki* or community leader was responsible for formal rituals of the annual horticulturally based calendar, we also have evidence for a second kind of spiritual practitioner, the *taaula*, who might be characterized more as a shaman or spirit medium. There is also evidence for a kind of secular ruler, a *sau*, who may have been the highest ranking *qariki* in the larger society that included multiple *kainanga*.[28]

The above reconstructions for APS are based on comparative lexical reconstruction of Proto Polynesian words, with semantic reconstructions augmented by careful comparative analysis of Polynesian ethnographic sources, in order to work out precise "semantic history hypotheses." However, direct archaeological evidence from at least thirty-one settlements radiocarbon dated to the period from about 2,500–1,800 years ago (B.P.) also adds important information on the nature of APS.[29] Settlements were typically small in scale (covering only a few hundred square meters) and frequently were located along the coastal plains and beach ridges that had ready access to both marine resources and garden land. The sizes of these settlements suggest spatial organization on the scale of individual hamlets to modest villages with multiple households, totaling perhaps 100 to 200 persons at most. There is no evidence for monumental public architecture, nor is there much material evidence for marked status differentiation.

From the sketch presented above, it should be evident that APS in the Polynesian homeland archipelagoes of Tonga and Samoa were relatively small-scale social formations, organized along principles of genealogical ranking and seniority of descent, but lacking elaborate social stratification or hierarchy. In the mid- to late first millennium A.D., the final phase of the great Polynesian diaspora into the eastern Pacific began with exploratory voyages out of these western homeland islands into the central eastern island groups including the Society Islands, Cook Islands, Austral Islands, and Marquesas. Mangaia, in the southern Cooks, was probably one of the first Eastern Polynesian islands to be discovered and colonized, no later than around A.D. 900. Recent radiocarbon dating of sites in the Marquesas Islands suggests initial settlement there at around the same time, ca. A.D. 700–900. The Hawaiian archipelago was probably discovered from a voyage originating in the Marquesas Islands, likely in the period A.D. 800–1000. Thus the founding groups in all three cases were closely related offshoots from the APS stock. Yet when we examine the ethnohistoric and ethnographic accounts of late eighteenth- and early nineteenth-century Mangaia, the Marquesas, and Hawaiian societies (including the accounts of Cook's voyages), the differences among these three—which had only diverged at most a millennium earlier—are quite remarkable.

Situated in the southern Cook Islands, Mangaia has a total land area of about 52 square kilometers and is estimated to have supported a total population of perhaps 5,000 persons at the time of initial contact with Europeans. The island's contact-period sociopolitical organization is known from extensive missionary accounts and from early twentieth-century "salvage" ethnography, especially by the famed Polynesian scholar Te Rangi Hiroa.[30] Mangaian society consisted of a chiefship, with a paramount chief (Te Mangaia) at the apex, and several other important chiefly titles. Rather than inheriting the paramountship by virtue of genealogical descent, however, each successive Te Mangaia came to power through military conquest. Not surprisingly, warriors *(toa)* also held positions of considerable power in this society.

The highly militaristic nature of late Mangaian society is closely linked to its physical and biotic environment. Mangaia is a geologically old island with highly weathered volcanic surfaces in the interior, surrounded by a 1- to 2-kilometer-wide rampart of largely infertile upraised limestone *(makatea)*. Most of the deeply weathered central volcanic, like the *makatea,* is not amenable to cultivation because of nutrient depletion through excessive leaching. The radial stream drainage pattern of the central volcanic cone dissects the interior slopes into several valleys with alluvial floors, which were the main focus of the island's economic production system.[31] These valley floors were terraced in a gridlike network of pondfields and irrigation canals, used to intensively cultivate taro *(Colocasia esculenta)*, the main staple crop. Although these irrigation systems covered a mere 2% of the island's land surface, they were responsible for the largest part of the staple food output.

Not surprisingly, these irrigation systems (*puna* lands) were highly prized and the object of continual dispute. Mangaian oral traditions[32] describe a lengthy series of intertribal wars for control of these *puna* lands. The victors took control of the irrigation systems, while the vanquished would be forced to eek out a living in the marginal *makatea* zone. The political system reflected this more-or-less continual state of war, with the paramount chief at any time being the supreme war leader, called Te Mangaia. The installation of a new Te Mangaia after a war of conquest of the *puna* lands required a human sacrifice to the god Rongo at his principal temple of Orongo. Rongo was both the god of war and the god of taro irrigation; his regular peacetime offerings were parcels of cooked taro. The ideological linkages between Rongo, war, taro, and human sacrifice were complex: Rongo assured both success in war and continued fertility of the taro fields, but these required continual sacrifices of both human bodies and taro in an endless cycle.

Archaeological research augments and elaborates the picture of late Mangaian society reconstructed from ethnohistory and salvage ethnography. Excavations in the deeply stratified Tangatatau Rockshelter site reveal a sequence, beginning about A.D. 1000, in which there was increasing depletion or severe impact on a range of natural food resources, including native bird populations and fish and shellfish stocks. Pigs, which had been introduced with the original Polynesian colonists, were eliminated by around A.D. 1500, presumably because they competed directly with humans for the limited food production of the gardens and irrigated pondfields. The principal terrestrial protein source thus became the diminutive Pacific rat *(Rattus exulans)*.[33] Marine resources had also become significantly impacted owing to the constant pressure of fishing on the narrow fringing reef.[34]

By around A.D. 1600, the Mangaians were living in sets of small hamlets constructed on earthen terraces dispersed on low ridges around the peripheries of their taro irrigation systems. The foci of these habitation complexes were small temples, called *marae*, each dedicated to a particular ancestral deity. Archaeologically, these *marae* sites are still visible, as terraces with pavements of coral gravel with upright stones (sometimes of limestone stalactites taken from caverns in the *makatea*) representing the individual deities. During the frequent periods of warfare, groups would retreat to refuge caves in the *makatea* limestone, where they could more readily defend themselves against raiding and the taking of sacrificial victims.

The Mangaian oral traditions of warfare and personal violence that permeated the late precontact society are also borne out by archaeological evidence. Excavations in the Keia Rockshelter revealed a specialized site function, with a series of earth ovens and a midden deposit containing almost exclusively human skeletal remains. A score or so individuals had been cooked in these ovens, their bodies dismembered, and based on the taphonomic treatment of the individual faunal parts, consumed. Evidence of such cannibalism was also found at several other sites, such as the Tangatatau Rockshelter.

In short, Mangaian society had followed a particular evolutionary history that was strongly influenced by the relatively restricted environmental potential of this geologically old and resource-limited island. The scale of Mangaian society remained not unlike that of its APS ancestor, and many aspects of APS can be recognized in late Mangaian sociopolitical organization. The term for the APS "house" leaders, *qariki*, continued in use as the term for Mangaian hereditary leaders. However, the principal chief, Te Mangaia, was no longer determined by hereditary descent but rather by victory in war. Moreover, the island's ritual system was not simply a horticulturally based set of annual rites to assure yam production. Rather, the ritual system emphasized the worship of Rongo, a Janus-like god of taro and of war. His principal temple, or *marae*, on the coast at Orongo, was the scene for human sacrificial offerings at the installation of each new Te Mangaia. Thus in Mangaia we see strong echoes of the APS pattern, but significantly changed and influenced by a history of increased resource depletion and pressure, one that led inexorably to a society based on terror and militaristic rule.

The Marquesas Islands lie between 7 and 10 degrees south of the equator, with a humid tropical climate (in contrast to subtropical Mangaia) well suited to the mix of root, tuber, and tree crops transferred by the early Polynesian voyagers out of their tropical Western Polynesian homeland. However, the cold Humboldt Current that sweeps from southeast to northwest across the ten major islands of the archipelago inhibits coral growth. This combined with coastal subsidence has prevented the development of significant coral reefs, other than small fringing reefs in places (such as Anaho and Ha'atuatua on Nuku Hiva Island). Thus the Marquesas are renowned for their rugged topography, the many deep bays set off by cliffs and rocky headlands; the interiors of the volcanic islands are deeply dissected by valleys, most of which are traversed by permanently flowing streams. The smallest island to have been permanently inhabited, Eiao, has a surface area of about 52 square kilometers (the same as Mangaia), whereas the largest, Nuku Hiva, has a land area of 335 square kilometers. In aggregate, the archipelago offers an order of magnitude greater land surface for human habitation and development of agrarian systems than does Mangaia. Nonetheless, the Marquesan environment did pose some challenges to the development of a robust economy, especially due to recurrent drought.[35] Drought years frequently resulted in failure of the breadfruit harvest and resulting famine. To help offset the impact of such droughts, the Marquesans developed particular food storage methods, but these methods had their limitations when drought persisted for more than a single year.

The social, economic, and political organization of the Marquesas at the time of contact with Europeans (which began earlier than elsewhere in Polynesia, with the initial Spanish voyage of Mendaña in 1595) has been extensively described by ethnographers such as E. S. C. Handy and anthropologically informed historians including Nicholas Thomas and Greg Dening.[36] The maximum population prior to the devastating effects of the European-introduced diseases has been a matter of debate, but in my view was not less than 50,000 and could well have been as high as 100,000. There was no archipelago-wide political integration of this population, however, and even the larger islands were typically subdivided into independent and frequently warring political units. 'Ua Pou seems to be the only island that had some degree of integration into a single chiefdom polity.

The primary social unit around which late precontact Marquesan society was organized was what Handy called the "tribe," a kin group tracing common ascent from a founding ancestor.[37] The term for this social group, *mata'eina'a,* is the Marquesan reflex of Proto Polynesian *\*kainanga* which, as we saw earlier, can be traced back to APS.[38] One or more of these *mata'eina'a* units occupying a main valley (perhaps with smaller subsidiary valleys) would form a Marquesan political unit. Significantly, the key Proto Polynesian term *\*kaainga* referring to the residential group with its estate, while retained in Marquesan as *aika,* had only the general meaning of "land" or "property," without its former reference to a primary social group. This semantic change hints at considerable social transformation and parallels a similar change in Hawai'i, to be discussed below.

The *mata'eina'a* leaders were *haka'iki,* a term that is cognate with Proto Polynesian *\*qariki. Haka'iki* were the genealogically senior members of the ascent line. However, the Marquesan *haka'iki,* though considered to be *tapu* or sacred, shared their power in an uneasy and fluid relationship with two other status roles: those of the inspirational priests *(tau'a)* and the warriors *(toa).* The *tau'a* (derived from Proto Polynesian *\*taaula*) were spirit mediums who were representative of a class found throughout Polynesian societies, but who in the Marquesas developed a particularly strong hold on the society, with their power rivaling or even surpassing that of the hereditary *haka'iki* leaders. *Tauʻa* resided in sepulchral temples *(meʻae)* typically situated in the isolated interior parts of the valleys, with massive stone foundations supporting pole-and-thatch structures strewn with human crania and bones. *Tauʻa* officiated at most of the critical rituals around which the yearly cycle revolved, they prescribed when to make war or raid neighboring tribes, and they were responsible for organizing major feasts requiring human sacrifice. The *tauʻa*'s bidding was carried out by the *toa,* warriors, who were not full-time specialists, but the leaders of prominent families holding land and other prerogatives. *Toa* were marked by their extensive tattoos and other material symbols of their status. A final marked status category in late Marquesan society was that of *tuhuna* (derived from Proto Polynesian *\*tufunga*), referring to persons with specialized knowledge, such as fishermen, stone carvers and builders, and tattoo experts.

The economic system underpinning this complex chiefdom society combined horticultural production of staple crops with animal husbandry (particularly of pigs) and marine exploitation. Although fishing and shellfish gathering were important, the lack of coral reefs limited the overall biomass available for exploitation in the Marquesan bays and inshore waters. Most important for subsistence was the production of two starch staples: breadfruit *(Artocarpus altilis)* and taro. The Marquesan climate is especially conducive for breadfruit trees, and nowhere else in tropical Polynesia did subsistence come to depend so much on this crop as in this archipelago. The valleys supported extensive breadfruit plantations, with smaller areas devoted to irrigated taro pondfields (as in Mangaia). When breadfruit harvests were plentiful, the excess fruit was stored in subterranean pits or silos, which underwent semianaerobic fermentation that preserved the starchy mass (called *ma*) up to several years. *Ma* pits were associated with house sites, but large communal pits were located in defensible positions within the valleys or on fortified ridgetops. When famine ensued during periods of drought and curtailed breadfruit harvests, those individuals with access to reserves of *ma* had the means to weather the food crisis. Early European visitors to the Marquesas frequently commented on the severe effects of such famines and on the importance of having access to preserved *ma*.

Perhaps not surprisingly in this unpredictable environment in which food was plentiful in some years, but scarce in others, the chiefdom polities occupying their separate valleys on individual islands were frequently in a state of hostility toward each other. Indeed, what is so striking about late precontact Marquesan society is the extent to which raiding and warfare had become endemic and intimately bound up with a cycle of feasting and ritualized cannibalism that I have elsewhere called "competitive involution."[39] Competition between *mata'eina'a* groups, which was critical to the prestige of the *tau'a* and *toa,* involved the undertaking of feasts *(ko'ina)* to celebrate a diversity of occasions, including the birth of the chief's heirs, the betrothal and marriage of high-ranking individuals, harvest, victory in war, but most importantly, the death and subsequent memorialization of leading *tau'a*. The memorial feasts for such *tau'a,* called *mau,* were more important and impressive than those for many hereditary *haka'iki.* Most importantly, *mau* required the taking of human sacrificial victims (and ritualized cannibalism), typically from neighboring tribes, thus fueling the endless cycle of raiding and retribution.

Clearly, late Marquesan society had developed from its APS origins in directions that were in many respects similar to those of Mangaia. Certainly, the emphasis on competition, warfare, and the cults of human sacrifice display many parallels. On the other hand, Mangaia's small scale permitted island-wide political integration, whereas the geographic dispersion and topographic isolation of Marquesan valleys lent itself to political fragmentation. Moreover, the economic production systems had developed along different trajectories, with the emphasis on taro irrigation in Mangaia and dominance of breadfruit arboriculture (and pit storage) in the Marquesas.

The Marquesan archaeological record is particularly rich and has been extensively investigated over the past half-century, providing considerable insight into the temporal process by which Marquesan society was transformed into the particular configurations sketched above.[40] The date of initial Polynesian discovery and settlement of the archipelago remains in dispute but is unlikely to have been much earlier than A.D. 700–800, based on the emerging record of radiocarbon dates. The earliest documented settlements consist of coastal hamlets and some rockshelters, and the artifact styles in these sites show close similarities to materials from the early levels at Tangatatau in Mangaia and other early Eastern Polynesian sites. This suggests that during the early phase of Polynesian settlement, there was considerable contact among pioneering communities across the central Eastern Polynesian region.

Major changes begin to be evident during what has been termed the Expansion Period of the Marquesan cultural sequence, originally dated by Suggs to A.D. 1100–1400, but more likely, as shown by on recent evidence, to have begun somewhat later, perhaps around A.D. 1200–1300. Whatever the exact dating turns out to be, the Expansion Period is marked by several trends: population increase as evidenced by large numbers of new sites; expansion of population into the interiors of the large valleys, and onto the drier, less favorable parts of the islands; increased pressure on natural food resources such as birds, fish, and shellfish, leading to resource depression; and evidence for increased pig production and development of agricultural production.

Of particular interest is the archaeological evidence for monumental architecture, since such architecture correlates closely with the ethnographically documented patterns of social status and ceremonial feasting described above. Marquesan landscapes are noted for several types of large stone constructions, including (1) *paepae*, or elevated house platforms; (2) *me'ae*, the stone foundations of temples used by the powerful *tau'a* priests; and (3) *tohua*, large terraces surrounded by *paepae* and often incorporating a *me'ae*, which were the ceremonial settings for the large feasts. The larger *tohua* sites are impressed constructions, sometimes covering hundreds of square meters and incorporating dozens of subsidiary *paepae* and other structures; they required not inconsiderable investments of labor to construct. Although only a few such *tohua* have had excavations conducted in them to date, the available evidence indicates that the first *tohua* began to be built during the Expansion Period. However, the phase of greatest construction activity was clearly what Suggs called the Classic Period, dating to the last century or two prior to European contact and overlapping into the early contact period. This was clearly the period during which the ethnographically attested pattern of "competition involution," marked by incessant raiding, production of ever grander feasts, and emphasis on human sacrifice, developed. It is presumably during this final phase of the precontact era, when population density was at its highest and the periodic effects of drought and famine were at their most pervasive, that the Marquesan sociopolitical system underwent the greatest transformations away from the Ancestral Polynesian pattern toward what Thomas has called its "fluid and competitive" social system.[41] The massive *tohua* terraces and other megalithic structures characteristic of this phase offer material witness to the struggles for prestige and power that were played out among the hereditary *hakaʻiki*, struggling to retain traditional status, and the *tauʻa* and *toa*, who found abundant opportunities for self-aggrandizement in the often precarious Marquesan environment.

When Captain James Cook sailed into Kealakekua Bay at Hawaiʻi Island on January 17, 1779, he not only encountered a greater aggregate population than he had witnessed anywhere else in Polynesia on his three extensive voyages of discovery, but a society that had recently undergone major transformations. Kealakekua Bay and the nearby royal seat of Hōnaunau were at the center of the Hawaiʻi Island Kingdom, which had first been unified around A.D. 1600 by the great war chief ʻUmi-a-Liloa, who conquered five previously independent chiefdom polities and brought them under his sole control. At roughly the same time, on the nearby island of Maui, another great chief, Pi'ilani, had similarly unified that island, also conquering and integrating the smaller islands of Lana'i, Kaho'olawe, and part of Moloka'i into his dominions. The ruling houses of Maui and Hawai'i each governed over populations that numbered between 60,000 and 100,000 persons. During the seventeenth and eighteenth centuries, leading up to Cook's dramatic (and for him, fatal) arrival in this previously isolated archipelago, significant economic, social, political, and religious changes took place—changes that ultimately made the Hawaiian branch of the Polynesian cultural tree stand out markedly from its sister cultures.

The Hawaiian archipelago, in striking contrast to resource-constrained Mangaia or the Marquesas, incorporates eight principal islands and many smaller islets, as well as a combined surface area of 16,700 square kilometers. The island chain has formed over a geologic "hot spot" (now situated under the island of Hawai'i) and displays an age progression due to tectonic movement of the Pacific Plate. Thus, although the large eastern island of Hawai'i is still geologically active, the islands to the west are progressively older and more eroded and display other corollaries of age, such as permanent stream drainages and developed coral reefs. Consequently, the resource base of individual islands varies considerably. In particular, the large, geologically young islands of Hawai'i and Maui mostly lack permanent streams (with a few exceptions), and the agricultural systems developed by Polynesians on these large islands had to depend primarily on rainfall. Vast agricultural field systems for the dryland cultivation of sweet potato (Ipomoea batatas) and taro, along with secondary crops such as sugarcane, were developed on these islands beginning around A.D. 1400. On the older islands from Moloka'i to Kaua'i, the presence of permanent streams allowed for the development of taro irrigation systems in the valley floors (as in Mangaia). In addition, the coastlines of the older islands, with their more developed fringing reefs, were conducive to the construction of numerous stone-walled fishponds, with aquacultural production of mullet and milkfish augmenting reef fishing and shellfish gathering.

On the older, westerly islands, extensive irrigation systems had begun to be developed by around A.D. 1200, and the network of fishponds began to be constructed by at least A.D. 1400.

Thus, by the time that 'Umi-a-Liloa on Hawai'i and Pi'ilani on Maui undertook their respective conquests and consolidation of power (around A.D. 1600), the economic bases of subsistence production had taken on a distinctive spatial pattern across the archipelago. On the older islands from Moloka'i to Kaua'i, the valleys and alluvial plains had been extensively terraced for irrigated taro production, while the coastlines were modified with the scallop-shaped stone walls of fishponds. On Maui and Hawai'i, however, irrigation works were confined to relatively limited zones, and the bulk of staple starch production was generated on vast upland slopes (in Kaupō, Kahikinui, and Kula on Maui; in Kohala, Kona, and Ka'ū on Hawai'i). Where the ideal combination of relatively young (and hence still nutrient rich) substrates and sufficient rainfall (at least 700 mm annually) permitted, these slopes had been converted into virtually continuous dryland agricultural field systems. The Kohala field system on Hawai'i Island, which has been well studied archaeologically, covers an area of at least 50 square kilometers and is marked by a reticulate grid of field walls and intersecting trail systems. Dotted within the field system are hundreds of residential structures and larger *heiau* or stone temple foundations.[42]

These two different kinds of agricultural production systems—irrigation and aquaculture on the older islands, dryland field systems on the younger islands—entailed different pathways of agricultural *intensification,* along with different levels of surplus production and of environmental risk.[43] Intensification is generally defined as the addition of inputs of labor, capital, or skills, up to the economic margin, measured against constant land. In the case of the irrigation systems, intensification entailed the construction of permanent facilities (canals, terraces), or what Harold Brookfield called "landesque capital intensification."[44] Although they required significant labor inputs for initial construction, once built these systems could be maintained with relatively low labor inputs. Moreover, they could yield substantial surplus beyond what was required to sustain the labor force. In contrast, the dryland or rain-fed field systems of Maui and Hawai'i followed a pathway of "cropping cycle intensification," much like that described by Esther Boserup in her classic work on agricultural intensification.[45] Here, increased yields are achieved by increasing the fallow time between crops and by defining ever smaller field plots; labor inputs are unrelenting, as the need for weeding and mulching becomes greater over time. Although the dryland systems have some potential for surplus production, this is not as great as in the irrigated systems, and yields may actually begin to decrease over time if increased cropping frequency leads to nutrient depletion.[46] Moreover, the dryland field systems were vulnerable to annual fluctuations in rainfall, especially periodic drought. Hawaiian oral traditions refer to devastating droughts, some of which led directly to political upheavals.

The loci for major sociopolitical transformations in late Hawaiian society, beginning around A.D. 1600, were the younger islands of Maui and Hawai'i, with their reliance on the dryland field systems. As these vast dryland cultivation zones were first developing, from around A.D. 1400, they permitted the growth of substantial populations, and yields were high enough to provide a steady stream of surplus to underwrite the ambitions of regional chiefs. Two centuries later, these now large populations were frequently contending with each other for territorial control, often driven by periodic droughts or simply the need to acquire more land. Out of this territorial competition emerged the great war leaders Pi'ilani and 'Umi-a-Liloa, who, respectively, consolidated power and moved the political system from one of chiefship to that of kingship.

This short essay does not permit a summary of all the other changes that accompanied the late Hawaiian political transformation, and so just a few will be mentioned here.[47] Most importantly, the very nature of hereditary leadership was radically altered. The APS term *qariki,* originally indexing the senior leader of a descent group, was continued in Hawaiian as *ali'i*, now referring to an internally ranked, largely endogamous elite class, with complex rules of intermarriage, including brother–sister unions at the highest ranks. The most highly ranked *ali'i* were regarded as divine kings, with genealogies that linked them to the gods. The newly acquired status of these exalted beings was confirmed through an elaborate set of sanctions (*kapu*, or taboo) for the isolation and protection of their persons, access to luxury foods, and material symbols (such as the justly famous capes and cloaks of yellow and red bird feathers, some of which were first collected on Cook's voyage of 1778–1779).

The social organization of the commoner class, and its rights to land and other property, were also transformed dramatically from the older APS patterns. Commoners were now known by the word *maka'āinana*, a cognate of the older Proto Polynesian word for the descent group, *\*kainanga* (and similarly reflected in the Marquesan term *mata'eina'a*) but which had now lost its original semantic content of genealogical descent. More telling, the Proto Polynesian word *\*kaainga*, which as we have seen originally referred to the core "house" residential group and its inalienable estate, now became Hawaiian *'āina*, meaning "land" in general. This major semantic shift went hand-in-glove with a transformation of the system of land tenure, in which the *ali'i* now held territorial segments of an island (called *ahupua'a*, or "pig altars") in exchange for supporting the king, and the commoners worked the lands within these territories. The commoners' rights to garden land and resources were thus validated by regular payment of labor and tribute, and they could be dispossessed from these lands for failure to produce what was demanded of them. This marked a radical change from the older Polynesian system in which one's rights to land were determined by birth and inclusion in a *\*kaainga* "house" group.

Finally, the religious system underwent extensive modifications, many of which we can detect archaeologically through study of the extensive stone foundations of temple sites found throughout the islands. The old APS concept of the chief's house and adjacent *\*malaqe* as the ritual center of the community was replaced by an elaborate hierarchy of functionally specific temples, called by an innovated Hawaiian word, *heiau*. The kings, aided by a class of priests (*kahuna*, from the older Proto Polynesian term *\*tufunga*), performed elaborate and costly ceremonies at war temples called *luakini*, these often requiring a human sacrifice. Across the agricultural landscapes, smaller temples dedicated to the gods of horticulture (Lono in the dryland zones, Kāne in the irrigated regions) served to ritually regulate the economic production system. On Hawai'i and Maui, the end of the main growing season for sweet potato in the field systems was marked by the annual rites of the *Makahiki*, whose onset was determined by the first visibility of Pleiades at sunset, around late November.[48] Then, a ritual procession of Lono priests and warriors would visit in turn each of the *ahupua'a* territories, collecting tribute. Thus, as in many other early state societies, taxation was deeply embedded in religious ideology.

Of the three Polynesian societies whose histories I have briefly surveyed here, Hawai'i took the transformations of society and the political economy the farthest from its roots in APS. As Sahlins once remarked, Hawai'i took "the primitive contradiction between the domestic and public economies to an ultimate crisis—revealatory [*sic*] it seems not only of this disconformity but of the economic and political limits of kinship society." [49] Fortunately, the power of comparative analysis, aided specifically by the kinds of detailed historical linguistic reconstruction that enable us to discern that the Hawaiian word for land (*'āina*) was a continuance of the ancient word for a residential kin group (*\*kaainga*), allows us to trace the highly evolved structures of late Hawaiian society back to their deep roots in APS. In the Hawaiian case, we actually see the emergence of a new form of sociopolitical structure—the archaic state—out of chiefdoms.

In the preceding pages I have attempted to indicate what can be achieved by applying a carefully formulated method of controlled comparison to the understanding of how several closely related societies have diverged and transformed from a common ancestor. This method, which involves the use of both a phylogenetic model and a triangulation approach, allows for (1) the reconstruction of many aspects of the ancestral societies from which the later, ethnographically attested "daughter" societies were derived, and (2) the specific ways in which aspects of individual societies changed over time. It is also important to note that this approach to historical anthropology makes full use of relevant data from comparative historical linguistics, comparative ethnography and ethnohistory, and archaeology. Thus the approach is both theoretically robust and empirically rich.

The three Polynesian societies examined in this essay all began their historical trajectories with essentially the same cultural base but ended up roughly 1,000 years later with remarkable differences. The method of controlled comparison allows us to delineate which aspects of each contact-era society were retentions from the ancestral pattern and which were innovations. That is, we can address the fundamental problem of disentangling homologous from analogous structures—only in this case these structures are cultural rather than biological. And where there were innovations, we can begin to ask if there were convergent similarities, responding perhaps to similar challenges or constraints. For example, the emergence of fluid sociopolitical structures in both Mangaia and the Marquesas, in which there was a continual vying for power among the hereditary chiefs, priests, and warriors, might well reflect similar conditions of resource depletion, high population density, and limits to the intensification of agricultural production in these islands. Certainly, this was not the pathway of cultural evolution in Hawai'i, which resulted in a totally different outcome, in which the hereditary chiefs elevated their own status to the point of inventing divine kingship, fully harnessing and keeping in check the potential power of the priesthood and warrior classes.

The differences resulting from these divergent pathways of cultural evolution can be assessed with special clarity through the lens provided by historical and comparative linguistics. Table 1.1 lists a

Table 1.1  Transformations of some key Proto Polynesian terms and concepts in Mangaia, the Marquesas, and Hawai'i

| Proto Polynesian term | Mangaia | Marquesas | Hawai'i |
|---|---|---|---|
| **Social organization terms** | | | |
| *kaainga, "house group" | kainga, residence and attached gardens | aika, general term for land or property | ʻāina, generalized term for land |
| *[mata]-kainanga, community | term is absent | mataʻeinaʻa, primary ascent group | makaʻāinana, generalized term for commoner |
| **Social status terms** | | | |
| *qariki, community leader | ariki, a hereditary title | hakaʻiki, hereditary chief | aliʻi, class of chiefly elites |
| *toa, warrior | toa, warrior | toa, warrior | koa, warrior |
| *taaula, priest, shaman | piʻa atua, priest | tauʻa, inspirational priest | kāula, prophet, seer |
| *tufunga, expert | taʻunga, craftsman, expert (secular) | tuhuna, craftsman, expert (secular) | kahuna, term for class of priests |
| **Terms for ritual spaces** | | | |
| *malaqe, open ceremonial space | marae, temple site with uprights | méʻae, sepulchral temples of the tauʻa | replaced with heiau, functionally diverse kinds of temples associated with specific cults |
| *qafu, sacred house mound | aʻu, to build or repair a marae | ahu, sacred place | ahu, altar, cairn. Component of the compound term ahu/puaʻa, "pig altar," for territorial land units |

few of the key Proto Polynesian terms referring to social organization, social status, and ritual structures, along with their cognate reflexes and semantic glosses in the Mangaian, Marquesan, and Hawaiian languages. Cultural conservatism is strongly indicated in the extent to which the root lexemes themselves persist over time. Indeed, the few cases where there have been lexical innovations (e.g., the Hawaiian terms *ahupua'a* and *heiau*) are strong indicators of major transformations. But more noteworthy are the semantic shifts—sometimes subtle and sometimes striking—that accompany the persistent vocabulary. By examining these shifts, we can most fully appreciate the ways in which these three Polynesian societies took a common ancestral pattern and transformed it in response to local conditions and historical contingencies. Let me then conclude this essay with a brief summation of those historical divergences.

In APS, communities were organized into two fundamental kinds of social groups, the residential *\*kaainga* and the larger *\*kainanga*. The *\*kaainga* was the basic unit of residence and of land-holding. For such a fundamental social concept to change, there must indeed have been major transformations in the sociopolitical fabric. Yet when I look at the three cases we have described in this chapter, only Mangaia retained something like the original meaning of the term. In the Marquesas, the residential unit lost its significance in the struggles for power and status, and the dominant social unit became the "tribe," the *mata'eina'a*, a transformed version of the ancient *\*kainanga*. But in Hawai'i the course of sociopolitical evolution went much further as the society was transformed from a small-scale chiefdom to an emergent archaic state. There, while the two ancient terms persist in linguistically recognizable form (PPN *\*kaainga* → HAW *'āina*; PPN *\*[mata]-kainanga* → HAW *maka'āinana*), the Hawaiian semantic values attached to these terms bear little resemblance to their original meanings. *'Āina* had come to signify land in the most general sense, without any specific reference to ownership by a specific group, since, of course, control of territorial units had now passed exclusively to the chiefly class. And in this highly stratified society, *maka'āinana* had come to reference a class of commoners in opposition to a class of elites. These differences allow us to see very clearly what is homologous (the retention of certain named categories) and what has been innovated in these social histories.

The next set of four lexical categories listed in Table 1.1 involves key social status positions, which were manifest in APS as *qariki,* the secular-sacred leader of community leader, *toa,* warriors, *taaula,* shaman or priest, and *tufunga,* expert of some kind. Again, the root lexemes themselves display strong persistence over time but with telling semantic transformations (only Mangaia innovated a new word for priest, *pi'a atua*). Late precontact Mangaian and Marquesan societies maintained the concept of *ariki* or *haka'iki* as the hereditary leader of an ascent group, but the role and functions of these leaders had diverged considerably from what we infer for APS. In Hawai'i, however, the cognate term *ali'i* had come to signify an entire class of elite persons, a "conical clan" of chiefly individuals all claiming descent from the gods while simultaneously asserting their distinctiveness vis-à-vis the class of commoners *(maka'āinana).* Indeed, in Hawai'i the *ali'i* distinguished among themselves at least nine grades of lexically marked chiefs and sub-chiefs, reflecting the emphasis this emergent archaic state placed on stratification.

All of these Eastern Polynesian societies retained the same Proto Polynesian term for warrior, *toa* or *koa,* a case of remarkable cultural conservatism. Of course, the specific roles of warriors in each society varied somewhat, as I have described earlier. When we turn to priests, however, considerable variation from the original APS model is in evidence. The *taaula* of Ancestral Polynesia was probably a minor player in the social fabric and remained so in its inherited versions in Mangaia and Hawai'i. Yet in the Marquesas the *tau'a* became the driving force in an involuted cycle of competitive raiding, feasting, and human sacrifice. The Mangaians innovated a new term for priest, *pi'a atua,* in keeping with the transformation of religion that accompanied the late precontact cult of Rongo. A much more pervasive transformation is reflected in the Hawaiian reflex of Proto Polynesian *tufunga, originally meaning a craftsman or expert, and retaining that meaning in Mangaia and the Marquesas. In Hawai'i, the *kahuna* became a formal priesthood, or virtual class of priests (usually drawn from the junior ranks of chiefs, or *ali'i*), highly specialized into a number of formal cults and functions (e.g., the cult of the war god Kū, of the god of dryland agriculture, Lono, or of the creator god and deity of irrigation, Kāne). This increased specialization rivaled the specialization with the class of *ali'i*, and together marked the emergence of administrative specialization within the emergent archaic state.

The final section of Table 1.1 lists two key terms relating to ritual spaces and their transformed variants in the three societies under consideration. The key Proto Polynesian term *malaqe*, signifying a simple ceremonial yard or court at which various rituals were performed, persists in both Mangaia and the Marquesas but is lost in Hawai'i. Mangaia retains the closest variant to the ancestral form, with architecturally simple courts, usually paved with coral gravel, delineated at one side with low uprights honoring various deified ancestors. In the Marquesas, the *me'ae* became a specialized kind of temple associated with the increasingly powerful *tau'a* or inspirational priests. The Hawaiians, however, abandoned the term entirely, substituting a new concept of *heiau* (probably derived from the word *hai*, to sacrifice). Archaeological evidence indicates a major increase in the construction of such *heiau* after about A.D. 1500, associated with the rise of the major island-wide polities. Moreover, *heiau* were functionally specialized and elaborated, with the largest *luakini*-type structures dedicated to the war god Kū, but other deities also having their own particular temple forms.[50] The late precontact Hawaiians also modified another old Polynesian term, *qafu*, originally the mound on which the chief's sacred house (at one end of the *malaqe*) was elevated. The Hawaiian reflex *ahu* was now combined with the word for pig *(pua'a)* to create the new compound term *ahupua'a*, with a literal meaning of "pig altar," but in fact signifying the radial land territories into which the Hawaiian divine kings now divided their island realms. The word seems to have originated with the practice of placing tribute (pigs, in particular, being the most valued flesh food in the islands) on stone altars at the boundaries of such territories. This practice became codified with the *makahiki* ceremonials carried out in the name of Lono, as described earlier. Thus in the Hawaiian case in particular, we see how transformations of APS concepts of social organization, social status, and ritual practice were all intimately bound up and radically transformed together in late prehistory.

In this chapter, I have endeavored to demonstrate by way of the empirically close comparison of three Polynesian cases how the application of a phylogenetic model and the use of triangulation allow for the disentangling of homology and analogy in cultural evolution. The varied ethnographic societies of Polynesia encapsulate a remarkable degree of variation in social organization, modes of production, political economy, and religion, while all remaining recognizably part of a larger cultural pattern. Indeed, in his classic work on Polynesian social stratification, Marshall Sahlins invoked the metaphor of biological evolution when he characterized the varied Polynesian cultures as "members of a single cultural genus that has filled in and adapted to a variety of local habitats."[51] Understanding how individual Polynesian societies diverged from their common ancestor and tracking their historical pathways of cultural evolution require a carefully constructed method of controlled comparison. Only by drawing on the power of such comparative analysis is it possible, with some degree of confidence, to distinguish what features of a particular ethnographically described society were carryovers from the older, ancestral cultural pattern and which were innovations. Distinguishing homologous from analogous traits is the critical first step to a broader understanding of the processes of historical change.

## NOTES

1. Cook himself did not use this term, although it had evidently been coined as early as 1756 by C. De Brosses in *Histoire des Navigations aux Terres Australes* (Paris, 1756).

2. James Cook, "Journal," in J. C. Beaglehole, ed., *The Journals of Captain James Cook, The Voyage of the* Resolution *and* Discovery, *1776–1780* (Cambridge, 1967), p. 279.

3. Marshall Sahlins, *Social Stratification in Polynesia* (Seattle, 1958); Irving Goldman, *Ancient Polynesian Society* (Chicago, 1970). Earlier comparative work on Polynesia included the massive three-volume study by R. W. Williamson, *The Social and Political Systems of Central Polynesia* (Cambridge, 1924). The value of a comparative approach in studying human history in Oceania is well argued by Ward H. Goodenough, "Oceania and the Problem of Controls in the Study of Cultural and Human Evolution," *Journal of the Polynesian Society* 66 (1957): 146–155.

4. On the comparative analysis of Polynesian sailing canoes, see Ben Finney, "Ocean Sailing Canoes," in K. R. Howe, ed., *Vaka Moana: Voyages of the Ancestors* (Auckland, New Zealand, 2006), pp. 100–153.

5. Douglas Oliver, *Oceania: The Native Cultures of Australia and the Pacific Islands,* 2 vols. (Honolulu, 1989).

6. The long history of Polynesian historical linguistics is well summarized in Jeff Marck, *Topics in Polynesian Language and Culture History,* Pacific Linguistics 504 (Canberra, 2000).

7. Stephen J. Gould, "Evolution and the Triumph of Homology," *American Scientist* 74 (1986): 60–69; Ernst Mayr, *The Growth of Biological Thought* (Cambridge, MA, 1982).

8. Two important books that discuss developments in the theory of a dual model of biological and cultural evolution are Peter J. Richerson and Robert Boyd, *Not by Genes Alone: How Culture Transformed Human Evolution* (Chicago, 2005) and Stephen Shennan, *Genes, Memes and Human History* (London, 2002). Shennan, in particular, integrates the theory of cultural evolution with the use of archaeological data to track such evolution over time.

9. Ernst Mayr, *This Is Biology: The Science of the Living World* (Cambridge, MA, 1997), p. 29.

10. A current overview of Polynesian archaeology and prehistory is presented in Patrick V. Kirch, *On the Road of the Winds: An Archaeological History of the Pacific Islands before European Contact* (Berkeley, CA, 2000).

11. Homologous traits are retentions from a common ancestral condition, whereas analogous traits have arisen after the breakup of an ancestral culture into descent groups, usually in response to similar conditions or challenges. Synologous traits are those that have been borrowed across cultural boundaries. For further discussion of these important distinctions and of the nature of "cultural phylogenies," see R. Boyd, M. B. Mulder, W. H. Durham, and P. J. Richerson, "Are Cultural Phylogenies Possible?" in P. Weingart, S. D. Mitchell, P. J. Richerson, and S. Maasen, eds., *Human by Nature: Between Biology and the Social Sciences* (Mahwah, NJ, 1997), pp. 355–386.

12. Patrick V. Kirch and Roger C. Green, *Hawaiki, Ancestral Polynesia: An Essay in Historical Anthropology* (New York, 2001). For original formulation of the phylogenetic model, see A. K. Romney, "The Genetic Model and Uto-Aztecan Time Perspective," *Davidson Journal of Anthropology* 3 (1957): 35–41. The methodological details of Romney's initial propositions were further developed by E. Z. Vogt, "The Genetic Model and Maya Cultural Development," in E. Z. Vogt and A. Ruz L., eds., *Desarrollo Cultural de los Mayas* (Mexico, D. F., 1964), pp. 9–48.

13. Peter Bellwood, *First Farmers: The Origins of Agricultural Societies* (Malden, MA, 2005).

14. Lexicostatistics involves the comparison of languages by means of statistical frequency of presumed "cognates." Although it has the advantage of allowing many languages to be compared rapidly, it is incapable of distinguishing cognates shared through inheritance from borrowings. Glottochronology applied a presumed regular rate of lexical change to lexicostatistical data in order to infer language chronology; this method is not widely accepted today.

15. Such a tree model for the Polynesian languages is provided by Kirch and Green, *Hawaiki, Ancestral Polynesia*, figure 3.5.

16. The Polynesian homeland region is sometimes described as including the Fiji archipelago, but this is inaccurate. Fiji, Tonga, and Samoa were all settled around 900 B.C. by peoples of the Eastern Lapita cultural complex. It was from one of the descendant communities of these Eastern Lapita peoples in the Tongan and Samoan archipelagoes (and including the smaller islands of Futuna and 'Uvea) that Ancestral Polynesian culture emerged later in the first millennium B.C. Thus while Polynesian cultures share immediate roots with Fijian, the Polynesian homeland, strictly speaking, does not extend to the Fijian islands.

17. Linguistically, this was marked first by the breakup of the original Proto Polynesian speech community into Proto Tongic and Proto Nuclear Polynesian groups, and later by the further breakup of Proto Nuclear Polynesian into Proto Ellicean and Proto Eastern Polynesian groups. The differentiation of Polynesian languages is treated in considerable detail by Marck, *Topics in Polynesian Language and Culture History.*

18. See Kirch and Green, *Hawaiki, Ancestral Polynesia,* pp. 42–44.

19. For details of this example, see Kirch and Green, *Hawaiki, Ancestral Polynesia,* pp. 149–153, table 6.2, figure 6.2.

20. New Zealand represents something of an anomaly in several respects: it is "subcontinental" in scale (and in geological terms a remnant of the ancient continent of Gondwanaland), and temperate in climate (whereas the rest of Polynesia is tropical or subtropical). Polynesian colonists arriving in New Zealand around A.D. 1200 had to adapt to these significant environmental differences in ways that resulted in Maori culture being more distinctive from other sister Polynesian cultures in many respects.

21. The initial date of Polynesian settlement for both Mangaia and Hawai'i has been the subject of considerable debate. Recent radiocarbon dating of sites throughout Eastern Polynesia, however, strongly suggests that Polynesian expansion into this region dates to around A.D. 900–1100.

22. Hawai'i and Mangaia were both among the islands visited by Captain James Cook on his famous Pacific voyages, both on Cook's fateful third voyage in 1777–1779.

23. The full reconstruction of Ancestral Polynesian social, political, and ritual organization is presented in Kirch and Green, *Hawaiki, Ancestral Polynesia,* pp. 201–276.

24. It is important to stress the plural "societies" here as there were multiple social communities occupying many islands distributed geographically from southern Tonga to Samoa.

25. C. Levi-Strauss, *The Way of the Masks* (Washington, DC, 1982), pp. 172–187.

26. The ranking among individual *kaainga or households was thought to have been more 'heterarchical' than strictly hierarchical in APS.

27. The Polynesian lunar calendar is discussed in Kirch and Green, *Hawaiki, Ancestral Polynesia,* pp. 267–276, and a diagrammatic summary of the ritual cycle is shown in figure 9.5.

28. On the problem of *sau and its meaning in APS, see the arguments in M. Taumoefolau, "From *Sau 'Ariki to Hawaiki," *Journal of the Polynesian Society* 105 (1996): 385–410.

29. A list of ancestral Polynesian settlement sites is provided in Kirch and Green, *Hawaiki, Ancestral Polynesia,* table 3.2.

30. Te Rangi Hiroa, *Mangaian Society,* Bernice P. Bishop Museum Bulletin 122 (Honolulu, 1934).

31. Mangaia is discussed more extensively in Patrick V. Kirch, *The Wet and the Dry: Irrigation and Agricultural Intensification in Polynesia* (Chicago, 1994), pp. 269–287. See also references cited therein.

32. These traditions are extensively discussed by Te Rangi Hiroa, *Mangaian Society,* pp. 26–83.

33. The early missionaries describe the hunting of these rats, and note that after the introduction of Christianity, Saturday became the principal rat-catching day so that there would be rats to accompany the Sabbath meal.

34. Virginia L. Butler, "Changing Fish Use on Mangaia, Southern Cook Islands," *International Journal of Osteoarchaeology* 11 (2001): 88–100.

35. The effects of drought on the Marquesan vegetation are described by A. M. Adamson, *Marquesan Insects: Environment,* Bernice P. Bishop Museum Bulletin 139 (Honolulu, 1936).

36. The classic ethnographic account of the Marquesas is Edward S. C. Handy, *The Native Culture of the Marquesas,* Bernice P. Bishop Museum Bulletin 9 (Honolulu, 1923). A reanalysis of Marquesan social organization is presented by Nicholas Thomas, *Marquesan Societies: Inequality and Political Transformation in Eastern Polynesia* (Oxford, 1990). Historical scholarship on the Marquesas owes a great debt to the works of Greg Dening, especially *Islands and Beaches: Discourse on a Silent Land, Marquesas 1774–1880* (Honolulu, 1980).

37. While anthropologists have typically called such social units "descent" groups, in the indigenous Polynesian concept they are "ascent" groups because following a botanical metaphor, the latest generation of offspring forms the tips of a branching genealogical structure, with the ancestors at the "trunk" or base. Hence one ascends from one's ancestral line.

38. This term has a slightly complex semantic history, the Proto Polynesian *\*kainanga* becoming *'eina'a* through regular sound shifts, including Proto Polynesian *\*k* and *\*ng* to Marquesan (glottal stop), and the addition of the prefix *mata*.

39. See Patrick Kirch, "Chiefship and Competitive Involution: The Marquesas Islands of Eastern Polynesia," in T. Earle, ed., *Chiefdoms: Power, Economy, and Ideology* (New York, 1991), pp. 119–145.

40. Key early works on Marquesan archaeology include Ralph Linton, *Archaeology of the Marquesas Islands,* Bernice P. Bishop Museum Bulletin 23 (Honolulu, 1925), and Robert Carl Suggs, *The Archaeology of Nuku Hiva, Marquesas Islands, French Polynesia,* American Museum of Natural History Anthropological Papers 49 (New York, 1961). For a more recent synthesis of Marquesan archaeology and cultural history, see Barry V. Rolett, *Hanamiai: Prehistoric Colonization and Cultural Change in the Marquesas Islands,* Yale University Publications in Anthropology 81 (New Haven, CT, 1998).

41. Thomas, *Marquesan Societies,* p. 175.

42. For recent archaeological studies of the Kohala field system, see T. N. Ladefoged, M. W. Graves, and R. P. Jennings, "Dryland Agricultural Expansion and Intensification in Kohala, Hawai'i Island," *Antiquity* 70 (1996): 861–880, and T. N. Ladefoged, M. W. Graves, and M. D. McCoy, "Archaeological Evidence for Agricultural Development in Kohala, Island of Hawai'i," *Journal of Archaeological Science* 30 (2003): 923–940.

43. Patrick V. Kirch, "Agricultural Intensification: A Polynesian Perspective," in Joyce Marcus and Charles Stanish, eds., *Agricultural Strategies* (Los Angeles, 2006), pp. 191–220.

44. Harold C. Brookfield, "Intensification and Disintensification in Pacific Agriculture: A Theoretical Approach," *Pacific Viewpoint* 13 (1972): 30–48. See also H. C. Brookfield, "Intensification Revisited," *Pacific Viewpoint* 25 (1984): 15–44.

45. E. Boserup, *The Conditions of Agricultural Growth: The Economics of Agrarian Change under Population Pressure* (Chicago, 1965). See also Kirch, "Agricultural Intensification," pp. 200–203, for a discussion of cropping cycle intensification.

46. Such depletion as a result of precontact cultivation practices has recently been demonstrated in the case of the Kahikinui, Maui, dryland agricultural system. See A. S. Hartshorn, P. V. Kirch, O. A. Chadwick, and P. M. Vitousek, "Prehistoric Agricultural Depletion of Soil Nutrients in Hawai'i," *Proceedings of the National Academy of Sciences* 103 (2006): 11092–11097.

47. For an overview of the emergence of an "archaic state" level of society in late precontact Hawai'i, see Patrick V. Kirch, *From Chiefdom to Archaic State: Social Evolution in Hawaii* (Provo, UT, 2005).

48. It was the arrival of Captain Cook at precisely this time, among other circumstances, that evidently prompted the Hawaiian priests to declare that he was the returning god Lono. See Marshall Sahlins, *Historical Metaphors*

and *Mythical Realities: Structure in the Early History of the Sandwich Islands Kingdom* (Ann Arbor, MI, 1981).

49. Marshall Sahlins, *Stone Age Economics* (Chicago, 1972), p. 141.
50. On the hierarchy of temples in ancient Hawaiʻi, see Valerio Valeri, *Kingship and Sacrifice: Ritual and Society in Ancient Hawaii* (Chicago, 1985).
51. Sahlins, *Social Stratification*, p. ix.

# 2

## Exploding Wests: Boom and Bust in Nineteenth-Century Settler Societies

### JAMES BELICH

This essay is, in part, yet another attempt to explain the remarkable growth of the American West. This hallowed quest dates back from the current fine crop of "New Western" historians, through Frederick Jackson Turner in the 1890s, to Alexis De Tocqueville in the 1830s. Such scholars sometimes sought to discover America's quintessence on its frontier, arguably a Holy Grail. But they also addressed a real macrohistorical problem: explosive growth. In 1790, the trans-Appalachian West contained 109,000 American settlers. In 1920, this figure had risen to 62 million.[1] These millions were not impoverished backwoodsmen, but among the richest people on the planet, with giant cities such as Chicago, which had grown from around 100 people in 1830 to 2.7 million ninety years later. This was probably the most explosive form of growth in human history, and American fascination with it is understandable. The American West had a forgotten twin, however, born at much the same time, to much the same parents, and growing at much the same remarkable rate. This was the British "West," later known as the "white dominions" of Canada, Australia, New Zealand, and South Africa. In 1790, this fragmented West contained about 200,000 European settlers, mostly French. By 1920, it had 24 million people, mostly British and Irish—fewer than the United States West but not bad for a forgotten twin.[2] The British West, too, had its mushrooming settler cities, Melbourne and Sydney, Toronto and Cape Town, and its white citizens also were among the richest people in the world.

From the 1870s, this new explosive form of long-range settlement extended beyond the Anglo-Wests. Manchuria, Uruguay, and parts of Brazil are possible examples, but Argentina and Siberia are the two clearest-cut cases. Despite exports of hides and wool, and a flurry of foreign investment in the 1820s, not until the 1870s did Argentina experience the growth that its own governing elite had expected. From that decade, however, the Pampas of central Argentina were explosively settled. Argentina's population quadrupled from 1.8 million in 1869 to almost 8 million in 1914, over 90% of them European.[3] The region in which growth was greatest (Buenos Aires city and province and Santa Fe province) grew eightfold. As in the Anglo-Wests both economic development and demographic growth took place. Argentina had a hybrid metropolis: Britain provided its money and later its markets; Italy and Spain provided its migrants.[4] But settlement was no less explosive for speaking Spanish. Buenos Aires, the "Paris of the Southern Hemisphere," had over 1.5 million people and a subway system in 1914. Argentina's aim "to be tomorrow what the US is today" was looking promising.[5]

Siberia, Russia's "Wild East," also grew exponentially. Between 1863 and 1914 its population more than tripled from 3.1 million people to 10 million, 80% Russian, with most of the growth concentrated in the 1890s and 1900s and in the southwest and southeast.[6] Again, urban development as well as population increase took place. Vladivostok, in the Russian Far East, grew sevenfold between 1885 and 1910; Blagoveshchensk, "the New York of Siberia," sixfold; Irkutsk, "the Paris of Siberia," threefold. With its opera house, cathedrals, museum, thirty-four schools, and electric lighting juxtaposed with wooden shanties, Irkutsk was "just like a mushroom city in Western America." "I tell you," said an American salesman of agricultural equipment in 1901, "Siberia is going to be another America," complete with gold rush "Californias" and a Chinese "Yellow Peril."[7]

This remarkable nineteenth-century explosive settlement was not a matter of steady expansion. Instead, it had a three-step rhythm of boom, bust, and "export rescue." A huge boom lasting five to fifteen years at least doubled the population of a large frontier area in a single decade. Booming frontiers were net importers, not exporters, of both goods and capital. Their markets were dynamic and highly commercialized, but local—last year's settlers made their money by supplying this year's settlers, and by preparing for next year's settlers. A dramatic bust, "crash," or "panic" followed, decimating growth rates and bankrupting around half of the boom-time farms and businesses. In the third step, which can be called "export rescue," a new socioeconomy was painfully created from the shards of the old, oriented to the mass export of staple products such as wheat, cotton, or timber to a distant metropolis. The economy recovered and continued to develop but at a much slower pace, and in some respects relations with the metropolis were tighter and more dependent than they had been during the boom.

The first full booms, featuring development as well as growth, money as well as migrants, and mushroom cities as well as rural settlement, began around 1815 in the American Old Northwest and Old Southwest and possibly in Upper Canada as well. Booms sometimes followed long periods of slower, steadier incremental settlement. Western Australia and British Columbia, for example, were founded in the 1820s and 1840s, respectively, but did not explode until the 1880s. Defining booms as at least the decennial doubling of a population from a not-insignificant base (say at least 20,000 people), most Western American states, most British settlement colonies, and some Argentine and Siberian regions experienced the full three-step rhythm of settlement at least once. Over two dozen cases are set out in Table 2.1. Some details may be contestable, but the evidence for the overall pattern is strong.

Booms were powered by mass transfers of people, money, goods, information, and skills from one or more metropolises to the relevant

*Table 2.1*  Settlement booms, busts, and "export rescues"

| Boom-bust dates | Region | Settler city | Export rescue |
|---|---|---|---|
| **United States** | | | |
| Boom One: 1815–1819 | Old Northwest, Old Southwest | Cincinnati, New Orleans | Cotton, cured pork |
| Boom Two: 1825–1837 | Old Northwest, Old Southwest | Cincinnati, St. Louis, New Orleans | Cotton, pork, grain |
| Boom Three: 1845–1857 | Old Northwest, Midwest, Texas, California | St. Louis, Chicago, San Francisco | Grain, pork, gold |
| Boom Four: 1865–1873 | Midwest | Chicago | Grain, pork, live cattle |
| Boom Five: 1878–1887/93 | Midwest, Far West, West Texas | Chicago, Denver, Minneapolis, | Grain, chilled beef |
| Boom Six: 1898–1907/13 | Far Northwest, Southern California, Oklahoma | Seattle, Los Angeles | Grain, timber, fruit |
| **Canada** | | | |
| Boom One: 1815–1819/21? | Eastern Townships? parts of Ontario | Montreal | Timber |
| Boom Two: 1829–1837/42 | Ontario, New Brunswick | Toronto, Saint John | Timber |
| Boom Three: 1844–1848 | Ontario | Toronto, Hamilton | Wheat, timber |
| Boom Four: 1851–1857 | Ontario | Toronto, Montreal | Wheat, cheese |
| Boom Five: 1878/85–1883/93 | Manitoba, British Columbia | Winnipeg, Vancouver | Wheat |
| Boom Six: 1898–1907/13 | British Columbia, Prairie Provinces | Regina, Saskatoon, Edmonton, Calgary | Wheat, timber |

## Australia

| | | | |
|---|---|---|---|
| Boom One: 1828–1842 | Tasmania, New South Wales | Hobart, Sydney | Wool |
| Boom Two: 1848–1867 | All except West Australia and Tasmania | Melbourne, Sydney, Adelaide | Wool, gold, wheat |
| Boom Three: 1872–1879/91 | Inland Victoria and NSW, Queensland | Brisbane | Wool, wheat, meat, dairy products |
| Boom Four: 1887?–1913 | Western Australia | Perth | Gold, wool, wheat |

## New Zealand

| | | | |
|---|---|---|---|
| Boom One: 1850–1867 | South Island | Dunedin | Wool |
| Boom Two: 1870–1879/86 | South Island, North Island | Auckland, Wellington | Meat and dairy products |

## South Africa

| | | | |
|---|---|---|---|
| Boom One: 1855–1865 | Cape | Port Elizabeth | Wool |
| Boom Two: 1870–1882 | Cape | Kimberley, East London | Diamonds |
| Boom Three: 1886–1899 | Cape, Natal, Transvaal | Cape Town, Johannesburg | Gold |

## Argentina

| | | | |
|---|---|---|---|
| Boom One: 1865–1873 | Buenos Aires | Buenos Aires, Rosario | Wool |
| Boom Two: 1878–1890 | Buenos Aires, Santa Fe | Buenos Aires | Grain |
| Boom Three: 1896–1913 | Buenos Aires, Santa Fe, La Pampa | BA, Cordoba, Mar Del Plata, Tucuman | Chilled beef |

## Siberia

| | | | |
|---|---|---|---|
| Boom One: c. 1885–1899 | Central and Eastern Siberia | Blagoveshchensk | Wheat |
| Boom Two: 1906–1914 | Eastern Siberia, Russian Far East | Chita, Vladivostok, Harbin | Butter |

frontier. They were therefore characterized by a sudden surge in the vectors of mass transfer—ships, wagon trains, or railroads; banks, newspapers, booster literature, and post offices; migration businesses and organizations. These were mostly urban-based activities. Unless there were large indigenous urban populations, as in Mexico City, normal settlement took a couple of centuries to create large cities. Explosive settlement, by contrast, took a couple of decades. Many of these precocious cities, such as Cincinnati or Winnipeg, later became famous as exporters but spent their boom decades primarily as inlets supplying imports to exploding frontiers, not outlets supplying exports to a distant metropolis. Chicago, the leader of the pack, did both at the same time, channeling out exports for a busted part of its hinterland while channeling in imports for a booming part, and this helps explain its super-high growth. Booming frontiers might have mushrooming inlet cities outside their political boundaries. The inlet city of booming Texas in the 1840s and 1850s was New Orleans in Louisiana. The inlet city of booming Upper Canada in 1815–1819 was Montreal in Lower Canada.[8]

During booms, old exports might continue and new exports might emerge, but a large export sector was not vital. The main economic game was actually growth itself: the encouragement, management, and renewal of inflows of people, goods, and money; the supply, housing, and support of immigrants; the stocking of new farms; the construction of towns, farms, and transport infrastructure; the supply and support of construction. The *progress industry* is a useful generic label for this cluster of activities, all involving growth through growth.[9]

The building of transport infrastructure was one leading element of the progress industry. Public or private, transport projects were generally funded by vast metropolitan loans or bond issues, but most of their other inputs were local: manpower, work animals, food for both, and raw materials such as wood. They therefore had a double effect. Once completed, they facilitated communications and access to markets. But they were also valuable as business boosters during the process of construction. In this latter sense, roads, canals, or railroads that proved to be unprofitable or were duplicated by local rivalries, were not wasted. In the 1830s, three different Lake Erie towns succeeded in persuading the Ohio Canal Board to make them termini of the same canal.[10] This tripled the cost and cut efficiency by two-thirds, but it also tripled the "progress"—the farm, manufacturing, and labor markets generated by canal construction. At the height of the 1880s boom in Argentina, "some twenty-one private companies and three state lines competed in chaotic fashion." By 1890, "after years of sacrifice, Argentina could claim a poorly-coordinated railway network containing three different gauges, with excessive construction in some areas and none in others."[11] Some observers attributed this dysfunction to Hispanic overexcitability. In fact Anglophone rail booms had the same characteristics, and in any case Britons were funding and planning most Argentine railroads.

Creating instant infrastructure in booms was a vast industry. Rail construction in Upper Canada in the 1850s may have directly occupied as much as 15% of the male workforce.[12] In the 1890s, the Trans-Siberian Railway suddenly "increased the capital value of Siberian industrial output by around 20 times."[13] In New Zealand between 1871 and 1900, rail construction accounted for over 40% of capital formation.[14] The Victorian economy's main game was, literally, building itself. At peak, in 1888, building housing absorbed "just over four-fifths of total private investment in the colony."[15] Melbourne used brick, but most settler cities were built of wood, usually more than once. "San Francisco burned and rebuilt itself at least four times."[16] According to one estimate there were 290 major urban fires in Canada and the United States between 1815 and 1915, and New Zealand and Siberian boomtowns also burned freely.[17] Fires were traumatic, but rebuilding these disposable cities boosted business still further.

Forestry, supplying construction and packaging materials and fuel for the local market, was another key element of the progress industry. Wood consumption was high in the nineteenth century, especially in settler societies and most particularly during booms. Only 10% of 4,000 American locomotives were coal fired in 1859; the rest burned wood.[18] The same was true of steamships and of Australasia, Canada, and Siberia. A population doubling in a decade needed several times the houses, town buildings, farm buildings, and fences of a region growing normally. Mining and transport projects were also big users of wood. Roads were sometimes made of planks and "corduroy" logs; bridges and telegraph poles were wooden; canals needed timber struts and the like; and iron rails needed wood too— for ties or sleepers, and for fences to keep animals off the track. A rail line required 2,640 wooden sleepers or cross-ties per mile, which had to be replaced every six years or so. When all this is added to the millions of trees that were simply cut and burned to clear farmland, we can see why settler booms ate forests. The American boom of the 1850s consumed an England-sized chunk of forest—40 million acres.[19] Boom-time forestry was a huge business, even when timber exports were modest.

A third leading element of the progress industry was boom-time farming and farm-making. In the booming 1850s, a quarter of the farm labor force in the American West was actually engaged in clearing land and constructing farm buildings—farm-*making* rather than farming proper.[20] Farmers with little capital frequently engaged in nonfarm work, on and off the farm, and booms meant that the jobs were available. "Farmers" were to be found working on the construction of roads, canals, or railways and even in manufacturing. Either they used their off-season for this work, or they left the actual farming to their families back home, led by sturdy yeowomen. Other farmers worked seasonally for wages in the lumber industry or supplied wood products themselves as a "sideline" to farming. It was the boom itself that provided the demand for farmers' nonfarm products and labor, and the same is true for their farm products.

Agricultural history tends to assume that settler agriculture went more or less directly from pioneer semi-subsistence to long-range exports. Sometimes, a brief "settler's market" or "shanty market" is acknowledged, but it is seldom accorded much significance. In fact, boom-phase farming was highly commercial and dynamic, but the market was local. It was also big and varied, and the boom could last up to fifteen years. Construction and forestry and their motley crews were huge consumers of meat, bread, liquor, and leather, as were urban populations and farm immigrants in the process of establishing themselves. The last also required breeding animals and seed in quantity—an immense "stocking" market. There was yet another whole dimension to boom-phase farming. A crucial, but strangely neglected, category of farm product was work animals and their feed. Over half of all work energy in the United States in 1850 was supplied by horses, which were raised on farms. The demand for horses and oxen was particularly strong on booming settler frontiers. Pre-boom New South Wales in 1821 had eight people to each horse. Booming New South Wales in 1851 had 1.5 people per horse.[21] The British ratio at this time was about twelve people to one horse.[22] In the nonboom state of South Carolina in 1860, the ratio of work animals to people was about 1 to 4.5. In the boom state of Texas, it was about one to one.[23] Siberia had eighty-five horses per 100 people, far more than in European Russia, and Argentina had 115.[24] Often, working animals could not graze much but required feed—oats, hay, and corn—and farmers provided this too. During booms, acreages of these crops often exceeded those of wheat. In effect, farmers in the nineteenth century were not just farmers, but also producers of the motor vehicle engines and oil fuels of the day.

Other elements or allies of the progress industry included the supply of money, immigrants, and imported goods, each in itself a big business. Extractive industries such as whaling and hunting for furs and hides might have predated the boom, but they intensified with it, often to the point of the local extinction of the prey—it was American Booms Four and Five that almost wiped out the bison. Rushes for valuable minerals, notably gold, often accompanied booms but seldom caused them. Victoria and the South Island of New Zealand were booming before their great gold discoveries of 1851 and

1861, and this is also true of various Siberian "Californias" in the 1880s and 1890s. Even in gold-rush California in 1848, mining began at Sutter's Mill, not milling at Sutter's Mine. War against indigenous peoples and European precursors was sometimes another ally of the progress industry, bringing dozens of forts, thousands of soldiers, and millions of dollars to further fuel booms.

Busts, also called crashes or panics, are the best-known aspects of the rhythm of settlement—the tips of the iceberg. The American West experienced at least five great rounds of boom, bust, and export rescue pivoting on the busts of 1819, 1837, 1857, 1873, and 1893. A further boom, busting in 1913, could arguably count as two, with another bust in 1907. Canada shared the earlier busts, then experienced only minor booms between the 1860s and 1890s, before exploding again with a vengeance on its western prairies during 1897–1913. South Africa crashed in 1865, 1882, and 1899; Australia in 1842, 1866, and the early 1890s; Argentina in 1873, 1890, and 1913. Siberia underwent at least one big crash in 1899–1900. There were local variations: the South Island of New Zealand busted in 1879–1880, the North Island in 1886. Few economic historians would deny the existence of these busts; indeed, some would add still more. But the busts do tend to be downplayed by the debates over whether or not they constituted technical depressions, in which real wages fall and economies actually shrink.[25] Often, we find that falling prices compensated for falling wages so that real per capita incomes held up, and we observe that modest growth persisted in the economy as a whole. But whether or not they were technical depressions, these busts were watersheds in their day. They decimated growth rates. Booming Milwaukee grew 44.5% in population in the three years 1855–1857, whereas busted Milwaukee grew 2.8% in the three years 1858–1960.[26] Farms and businesses went broke in droves.

The bust of 1819 killed off half of the hundreds of American single-unit banks founded in the 1810s.[27] The Australian bust of 1891 forced 54 of 65 large banks to close, 34 of them permanently.[28] The

American bust of 1893 closed 573 banks and 8,105 major businesses.[29] After a bust in 1865, claimed contemporaries, "the whole of South Africa was in a state of bankruptcy."[30] Some 400 Argentine and Anglo-Argentine companies went bankrupt in 1873–1877, and at least another 300 kicked the bucket after the bust of 1890.[31] The 1900 bust knocked out at least fifty-five major Siberian enterprises.[32] As for farmers, the Midwest between 1830 and 1890 experienced four busts. "No matter the age of the community, between 50% and 80% of any new group of farmers were gone ten years later."[33] In the Maritime Provinces of Canada, about half the farmers in some areas were forced off their farms by the bust of the early 1840s.[34] Towns, too, became ghost towns in hordes. "Of more than 100 towns platted from 1884 to 1888 in Los Angeles County, 62 no longer exist except as stunted country corners, farm acreages, or suburbs."[35] Some see ghost towns as uniquely American, but New Zealand has 240 of them.[36]

Bust phases lasted from two to ten years, during which the shattered shards of the economy were usually reassembled into a new system that was more modest but steadier and based firmly on "export rescue." The economy's main game switched from growth itself to the mass export of one or two staples to one or two metropolitan markets. A great reshuffle took place. Small farmers who survived the bust bought up the holdings of neighbors who had not, while large holdings were broken up, with both processes creating more viable, medium-sized, units. While production dispersed, the processing and distribution of staples tended to concentrate into giant meatpacking, milling, rail and shipping companies, and combines. In production and in processing/distribution alike, success was to some extent built on the failure of others during the bust. Their assets could be bought for a song. This double investment meant that explosive settlement was bust-driven, as well as boom-driven.

Export rescue sometimes took the form of a huge surge in long-standing exports, with increased volumes compensating for lower prices. Timber exports from Canada to Britain, already quite high in 1842 at 265,000 tons, surged after the bust of that year to 608,000 tons in 1845.[37] Cotton production in the American South was less than 60,000 tons in 1818, then shot up with the bust of 1819 to 166,000 by 1826. Sometimes, new exports were developed, as with the railed livestock that poured in from the American Midwest to the East after 1857, or the refrigerated meat that streamed in from Australasia to Britain from the 1880s. The production, processing, and transport of staples now dominated the settler economy. Unlike booms, which began and ended, export rescue phases were indefinite and cumulative. The Midwest experienced four successive types of exporting to the Northeast. After 1819, it began sending cured pork and grain via New Orleans; after 1837, wheat, by canal and the Great Lakes; after 1857, livestock, by rail; after 1873, dead meat in iced railcars. Australia successively pumped wool, wheat, and meat to Britain after its three busts, and Argentina went through much the same series. Each new export supplemented rather than displaced its predecessors. Growth rates were far lower under export rescue than during booms, but could still be quite respectable, and average real incomes tended to grow after the worst of the bust was over.

Export rescue was seldom easy or preordained but had to overcome numerous problems: low prices, inconsistency, bulk, decay, and distance. Low prices were dealt with by increased volumes. Inconsistency was inevitable in the production of farm-made dairy products and cured meats. Export rescue therefore corresponded with the advent of meatpacking plants and butter and cheese factories, together with improvements in grading and quality control. Bulk was handled in various ways—improved presses compressed cotton and wool, and silos and elevators improved the handling of grain. Decay was always a difficult matter with meat exports, but problems were resolved by better salt and curing techniques for pork in the 1820s; the railcars' use of natural ice to chill beef in the 1870s; and shipboard mechanical refrigeration of mutton and lamb in the 1880s. Staples also had to be packaged, presented, and timed in the way the market wanted them. Londoners expected New Zealand spring lamb to arrive in their spring, not New Zealand's.[38] Canada produced "Cheddar" cheese and "Wiltshire" bacon for the British market.[39]

A core feature of export rescue was the conquest of distance. Booms bequeathed an excess of rail routes and shipping lines. After the bust, rail and shipping companies engaged in cutthroat cost-cutting, which typically halved freight rates. Examples include steamboats on the Mississippi after the bust of 1837, railroads in the United States after the busts of 1873 and 1893, and ocean shipping after the Australian busts of 1842 and 1891. This tendency combined with technical developments, such as improvements in hulls and engines, which enabled steamships to burgeon in size. The links between frontier and metropolis thickened into a virtual bridge, permitting a new order of mass transfer. London and New York were the biggest cities in the world in 1900 partly because of the new far-flung virtual hinterlands provided by explosive settlement and export rescue. They were not looking out west merely for luxury or discretionary foods, or for top-ups in years of bad harvests, but literally for daily bread—and meat. The supply had to be completely reliable and intimately attuned to demand. The two ends of the system had to dovetail perfectly, like the two halves of a neatly broken glass. As various American founding fathers had predicted when they spoke of the "cement of interest" reinforcing the bonds of union, economic integration facilitated other forms of integration and vice versa. But such bonds could stretch over the Atlantic, the Pacific, and the Urals as well as over the Appalachians. Vast and regular staples exports, and reverse flows of print and manufactures, linked Britain quite tightly to its fragmented West, creating an informal but real "Greater Britain," circa 1850–1950. Its dominion denizens believed they were co-owners of the British Empire, not mere subjects, and their high living standards and easy access to London money, job, and food markets suggest they had a point.

How have historians handled explosive settlement and its strange rhythm? Economic historians, notably Simon Kuznets, have long noted the "cyclical" character of development in the American West. Kuznets suggested the pattern echoed that of well-attested three- to four-year business cycles, but on a larger scale and a longer time frame of fifteen to twenty-five years, which accords well with our rhythm of settlement. Supply and demand chased each other's tails, but it was the supply and demand of capital infrastructure, such as rail-building, not consumer goods as with short business cycles. Booms occurred as the supply of these expensive items strove to catch up with demand. Busts occurred when supply overshot demand— something that happened easily when construction projects could take five years or more. But Kuznets believed that his cycles began in the 1840s and were restricted to the United States, and he had little to say about either causation or export rescue. Other scholars did address exports, most notably the Canadian economist Harold Innis, a founder of the "staples thesis."[40] The essence of the thesis is that economic development in settler societies was driven by the export of one or two staple commodities to the metropolis. Exports varied in their "linkage effects"—their propensity to generate spin-offs in the economy at large, such as industrialization and urbanization. If linkages were poor, as in the fur trade and the cod trade, there was little such development in the settler society. If they were good, as in the wheat and meat trades, there was a lot. But staples approaches have little to say about booms and busts. Both cycles and staples approaches are helpful on one or two steps in the rhythm of settlement, but neither tells us much about all three or, therefore, about the rhythm itself.

Social historians of settler societies often mention booms and busts but do not define them consistently or recognize their full effects or overall rhythm, and they tend in general to sideline economic history. Recent decades have witnessed welcome developments in the historiography of the biggest west, the American. A series of "new western" historians, whether "regionalists" emphasizing place or "neo-Turnerians" emphasizing process, have shown that the U.S. West was not populated solely by white males. In some cases they have also transcended American exceptionalism and compared their frontier with others. Some particularly exciting studies, by the likes of William Cronon, Richard White, Elliott West, and the remarkable historical geographer D. W. Meinig, take a rich cross-disciplinary "ecological" approach and have even ventured into economic history, which is in fact too important to be left solely to economists.[41] Yet it seems that even these scholars are still a little deficient in the rhythm section. Booms, busts, export rescues, and the sequence and resonances of all three, under these names or others, do not feature as much as they should.

The rhythm of settlement matters, even to noneconomic historians, because booms, busts, and export rescues were not solely matters of economics; they had major effects on society, culture, ethnicity and gender. During booms, for example, town and farm sectors were joined by a camp sector, housing the wandering single men who staffed the progress industry: lumbermen, navvies, miners, soldiers, boatmen, and the like. These people had their own rowdy and volatile but not wholly disorderly subculture, which I have described elsewhere as "crew culture."[42] After busts, the relative importance of crews diminished, and they tended to be reined in by social evangelist causes such as temperance movements, which themselves were motivated partly by a bust-induced sense of sin. Another example of the noneconomic impact of booms involves the implications they had for indigenous peoples. A surprisingly wide range of tribal peoples adapted quite well to normal European settlement, either interacting with it or resisting on the basis of some parity. Their autonomy tended to end when booms came along. The Sioux, Comanche, Modoc, and Nez Perce of the United States, the Métis of Canada, the Maori of New Zealand, the Aboriginals of Tasmania and Queensland, the Xhosa of South Africa, the Araucanians of the Argentine Pampas are all cases in point. These peoples could handle normal European settlement. It was *explosive* settlement that proved too much for them, and to underestimate the human tsunami they faced does their resistance less than justice. Histories of settler societies and their indigenous rivals that ignore boom, bust, and export rescue are like histories of sailing without the wind or of farming history without seasons.

Recognizing the rhythm of settlement is important because it can recontextualize the history of nineteenth-century settlement and help us understand *how* explosive settlement occurred. It does not tell us *why*. Why did long-range settlement quite suddenly change gear around 1815? Why did it take the form of spasmodic rounds of boom, bust, and export rescue? Why did it begin in Anglophone North America and continue to be Anglo-*prone,* though not exclusively Anglophone? Half a short essay cannot answer such questions comprehensively. What we can do, however, is briefly consider a trio of the more obvious causal factors, namely, institutions, staples exports, and industrialization, and then add another trio of less obvious factors to the mix.

Before addressing possible explanations, we need to confront the perils of Anglocentrism on the one hand and the hard fact that explosive settlement does appear to have favored Anglophones on the other. Past generations of British and American writers indulged themselves in triumphalist trans-Atlantic explanations of success in settlement, as in other things. Such explanations ranged from racial Anglo-Saxonism to Churchillian celebrations of the English-speaking peoples and can no longer be taken seriously. Yet, while explosive settlement was by no means exclusively Anglophone, it was Anglo-prone. Individual Siberian and Argentine booms and busts were fully equal to Anglophone ones, and until 1917 so was Siberian "export rescue." Millions of tons of wheat and butter were pumped into industrializing St. Petersburg around 1914 in much the same way as the American West fed New York and the British dominions fed London. As an "adopted dominion," Argentina also fed London until the Ottawa Agreement of 1933 revealed that it was a Cinderella in the dominion sisterhood. But the Argentine and Siberian booms started later and there were fewer of them than the Anglo ones, while their "export rescues" ended earlier. We need explanations that neither deny nor exaggerate nor celebrate the prominent Anglophone role in the nineteenth-century settler explosion.

Institutional explanations are especially vulnerable to tarring with the brush of Anglocentrism, and a few may deserve it. On the whole, however, we need to take seriously the possibility that a peculiarly growth-prone set of institutions emerged in Britain and was successfully transferred to its settlement colonies. The package would include the common law, with its protection of property rights, the recovery of debt, and eventually patent law; representative government, which even with limited male suffrage diminished autocracy, increased consent, and allowed for the co-option of emerging groups; and perhaps nonconformist Protestantism, which had an unusual savings ethic, if not a work ethic, and which was more cellular and reproducible in organization than either Catholicism or Anglicanism. One might add the propensity of English settlement to "clone" into small new autonomous polities rather than to extend large old ones. Without necessarily accepting the argument that English expansion was intrinsically less change-averse than Spanish expansion,[43] there is a clear and early structural difference between the two. Spanish America was centralized into two and later three great vice-regalities; English settlement was highly decentralized into dozens of colonies. Thus representative government had more play, while relatively easy access to freehold land expanded suffrage based on land ownership. In the nineteenth century, decentralization enabled newly autonomous territories, states, and colonies to borrow for their own development and gave them a separate brand to boost. Institutions may well have mattered; the question is how much. Again, we cannot answer this question here, but we can short-circuit it by appealing to the non-Anglo Wests. No one has yet accused late nineteenth-century Tsarist Russia of a sudden injection of common law, representative government, Protestantism, or regional autonomy, let alone all four. English institutions may have helped to better convert booms and export rescue into long-term stability and prosperity. But they cannot explain the settler explosion itself.

Another explanation is implicit in the staples thesis. After 1815, demand for staple commodities was boosted by industrialization and urbanization in Britain and the American Northeast. Noticing this, the staples thesis would argue, rational settlers and investors poured themselves and their money into the Anglo-Wests to provide the needed staples. Staples exports were obviously crucial to export rescue. But the notion that booms were the planned development phase of staples exporting presents some problems. For one thing, export rescues were more often than not dependent on technical innovations and changes in metropolitan demand that must have been hard to predict. Is it really conceivable that the settlers who surged into the Old Northwest from 1815 predicted the decline of wheat production in their Northeastern metropolis, the mass advent first of canals and then of railroads that linked them to it, and the advent of silos and elevators that lubricated the links? Did they predict the British repeal of the Corn Laws in 1846 that gave them an important supplementary market? In fact, boom-phase farmers usually did not worry much about exports because the dynamic local market made that concern unnecessary. The bust stimulated desperate experimentation and innovation that ultimately facilitated export rescue. Thus booms created busts, which stimulated export rescue. Exports, or the planned prospect of them, seldom drove booms, with the possible exception of cotton in America's Old Southwest. Busts themselves are another problem for notions of the rational pursuit of staples exports. Exports rescued settler economies as a whole, but not before busts wiped out up to half of all boom-time farms and businesses. Settler economies were built on layers of fiscal corpses, resembling coral insects more than rational actors.

A more promising explanation for the nineteenth-century settler explosion is the intersection of vast, potentially rich frontiers and the Industrial Revolution. This caters well for the Anglophone bias of the explosion and its non-Anglo latecomers. Russia and Spanish America had vast frontiers but not early Industrial Revolutions. France and Belgium had early Industrial Revolutions but not vast frontiers. Only the Anglophones had both. From the 1870s in Argentina, and from the 1880s in Siberia, industrial transport technology in the form of rail enabled these areas to explode too. History being an irritating beast, this neat explanation does not quite work. The beginning of the settler explosion clearly predates the first mass advent of rail in the West—in the Old Northwest in the 1850s. At first sight, one can rescue the industrialization hypothesis by turning from rail to steamboats. Steamers first appeared on the Mississippi and the St. Lawrence around 1815, when the settler explosion began, and their potential effect was considerable. Before steam, navigable rivers were largely one-way highways; upriver navigation against the current was very difficult. Steamers made rivers two-way, permitting easy ingress as well as egress, and opening up vast tracts of land around navigable waterways that had hitherto been inaccessible, at least to high-volume inflows. Inland expansion became possible, and the advent of rail from the 1850s only freed it from dependence on waterways.

The timing is almost right, but not quite. Three steamboats were operating out of New Orleans by 1815, but the first steamer did not reach St. Louis until August 1817, when that town was already booming.[44] "Prior to 1817 no steamboat had conclusively demonstrated the practicability of upstream navigation."[45] Early vessels had weak engines and were prone to grounding and accident. Steamboats had become the key to the Mississippi transport system by the mid-1820s, and arguably by 1818, but they had not done so by 1815, when the boom began. The story in Canada and Australia is similar. Steamers appeared on the St. Lawrence as early as 1809, but they were novelties for several years and did not make it to Lake Ontario until 1817, and then only as a promise of things to come. "Although steamboats had plied Lake Ontario since 1817, it was not until the mid-1820s that the lake was reliably serviced by some five to six boats."[46] Again, steamers arrived in Australia during its first boom, in 1831, but not at the beginning of it, in 1828, and in numbers too small (six by 1839) to have much effect anyway.[47] Steam transport was a factor in triggering later booms and was also crucial to some export rescues, but it is not the explanation for the earliest settler booms. Industrialization supercharged the settler explosion but did not cause it.

What did cause the settler explosion? Here, my attempt at an answer must remain brief, partial, and tentative. It posits the interaction of three shifts, each beginning around 1815. The first, the *Peace Bonus* of 1815, was a transitional moment in geopolitics, coming with the end of the Napoleonic Wars and coinciding with the end of four decades of British-American hostility. The second was the *rise of mass transfer*, a shift as much in *non*industrial as in industrial technology. The third was a *settler transition*, an upturn in the image of emigration in Britain and the United States.

For Europe and its offshoots, 1815 marked the end of 125 years of endemic warfare. The devastating French Revolutionary and Napoleonic Wars of the last quarter-century happened to have some positive effects for the English speakers. In the United States, the wars proved a boost to Northeastern proto-industrialization, fiscal institutions, and international trade. In Britain, they consolidated the leadership of European industrialization and left the country mistress of the seas. War also prompted the birth of intercontinental *mass* transfer, a development that was initially quite independent of industrialization. In 1808, Napoleon's "Continental Blockade" closed the Baltic to British trade, cutting off Britain's main source of timber. Britain turned to its North American colonies for alternative supplies. Between 1805 and 1812, New Brunswick's timber exports shot up from 5,000 to 100,000 tons. The new trade not only survived the Peace in 1815 but also profited from it. By 1819, the flow of timber to Britain weighed 240,000 tons[48]—more than the total flow of all goods from all of North America a few decades earlier—all without a steamship in sight. As generations of Canadian scholars have noted, empty timber ships returning to North America reduced the cost and difficulty of emigration.

The Peace of 1815 itself gave a further boost to mass transfer. Before 1815, merchant ships had to carry heavy guns as defense against privateers, numerous crews to work them, and costly insurance. After 1815, these costs suddenly dropped dramatically, as did the cost of shipbuilding.[49] The ancient technology of wind-powered ships also improved greatly from about 1815. Regular commercial packet services began in 1818, between New York and London, and packet ships continued to grow in size and numbers.[50] Big, fast sailing clippers were developed by the Americans in the 1840s but were also used by the British. In 1852, a 1,625-ton clipper carrying 960 emigrants made the trip between Britain and Melbourne in sixty-eight days.[51] The worldwide long-range shipment of goods may have amounted to a million tons annually in 1790. By 1840, it had reached 20 million tons.[52] The Anglophones had more than their fair share of the newly augmented but still sail-dominated sea lanes. The British merchant fleet was the world's largest throughout the nineteenth century and, until their Civil War, the Americans' fleet was second.[53]

Transport arteries burgeoned inland as well as on the oceans, using nonindustrial as well as industrial technology. Replacing a mere trail with even a modest road allowed the replacement of oxen with more efficient horses. Replacing modest roads with good roads halved the traveling time of coaches and doubled the loads of wagons.[54] "Turnpike mania," the rapid building of good quality toll-roads, swept the United States in the early nineteenth century. Turnpikes cost Americans $24.5 million between 1800 and 1830, dwarfing previous expenditures on roads.[55] The British West also spent heavily on roads and bridges—£4.8 million in Victoria alone between 1851 and 1861.[56] Water carriage remained best for bulk, however. New York's famous Erie Canal linked the Atlantic to the Great Lakes in 1825. The Erie became famous as an outlet for Western produce, but for its first seventeen years its primary importance to the West was as a new inlet for goods and people.[57] Various Canadian canals performed the same service. These developments surrounded eastern North America with a great circle of water transport. It was advances in water transportation, at least as much as the good old covered wagon, which opened up the American Midwest. In southeastern Australia and New Zealand, with their islands and indented coastlines, the sea served as internal transport as well as long-range link. The default highway was the beach. The forgotten role of the non-industrial revolution extended still further, beyond the 1815–1840s period. On the exploding frontiers, lumber was moved by gargantuan river rafts of up to twelve acres in extent, and by huge timber dams that used the pent force of water to wash along 10,000 logs. Horses, as we have seen, powered much of the settler explosion, and, as was true of machine technology, their quality as well as their quantity improved over time. Selective breeding meant that American draft horses were 50% bigger in 1890 than in 1860.[58]

Comparable improvements took place from about 1815 in the mass transfer of information and money. Banks proliferated on both sides of the Atlantic, both sides of the Appalachians, and in Australia from the 1820s.[59] There was a shift in lending practices. "While the older more conservative banks confined their loans to short-term commercial ventures . . . the newer banks made short-term loans for long-term investment with the expectation that they would be renewed indefinitely."[60] British overseas investment grew explosively, as did Northeastern investment in the West. One could date the first mass migration of money to 1816. In that single year total British overseas investment is calculated to have increased 150%.[61] Between 1775 and 1815, American Western settlement was not consistently reinforced by British migrants, goods, and money. This changed after 1815, marking a neglected but important shift. Majority literacy emerged on both sides of the Atlantic, postal services proliferated, and printed material burgeoned and became cheaper—in this case with some help from industrial technology.[62] Of 3,168 newspapers in the world in 1828, about half were in English.[63] The average circulation of newspapers per capita in the United States rose from one in 1790 to eleven in 1840.[64] In 1810, about 21 million individual newspapers a year were produced in the British Isles; and roughly the same number in the United States. By 1821, the figures were 56 million and 80 million, respectively.[65] In 1840, Britain had 2.5 times as many post offices as France, and the United States five times as many.[66]

Lewis Mumford's well-worn classification of technologies helps place these changes, nonindustrial as well as industrial, in their context. He posits three successive suites of modern technologies: eighteenth-century eotechnic—water, wind, wood, and work animals; nineteenth-century paleotechnic—steam, coal, iron, and rail; and twentieth-century neotechnic—petroleum, steel, electricity, and automobiles.[67] We tend to assume that each new stage displaced the other, and it is true that the neotechnic largely replaced the paleotechnic in the twentieth century. But the paleotechnic did not *replace* the eotechnic in the nineteenth. The two actually flowered together, and they did so most on settler frontiers. Here, the abundance of land, wood, water, wind, and work animals created a *non*-industrial revolution, which coexisted with the transfer of the industrial one. The use of two full suites of technology, eotechnic and paleotechnic, doubled the action.

This eotechnic and Anglo-prone rise of mass transfer was accompanied by a great shift in attitudes to emigration, helped by the explosion of print. Before about 1800, Anglophones on both sides of the Atlantic tended to see long-range migration as the last resort of the desperate. This attitude is well attested for Britain and is generally believed to have been overcome by a "revolution in colonial thought" around 1830 associated with the settlement evangelist Edward Gibbon Wakefield. Given the prominence of the frontiersman as an American archetype, it is surprising to find that negative attitudes to long-range settlement were also quite prominent in the United States. American officials in the 1780s and 1790s repeatedly referred to early Western settlers as "semi-savages," "lawless banditti and adventurers,"[68] "banditti whose actions are a disgrace to human nature." "The most abandoned, malicious, deceitful, plundering, horse-thieving rascals on the continent . . . the most vile and abandoned criminals."[69] The west was "a grand reservoir for the scum of the Atlantic states." As late as the 1820s, it was said that "the people of the Atlantic States have not yet recovered from the horror inspired by the term backwoodsman."[70] Well into the nineteenth century, "eastern fears of regression to primitivism among western settlers" remained "strong enough to stimulate missions, and the formation of Bible and tract societies, and other efforts to reclaim the migrants for a decent Christian order."[71]

Negative images of emigration were transformed into positive ones, not by Wakefield in 1830, but by a much broader trans-Atlantic ideological transition around 1815. Its semiotic shape was the partial displacement of the word "emigrant" by more positively loaded words. According to David Hackett Fischer and James C. Kelly, "before 1790, Americans thought of themselves as *emigrants,* not *immigrants.* The word immigrant was an Americanism probably invented in that year. It had entered common usage by 1820." Related terms also emerged in the 1810s. "*Pioneer* in the western sense first appeared in 1817"; "Words such as *mover* (1810), *moving wagons* (1817), *relocate* (1814), even the verb *to move* in its present migratory sense, date from this period." This was indeed a "radical transformation . . . a new language of migration."[72] But Fischer and Kelly fail to note that it was not solely American and that *settler,* not *immigrant* or *pioneer,* was its main manifestation. In Britain, *settler* was used in its current meaning at least as far back as the seventeenth century, but it was used infrequently. By the early nineteenth century, it had connotations of a higher status than "emigrant." Settlers were distinct from sojourners, slaves, or convict emigrants, and initially even from lower-class free emigrants. In Australia, "'Settlers' were men of capital and, in the 1820s, regarded as the true colonists, to be distinguished from mere laboring 'immigrant' . . . though eventually all Australia's immigrants were termed 'settlers.'"[73]

The contest between "settler" and "emigrant" can be traced through the fully searchable newspaper databases such as that of the *Times* of

London. The *Times,* of course, was an elite newspaper. But it did seek to use the conceptual language of its large number of readers and to speak the jargon of current public discourse. "Settler" was used very rarely in the *Times* before 1810, but the term surged thereafter to between half and two-thirds of "emigrant" usage, where it remained. *Blackwood's Edinburgh Magazine,* which is fully searchable between 1843 and 1863, used "emigrant" and "settler" equally in these years (124 usages to 126).[74] No long-running serial database equivalent to the *Times* seems to be available for the Unites States before 1851, and change over time is less easy to trace. But the *Plattsburgh Republican* of upstate New York used "settler" 2.5 times as often as it used "emigrant" between 1811 and 1820.[75] The massive "Making of America" database, consisting of 9,612 books and 2,457 volumes of journals published throughout the nineteenth century in the United States, features about 40,000 usages of "settlers," 18,500 of "emigrants," and only 7,500 of "immigrants." This "settler transition" was not primarily a matter of nationalism. British boosters begged prospective migrants to go to the settlement colonies rather than the United States, but without much success. The United States was the main destination for British immigrants, let alone Irish, for most of the nineteenth century. Americans returned the favor in the 1810s and 1900s by emigrating to Canada. Settler status was more a matter of virtual metropolitan standing, as a full citizen of a first-world society. But shared language and shared notions of racial kinship clearly did help enable British and American "invisible immigrants" to merge into each other's societies with "scarcely a ripple."[76] To some extent, settlement in the two Anglophone societies was mutually reinforcing.

Argentina and Siberia also benefited from the nonindustrial, eotechnic, revolution but, because they exploded late, industrial technology in the form of steam transport was a more important boomstarter. Did they, too, experience a settler transition? The evidence for Argentina is mixed. Between 1890 and 1914, 1.25 million Spanish migrated to Argentina, of whom 37% returned home. Initially, Argentina was surprisingly hostile to this immigration, which tended to be from Galicia rather than Andalusia, home of the original Argentine settlers. But at least rhetorically, Argentines began embracing the Spanish as kin from the 1880s, and Spanish immigration mounted— making a case for a settler transition. On the other hand, 1.5 million Italians entered during the period, of whom 55% returned home. Neither Spanish nor Italian immigrants took up Argentine citizenship: "only 2 per cent of all immigrants were naturalized between 1870 and 1920."[77] This suggests a "sojourner ethos" rather than a "settler ethos."

The signs of a settler transition for Siberia are stronger. For much of the nineteenth century, Siberia was seen as "a domain of eternal wind storms and snow . . . a dank and barren land, with gloomy penal mines."[78] In the 1880s, government policy toward the settlement of Siberia changed from vacillation to consistent support. The state distributed a vast mass of booster literature, aimed at the peasants of European Russia, who were experiencing a sharp upturn in literacy. Private merchants began flooding into Siberia, to the tune of 8,000 by 1897.[79] Oral peasant folk culture now depicted Siberia "as a place of utopian freedom *(volia)* and abundance *(privol'e),* where peasants got away from the world of lords and scarcity and lived as they were supposed to." There is a striking similarity to Anglophone folk images of settlement earlier in the century, right down to an emphasis on natural abundance. Siberian land was so fertile that wheat grew "taller than a man's head," and berries were "so plentiful . . . that a bucket tied to the neck of a grazing cow would fill up on its own."[80] Just as American Westerners saw themselves as Better Americans, and the denizens of the Dominions saw themselves as Better Britons, Siberians saw themselves not only as Russians but as Better Russians. They were considered to be healthier, tougher, more self-reliant, and more egalitarian than the metropolitan version. Where have we heard this before?

The settler transition was part of a wider nineteenth-century Anglophone ideological shift that can scarcely be touched on here. Historians of Protestantism posit a turn from Calvinist predestination to

Arminian self-determination at around the same time. The period also witnessed the rise of Methodism on both sides of the Atlantic, and Methodists were often leaders of Anglophone migrations. In secular ideology, this was the period in which finite notions of Progress, whereby even the greatest empires fell as well as rose, were replaced by ideas of Infinite Progress, in which the Fall need never come. For individuals, change ceased to be something rare and usually negative, and became common and often positive. The period also witnessed the rise of evangelism, socialism, and racialism, as well as "settlerism." As emigration lost its stigma, it became more imaginable, and it became more practicable with the rise of mass transfer, triggered by the geopolitics of 1808–1815 and supercharged by industrial technology. Other European and Asian peoples moved by the millions in the nineteenth century, but they did so later and less permanently than the Anglophones, and they often went to regions that were culturally alien. Argentina and Siberia demonstrate that Wests did not have to speak English to explode, but, especially before the 1870s, it did help.

Both the rise of mass transfer and the settler transition were part of a particular, as well as a general, phenomenon. The broad upturn in mass transfer dates from about 1815, but there was also a series of specific surges, enhancing flows of people, information, or money to particular frontiers at particular times, thereby sparking booms. Two examples are the completion of the Erie Canal in 1825 and the arrival of banks in Tasmania at about the same time. The settler transition also was both general and particular. It involved a general improvement in the image of emigration and conversions of particular frontiers from hell to heaven on earth in the minds of prospective migrants and investors, itself a potential trigger for a boom. The harsh, alien, convict-ridden climes of Australia and Siberia; the Cannibal Isles of New Zealand; the "Great American Desert" of the American West; the frozen wastes of western Canada; and the wild "Desert" of the Argentine Pampas, haunted by lethal Indian lancers— all were ideologically transubstantiated into promised lands. Ideology joined technology in generating explosive settlement.

## NOTES

Portions of this chapter appeared in different form in James Belich, *Replenishing the Earth: The Settler Revolution and the Rise of the Anglo-World*, published by Oxford University Press, 2009, used here by permission of Oxford University Press, Inc.

1. Margaret Walsh, *The American West: Visions and Revisions* (New York, 2005), p. 46.
2. This, and all statistics unless otherwise specified, are from the various volumes of B. R. Mitchell's magisterial *International Historical Statistics*, 4th ed., 3 vols. (London, 1998).
3. Peter Bakewell, *A History of Latin America: Empires and Sequels, 1450–1930* (Oxford, 1997), p. 460.
4. Rory Miller, *Britain and Latin America in the 19th and 20th Centuries* (London, 1993), pp. 106–107; Alistair Hennessy and John King, eds., *The Land that England Lost: Argentina and Britain, a Special Relationship* (London, 1992); Donald C. Castro, *The Development and Politics of Argentine Immigration Policy, 1852–1914: To Govern Is to Populate* (San Francisco, 1991); Jose C. Moya, *Cousins and Strangers: Spanish Immigrants in Buenos Aires, 1850–1930* (Berkeley, CA, 1998). On the economic growth of Argentina see Jeremy Adelman, *Frontier Development: Land, Labor, and Capital on the Wheatlands of Argentina and Canada, 1890–1914* (New York, 1994); Samuel Amaral, *The Rise of Capitalism on the Pampas: The Estancias of Buenos Aires* (Cambridge, 1997); Alan M. Taylor, "Peopling the Pampa: On the Impact of Mass Migration to the River Plate, 1870–1914," *Explorations in Economic History* 34 (1997): 100–132; Gerardo della Paolera and Alan M. Taylor, eds., *A New Economic History of Argentina* (New York, 2003).
5. D. C. M. Platt, "Canada and Argentina: The First Preference of the British Investor," *Journal of Imperial and Commonwealth History* 123 (1985): 77–92.
6. Nicolas Spulber, *Russia's Economic Transitions: From Late Tsarism to the New Millennium* (New York, 2003), p. 7. Also see Igor V. Naumov, *The History of Siberia*, ed. David N. Collins (London, 2006); Steven G. Marks, *Road to Power: The Trans-Siberian Railway and the Colonization of Asian Russia, 1850–1917* (Ithaca, NY, 1991); Alan Wood, ed., *The History of Siberia: From Russian Conquest to Revolution* (London, 1991); James Forsyth, *A History of the Peoples of Siberia: Russia's North Asian Colony 1581–1990* (New York, 1992).

7. T. S. Fedor, *Patterns of Urban Growth in the Russian Empire during the 19th Century* (Chicago, 1975); John Foster Fraser, *The Real Siberia, Together with an Account of a Dash through Manchuria* (London, 1902), pp. 85–87, 38; Mark Gamsa, "California on the Amur, or the 'Zheltuga Republic' in Manchuria (1883–1886)," *Slavonic and Eastern European Review* 81 (2003): 236–266; Eva-Maria Stolberg, "The Siberian Frontier between 'White Mission' and 'Yellow Peril,' 1890s–1920s," *Nationalities Papers* 32 (2004): 165–181.

8. J. P. Baughman, "The Evolution of Rail-Water Systems of Transportation in the Gulf Southwest 1826–1890," *Journal of Southern History* 34 (1968): 357–381; Annie Germain and Damaris Rose, *Montreal: The Quest for a Metropolis* (Chichester, 2000), p. 24.

9. For a fuller description of a particular "progress industry," see James Belich, *Making Peoples: A History of the New Zealanders from Polynesian First Settlement to the End of the 19th Century* (Auckland, 1996), chapter 14.

10. Harry N. Scheiber, *Ohio Canal Era: A Case Study of Government and the Economy, 1820–1861* (Athens, Ohio, 1969), pp. 121–123.

11. Alejandro Bendana, *British Capital and Argentine Dependence, 1816–1914* (New York, 1988), pp. 161, 143.

12. Douglas McCalla, *Planting the Province: The Economic History of Upper Canada, 1784–1870* (Toronto, 1993), p. 207.

13. Leonid M. Goryushkin, "The Economic Development of Siberia in the Late 19th and Early 20th Centuries," *Sibirica* 2 (2002): 12–20.

14. G. R. Hawke, *The Making of New Zealand: An Economic History* (Cambridge, 1985), pp. 68–69.

15. E. A. Boehm, *Prosperity and Depression in Australia, 1887–1897* (Oxford, 1971), p. 138.

16. J. S. Holliday, *Rush for Riches: Gold Fever and the Making of California* (Berkeley, CA, 1999), p. 183.

17. By J. G. Smith, cited in Frederick H. Armstrong, *City in the Making: Progress, People and Perils in Victorian Toronto* (Toronto, 1988), p. 253; Rollo Arnold, *New Zealand's Burning: The Settlers' World in the Mid-1880s* (Wellington, New Zealand, 1994); W. Bruce Lincoln, *The Conquest of a Continent: Siberia and the Russians* (Ithaca, NY, 1994), p. 263.

18. Michael Williams, *Americans and Their Forests: A Historical Geography* (New York, 1989), p. 156.

19. David E. Nye, *America as Second Creation: Technology and Narratives of New Beginnings* (Cambridge, MA, 2003), p. 193; Williams, *Americans and Their Forests*, pp. 344–347, 354.

20. Lance E. Davis and Robert E. Gallman, "Capital Formation in the United States during the Nineteenth Century," in Peter Mathias and M. M. Postan, eds., *The Cambridge Economic History of Europe* (Cambridge, 1978), p. 56.

21. Glen McLaren, *Big Mobs: The Story of Australian Cattlemen* (Fremantle, Australia, 2000), p. 115; Malcolm J. Kennedy, *Hauling the Loads: A History of Australia's Working Horses and Bullocks* (Melbourne, 1992), p. 67.

22. F. M. L. Thompson, "Nineteenth-Century Horse Sense," *Economic History Review*, new series, 29 (1976): 60–81.

23. R. B. Lamb, *The Mule in Southern Agriculture* (Berkeley, CA, 1963).

24. Fraser, *The Real Siberia*, p. 50; Roy Hora, *The Landowners of the Argentine Pampas: A Social and Political History, 1860–1945* (Oxford, 2001), pp. 59–60.

25. For an Australian example of such debates see Philip McMichael, *Settlers and the Agrarian Question: Foundations of Capitalism in Colonial Australia* (New York, 1984), pp. 175–180, and Barrie Dyster, "The 1840s Depression Revisited," *Australian Historical Studies* 25 (1993): 589–607. For a New Zealand example see James Belich, *Paradise Reforged: A History of the New Zealanders from the 1880s to the Year 2000* (Auckland, New Zealand, 2001), pp. 32–38. For a U.S. example, see Charles W. Calomiris and Larry Schweikart, "The Panic of 1857: Origins, Transmission, and Containment," *Journal of Economic History* 51 (1991): 807–834.

26. Douglas E. Booth, "Transportation, City Building, and Financial Crisis: Milwaukee, 1852–1868," *Journal of Urban History* 9 (1983): 335–363.

27. Thomas Cochran, *Frontiers of Change: Early Industrialization in America* (New York, 1981), p. 31.

28. S. J. Butlin, "British Banking in Australia," *Royal Australian Historical Society Journal and Proceeding* 49 (1963): 81–99.

29. Caroll Van West, *Capitalism on the Frontier: Billings and the Yellowstone Valley in the 19th Century* (Lincoln, NE, 1993), p. 196.

30. Quoted in Henry Slater, "Land, Labour and Capital in Natal: The Natal Land and Colonisation Company, 1860–1948," *Journal of African History* 16 (1975): 257–283.

31. Lance E. Davis and Robert E. Gallman, *Evolving Financial Markets and International Capital Flows: Britain, the Americas, and Australia, 1865–1914* (Cambridge, 2001), pp. 653–654; Donna J. Guy, "Dependency, the Credit Market, and Argentine Industrialization, 1860–1940," *Business History Review* 58 (1984): 532–561.

32. Goryushkin, "The Economic Development of Siberia."

33. Allan G. Bogue, "Farming in the Prairie Peninsula, 1830–1890," *Journal of Economic History* 23 (1963): 3–29.
34. T. W. Acheson, "The 1840s: Decade of Tribulation," in Phillip A. Buckner and John G. Reid, eds., *The Atlantic Region to Confederation. A History* (Toronto, 1994), p. 311.
35. Glen S. Dumke, *The Boom of the Eighties in Southern California* (San Marino, CA, 1944), p. 175.
36. Darrel E. Bigham, *Towns and Villages of the Lower Ohio* (Lexington, KY, 1998), p. 4; David McGill, *Ghost Towns of New Zealand* (Wellington, New Zealand, 1980).
37. D. L. Burn, "Canada and the Repeal of the Corn Laws," *Cambridge Historical Journal* 2 (1929): 252–272.
38. Belich, *Paradise Reforged,* chapter 2.
39. Robert Ankli, "Ontario's Dairy Industry, 1880–1920," *Canadian Papers in Rural History* 8 (1992): 261–275; Derrick Rixson, *The History of Meat Trading* (Nottingham, UK, 2000), p. 264.
40. Harold Innis, *Staples, Markets and Cultural Change: Selected Essays,* ed. Daniel Drache (Montreal, 1995).
41. Richard White, *"It's Your Misfortune and None of My Own": A History of the American West* (Norman, OK, 1991); Elliott West, *The Contested Plains: Indians, Goldseekers, & the Rush to Colorado* (Lawrence, KS, 1998); D. W. Meinig, *The Shaping of America: A Geographical Perspective on 500 Years of History,* 4 vols. (New Haven, CT, 1986–2004); William Cronon, *Nature's Metropolis: Chicago and the Great West* (New York, 1991).
42. Belich, *Making Peoples,* chapter 16.
43. Claudio Veliz, *The New World of the Gothic Fox: Culture and Economy in English and Spanish America* (Berkeley, CA, 1994); J. V. Fifer, *The Master Builders: Structures of Empire in the New World* (Durham, UK, 1996); J. H. Elliott, *Empires of the Atlantic World: Britain and Spain in America, 1492–1830* (New Haven, CT, 2006), e.g., p. 206.
44. Wallace Carson, "Transportation and Traffic on the Ohio and Mississippi before the Steamboat," *Mississippi Valley Historical Review* 7 (1920): 26–38; Jeffrey S. Adler, *Yankee Merchants and the Making of the Urban West: The Rise and Fall of Antebellum St. Louis* (New York, 1991), p. 23.
45. W. J. Petersen, *Steamboating on the Upper Mississippi* (Iowa City, 1937), p. 73.
46. Peter Baskerville, "Donald Bethune's Steamboat Business: A Study of Upper Canadian Commercial and Financial Practice," *Ontario History* 67, no. 3 (1975): 135–149; Gerald Tulchinsky, *The River Barons: Montreal Businessmen*

*and the Growth of Industry and Transportation, 1837–1853* (Toronto, 1977), p. 38. Also see R. F. Palmer, "First Steamboat on the Great Lakes," *Inland Seas* 44 (1988): 7–20, and Walter Lewis, "The First Generation of Marine Engines in Central Canadian Steamers, 1809–1837," *The Northern Mariner* 7 (1997): 1–30.

47. Edgar Dunsdorfs, *The Australian Wheat-Growing Industry, 1788–1948* (Melbourne, 1956), p. 69. Also see Frank Broeze, "Distance Tamed: Steam Navigation to Australia and New Zealand from Its Beginnings to the Outbreak of the Great War," *Journal of Transport History* 10 (1989): 1–21.

48. Graeme Wynn, *Timber Colony: A Historical Geography of Early 19th-Century New Brunswick* (Toronto, 1981), p. 33.

49. Ronald Hope, *A New History of British Shipping* (London, 1990), pp. 261–263; James Watt, "The Influence of Nutrition upon Achievement in Maritime History," in Catherine Geissler and Derek J. Oddy, eds., *Food, Diet and Economic Change Past and Present* (Leicester, UK, 1993), p. 77.

50. Yrjo Kaukiainen, "Shrinking the World: Improvements in the Speed of Information Transmission, c. 1820–1870," *European Review of Economic History* 5 (2001): 1–28.

51. Eric Richards, *Britannia's Children: Emigration from England, Scotland, Wales, and Ireland since 1600* (Hambledon, UK, 2004). Also see Frank Broeze, *Island Nation: A History of Australians and the Sea* (Sydney, 1998); "British Intercontinental Shipping and Australia, 1813–1850," *Journal of Transport History* 4 (1978): 189–207; and "The Costs of Distance: Shipping and the Early Australian Economy, 1788–1850," *Economic History Review* 28 (1975): 582–597.

52. Erik Banks, *The Rise and Fall of the Merchant Banks* (London, 1999), p. 92.

53. C. E. McDowell and H. M. Gibbs, *Ocean Transportation* (New York, 1954), p. 35.

54. Dorian Gerhold, "The Growth of the London Carrying Trade, 1681–1838," *Economic History Review,* new series, 41, no. 3 (1988): 406.

55. Daniel B. Klein and John Majewski, "Turnpikes and Toll Roads in Nineteenth Century America," in EH.Net Encyclopedia, edited by Robert Whaples. February 10, 2008, http://eh.net/encyclopedia/article/Klein.Majewski.Turnpikes.

56. D. Urlich Cloher, "Integration and Communications Technology in an Emerging Urban System," *Economic Geography* 54 (1978): 1–16.

57. Ronald E. Shaw, *Erie Water West: A History of the Erie Canal* (Lexington, KY, 1990), p. 261 and passim.

58. Clay McShane and Joel Tarr, "The Decline of the Urban Horse in America," *Journal of Transport History* 24 (2003): 177–198.

59. Howard Bodenhorn, *A History of Banking in Antebellum America* (New York, 2000); Hugh Rockoff, "Banking and Finance," in Stanley L. Engerman and Robert E. Gallman, eds., *The Cambridge Economic History of the United States*, vol. 2: *The Long Nineteenth Century* (Cambridge, 2000); Davis and Gallman, "Capital Formation in the United States during the Nineteenth Century," p. 63; J. Van Fenstermaker, "The Statistics of American Commercial Banking, 1782–1818," *Journal of Economic History* 25 (1965): 400–413; Peter L. Rousseau and Richard Sylla, "Emerging Financial Markets and Early US Growth," *Explorations in Economic History* 42 (2005): 1–26; Alice Techova et al., eds., *Banking, Trade, and Industry: Europe, American and Asia from the 13th Century to the 20th Century* (Cambridge, 1997); Iain S. Black, "Money, Information and Space: Banking in Early-Nineteenth Century England and Wales," *Journal of Historical Geography* 21 (1995): 398–412; Banks, *Rise and Fall of the Merchant Banks*; Geoffrey Jones, *British Multinational Banking, 1830–1990: A History* (Oxford, 1993); Lance Davis and Robert Huttenback, *Mammon and the Pursuit of Empire: The Economics of British Imperialism*, abridged edition (Cambridge, 1988).

60. Charles Sellers, *The Market Revolution: Jacksonian America, 1815–1846* (New York, 1991), p. 135.

61. Davis and Gallman, *Evolving Financial Markets*, pp. 55, 64. For Northeastern investment in the West, see John Denis Haeger, *The Investment Frontier: New York Businessmen and the Economic Development of the Old Northwest* (Albany, NY, 1981); Naomi R. Lamoreaux, *Insider Lending: Banks, Personal Connections and Economic Development in Industrial New England* (New York, 1994); Lance E. Davis and Robert J. Cull, "International Capital Movements, Domestic Capital Markets, and American Economic Growth, 1820–1914," in Engerman and Gallman, eds., *Cambridge Economic History of the US*, vol. 2, 733–812.

62. David Vincent, *Literacy and Popular Culture in England, 1750–1914* (Cambridge, 1989) and *The Rise of Mass Literacy: Reading and Writing in Modern Europe* (Malden, MD, 2000); Jon P. Klancher, *The Making of English Reading Audiences, 1790–1832* (Madison, WI, 1987); Patricia Anderson, *The Printed Image and the Transformation of Popular Culture, 1790–1860* (Oxford, 1991); Yrjo Kaukianen, "Shrinking the World: Improvements in the Speed of Information Transmission, c. 1820–1870," *European Review of Economic History* 5 (2001): 20; Allan R. Pred, "Urban Systems Development and the

Long-Distance Flow of Information through Pre-electronic US Newspapers," *Economic Geography* 47 (1971): 498–524.

63. C. A. Bayly, *The Birth of the Modern World, 1780–1914: Global Connections and Comparisons* (Oxford, 2004), p. 19; Daniel R. Headrick, *The Tentacles of Progress: Technology Transfer in the Age of Imperialism, 1850–1940* (New York, 1988) and *When Information Came of Age: Technologies of Knowledge in the Age of Reason and Revolution, 1700–1850* (Oxford, 2000).

64. Stuart M. Blumin, "The Social Implications of US Economic Development," in Engerman and Gallman, eds., *Cambridge Economic History of the US*, vol. 2, p. 828.

65. Charles G. Steffen, "Newspapers for Free: The Economics of Newspaper Circulation in the Early Republic," *Journal of the Early Republic* 23 (2003): 381–419.

66. Headrick, *When Information Came of Age*, p. 190.

67. Lewis Mumford, *Technics and Civilization* (London, 1934), pp. 109–110.

68. Peter S. Onuf, *Statehood and the Union: A History of the Northwest Ordinance* (Bloomington, IN, 1987), pp. 1, 33; R. A. Billington, *Westward Expansion: A History of the American Frontier*, 3rd ed. (New York, 1967), p. 210. Also see Andrew R. L. Cayton, *The Frontier Republic: Ideology and Politics in the Ohio Country, 1780–1825* (Kent, Ohio, 1986), pp. 7–9.

69. Quoted in Francis S. Philbrick, *The Rise of the West* (New York, 1965), p. 357.

70. Timothy Flint, *Recollections of the Last Ten Years in the Valley of the Mississippi* (1826, reprint ed. Carbondale, IL, 1968), p. 128.

71. Stuart M. Blumin, "The Social Implications of US Economic Development," in Engerman and Gallman, eds., *Cambridge Economic History of the US*, vol. 2, p. 837.

72. David Hackett Fischer and James C. Kelly, *Away, I'm Bound Away: Virginia and the Westward Movement* (Richmond, VA, 1993).

73. Richards, *Britannia's Children*, p. 109.

74. The Times Digital Archive, 1785–1985, http://infotrac.galegroup.com.helicon.vuw.ac.nz/itw/infomark/111/1/1/purl=rc6_TTDA?sw_aep=vuw; Internet Library of Early Journals, http://www.bodley.ox.ac.uk/ilej/.

75. Northern New York Historical Newspapers, http://gethelp.library.upenn.edu/guides/hist/onlinenewspapers.html.

76. Charlotte Erickson, *Invisible Immigrants: The Adaptation of English and Scottish Immigrants in Nineteenth-Century America* (London, 1972); Randy W. Widdis, *With Scarcely a Ripple: Anglo-Canadian Migration into the United States and Western Canada, 1880–1920* (Montreal, 1998), p. 199.

77. Michael Johns, "Industrial Capital and Economic Development in Turn of the Century Argentina," *Economic Geography* 68 (1992): 188–204. Also see Adelman, *Frontier Development*, pp. 109–112; Moya, *Cousins and Strangers*.

78. Mark Bassin, "Inventing Siberia: Visions of the Russian East in the Early Nineteenth Century," *American Historical Review* 96 (1991): 763–794.

79. Boris N. Mironov, "The Development of Literacy in Russia and the USSR from the Tenth to the Twentieth Centuries," *History of Education Quarterly* 31 (1991): 229–252; V. A. Skubnevskii and I. M. Goncharov, "Siberian Merchants in the Latter Half of the Nineteenth Century," *Sibirica* 2 (2002): 21–42.

80. Willard Sunderland, "Peasant Pioneering: Russian Peasant Settlers Describe Colonization and the Eastern Frontier, 1880s–1910s," *Journal of Social History* 34 (2001): 895–922. Also see Sunderland, "Peasants on the Move: State Peasant Resettlement in Imperial Russia, 1805–1830s," *Russian Review* 52 (1993): 472–485, 478, and footnote 27, and "An Empire of Peasants . . . ," in Jane Burbank and David L. Ransel, eds., *Imperial Russia: New Histories for the Empire* (Bloomington, IN, 1998); David Moon, "Peasant Migration and the Settlement of Russia's Frontiers, 1550–1897," *Historical Journal* 40 (1997): 859–893.

# 3 Politics, Banking, and Economic Development: Evidence from New World Economies

STEPHEN HABER

This essay has a simple premise: historians, political scientists, and economists have far more to teach one another than they usually suppose. In order to illustrate how insights from economics and political science may enrich the historical enterprise, and how insights from history may enrich economics and political science, this essay focuses on a topic that is not only of interest to all three disciplines but that has obvious real-world, practical implications for social welfare—the conditions under which societies create banking systems that allocate credit to broad segments of their populations.

Economists and political scientists have long sought to understand why some countries have large banking systems that allocate credit broadly, permitting rapid growth, while other countries scarcely have any banks at all, which constrains growth and limits social mobility.[1] Some comparative data gives a sense of the vast differences across countries: in 2005, private banks made loans to firms and households that equaled 98% of gross domestic product (GDP) in Japan, 131% in Spain, and 155% in the United Kingdom; in that same year private banks allocated credit equal to only 4% of GDP in Sierra Leone, 8% in Cambodia, and 15% in Mexico.[2] Economists and political scientists have proposed various explanations to account for these divergent outcomes, but the one that has gained favor in recent years focuses on differences across countries in terms of their degree of democratic governance: more democratic institutions correlate with ease of obtaining a bank charter and fewer regulatory restrictions on the operation of banks.[3] What is not fully understood, however, are the mechanisms undergirding these correlations: why, exactly, do democracies and autocracies treat banks differently?

There are well-known limits to the causal inferences that can be drawn through econometric analysis alone—and the study of political institutions and banking is not an exception to this general rule. A more complete understanding of the mechanisms requires scholars to look in detail at how banking systems develop *over time* within cases as political institutions varied, which is to say that the comparative questions posed by political scientists and economists can be answered by employing historical evidence and narrative. But not just any historical case studies will do. Because we want to know how variance in political institutions affected the substance of bank regulatory policies, and how those regulatory policies in turn affected the size and structure of banking systems, we need to select cases that varied in terms of their political institutions over time, and we need to be able to control for the level of banking development in each case prior to the period under study. This essay therefore looks at the natural experiment created by the development of the banking systems of three New World economies, the United States, Brazil, and Mexico, during the long nineteenth century—roughly from their independence until the outbreak of World War I. All three countries began their existence as independent nations without preexisting banking systems because their colonial powers did not permit the chartering of banks. All three obtained independence within a few decades of one another, and all three new governments needed banks in order to finance their operations.

Let us be clear about what these comparisons are intended to show—and what they are not intended to show. It would take a heroic—indeed reckless—effort to show that the only dimension on which the United States, Brazil, and Mexico differed was their political institutions. The United States was far wealthier and had a more equal distribution of income than Brazil or Mexico—and those differences had an impact on the demand for credit, and hence the number and size of banks. The comparison that we are drawing is about countries against themselves over time. The United States was founded as a federal republic, but one in which suffrage was initially restricted. Over time, not only did the suffrage become broader, but the number of states in the federation grew dramatically. Brazil was founded as a constitutional monarchy but transitioned to a federal republic in which suffrage was tightly controlled. Mexico was initially constituted as a centralized monarchy, but it quickly dissolved, giving rise to decades of political anarchy. When Mexico finally achieved political stability during the last decades of the nineteenth century it was through the creation of a long-lived dictatorship.

Let us also be clear about the argument advanced in this essay. The development of banking systems that allocate credit broadly is not the product of public-spirited political elites. In all three cases under study, political elites were motivated first and foremost by the need to create stable sources of state finance—and thus the central governments of all three countries tried, at various times, to constrain the number of banks. The development of broadly based banking systems is also not a product of political elites being forced to share power with bankers: Bankers and politicians can form coalitions that provide bankers with protected markets and monopoly profits, and politicians with a stable source of state finance. A broadly based banking system, which is to say one that funds projects based on whether they offer a risk-adjusted rate of return above the cost of capital, occurs under a unique set of political conditions—and those conditions are associated with political institutions that simultaneously limit the authority and discretion of public officials, allow the users of credit the right to vote, and provide the owners of financial assets with the ability to veto the redistributionist urges of voters. Even then, there is no guarantee that coalitions will not form that work against the owners of the banks. Banking systems are, in short, fragile plants.

Finally, let us be clear that we advance this argument tentatively. A more complete test than we offer here would require the historical analysis of far more than three cases. History is not, however, an enterprise characterized by increasing returns: the more cases the historian analyzes, the less he or she is likely to have mastered the facts of each case. Thus, this essay should be read not as the final word, but as an invitation to further research by historians and historically minded economists and political scientists.

The central role played by political institutions in the development of banking systems is perhaps nowhere more clearly apparent than in the nineteenth-century United States. America's political institutions gave rise to a banking system like no other in the world: the U.S. banking system was huge (indeed, it was far larger than that of Great Britain, which is usually considered the financial leader of the nineteenth century), and it was composed of tens of thousands of small banks that were prohibited from opening branches. Equally remarkable, for most of the period under study the U.S. banking system was not governed by a quasi-central bank that served as the government's fiscal agent. Indeed, the United States was unusual in that it created a quasi-central bank and then revoked its charter. For most of the nineteenth century, the U.S. banking system was self-regulating or was regulated by state governments.[4]

Driving the peculiar history of the United States banking system were the political institutions built into the Constitution of 1789. On the one hand, these institutions limited the authority and discretion of public officials by providing for a bicameral legislature, an indirectly elected president who could veto legislation, and a federal system that delegated wide authority to states. On the other hand, these institutions limited the political power of the common people by providing for indirect election of the president and the Senate. Further limiting their influence were state laws that gave the right to vote solely to property owners. These institutions themselves reflected the interest groups that dominated American politics in the decades after independence. Federalism reflected the fact that the colonies had been organized as thirteen independent entities, each of which had a colonial legislature. Indirect election and property qualifications for the suffrage suggested the nervousness of Federalist political elites about the way that populists could tap the redistributive urges of the common people.[5]

This set of political institutions—a central government whose authority and discretion were limited, coupled to limits on suffrage—produced an initial organization of America's banking system that was strikingly different from the system that exists today. The federal government lost little time in chartering a monopoly bank—the Bank of the United States (BUS), founded in 1791. The BUS was a commercial bank, owned and operated by wealthy Federalist financiers, that was fully capable of taking deposits and making loans to private parties. It was also the federal government's fiscal agent. The federal government subscribed 20% of the BUS's capital, without paying for these shares: instead, it received a loan from the bank and then repaid the loan out of the stream of dividends it received as a shareholder in the bank. In exchange, the BUS received a set of valuable concessions: the right to limited liability for its shareholders; the right to hold federal government specie balances; the right to charge the federal government interest on loans from the bank (notes issued by the bank to cover federal expenses); and the right to open branches throughout the country.

Had America's political institutions granted the federal government the sole right to charter banks, the BUS might have maintained a monopoly for a long time, much in the same way that the Bank of England was that country's sole joint-stock, limited-liability bank from 1694 to 1825. America's political institutions prevented that from happening, however. The Constitution provided that any power not explicitly delegated to the federal government could be exercised by the states. Under the Constitution, the states lost both the right to tax imports and exports and the right to issue paper money. Both of these powers were vested with the federal government, in exchange for which the federal government assumed the considerable debts that the states had amassed under the Articles of Confederation. Having been denied their traditional sources of finance, the states began to search for alternative sources of revenue. The Constitution said nothing about the state's right to charter banks of issue, whose banknotes would circulate as currency. States, therefore, had every incentive to sell bank charters so that they could fill their treasuries, and every incentive to own stock in those same banks. In fact, virtually all state governments in the early nineteenth century were major owners of bank stock. Circa 1810–1830, bank dividends and bank taxes often accounted for one-third of total state revenues.[6]

Just as the federal government had an incentive to maintain a federal monopoly (the BUS), state governments had incentives to constrain the growth of the banking systems within their own borders. New banks could compete away the monopoly rents earned by the incumbent banks, thereby reducing the dividend stream paid to the state treasuries. In fact, incumbent banks often offered "bonuses" to state legislatures to deny the charter applications of potential competitors.[7] Banking in the Early Republican United States therefore tended to be characterized by segmented monopolies. The four largest cities in the United States in 1800—Boston, Philadelphia, New York, and Baltimore—had only two banks apiece. Smaller markets typically had only one bank, if they had a bank at all. In 1800 there were only twenty-eight banks (with a total capital of only $17.4 million) in the entire country. These banks, it should be pointed out, did not lend to all comers: they discriminated on the basis of profession, social standing, and political party affiliation.[8]

The system of a single national bank and segmented state monopolies was not stable given American political institutions. One crucial source of friction was the different incentives that faced the states and the central government. Bankers with state charters, and hence state legislatures, had opposed the BUS from the time of its initial chartering in 1791. The reason for their opposition was straightforward: branches of the BUS undermined local banking monopolies. Once the Federalist Party went into decline, these state bankers were able to form political coalitions with the Jeffersonians, who were ideologically opposed to chartered corporations and "aristocratic" bankers. Some states even tried (unsuccessfully) to tax the banknotes of the BUS in order to constrain it from competing against their own banks. Not surprisingly, when the BUS charter expired in 1811, Congress, whose members represented state interests, did not renew it.[9] The War of 1812 demonstrated, however, the importance of a bank that could serve as the financial agent of the federal government, and thus a new charter (for a Second Bank of the United States) was granted in 1816. The Second Bank of the United States was founded on the same principles as the first bank, and it met the same fate when Andrew Jackson successfully vetoed the renewal of the bank's charter, forcing it to close in 1836. In fact, the closing of the Second BUS was the product of a very curious political coalition: bankers with state charters allied to populists who were opposed to banks of any kind.[10]

Changes in America's political institutions—most particularly an increase in the number of states as the country expanded westward coupled with relaxation of limits on suffrage—gave rise to a second source of friction: an expanding frontier led to competition between states for business enterprise and population. State legislatures therefore sought to construct canals that would funnel commerce through the state. State legislatures, however, generally did not have the ability to fund public works projects out of their meager tax revenues. One state response was to issue bonds (which caused a rash of state debt defaults), but another response was to charge a "charter bonus" on new bank charters. Such charter bonuses created an incentive for state legislatures to renege on the monopoly deals that they had already made with the incumbent banks.[11]

Competition over capital and labor also drove states to expand the suffrage, which undermined the coalitions that had supported restrictions on the number of bank charters. New states, eager to attract population, eliminated or reduced voting restrictions, forcing the original thirteen states to ratchet their voting restrictions downward. By the mid-1820s, property qualifications had been dropped or dramatically reduced in virtually all of the original states.[12] The extension of the suffrage, in turn, allowed citizens to bring pressure to bear on legislatures, voting in legislators who were willing to remove constraints on the chartering of banks.

Political competition within and among states undermined the incentives of state legislatures to constrain the number of charters they granted. Massachusetts began to increase the number of charters as early as 1812, abandoning its strategy of holding bank stock as a source of state finance and instead levying taxes on bank capital. Pennsylvania followed Massachusetts's lead with the Omnibus Banking Act of 1814. The act, passed over the objections of the state's governor, ended the cozy Philadelphia-based oligopoly that, until then, had dominated the state's banking industry. Rhode Island also followed Massachusetts's lead: in 1826 it sold its bank shares, increased the number of charters it granted, and began to tax bank capital as a replacement for the income it had earned from dividends. It soon became, on a per capita basis, America's most heavily banked state.

Although the rate at which states reformed varied—with Southern states lagging behind the Northeast by a wide margin—the U.S. banking system grew remarkably quickly. In 1820 there were 327 banks in operation with $160 million in capital—roughly three times as many banks and four times as much bank capital as in 1810. By 1835, there were 584 banks, with $308 million in capital—a nearly twofold increase in just fifteen years. At this point, larger cities often had a dozen or more banks, while small towns had as many as two or three.[13] In 1825, the United States had roughly 2.4 times the banking capital of England—usually thought of as the world's financial leader in the nineteenth century—even though the United States had a smaller population.[14] As the density of banks increased, competition among them increased as well, so much so that they began to extend credit to an increasingly broad class of borrowers. The result was that banks, particularly in the Mid-Atlantic states, lent funds to a wide variety of merchants, artisans, and farmers.[15]

By the late 1830s, the Northeast's de facto policies granting virtually all requests for bank charters became institutionalized in a series of laws known as free banking. Under free banking, bank charters no longer had to be approved by state legislatures. Rather, individuals could open banks provided that they registered with the state comptroller and deposited state or federal bonds with the comptroller as a guarantee of their note issues. Readers may wonder how such a system of free entry could have been compatible with the fiscal needs of state governments. The answer lies in the fact that under free banking all bank notes had to be 100% backed by high-grade securities that were deposited with the state comptroller of the currency. In essence, free banks were forced to grant a loan to the state government in exchange for the right to operate.

The first state to make the switch to de jure free banking was New York in 1838, and this changeover was without doubt the result of changes in the state's political institutions. From the 1810s to the late 1830s, bank chartering in New York was controlled by the Albany Regency—a political machine run by Martin Van Buren. Bank charters were only granted to friends of the Regency, in exchange for which the legislators received various bribes, such as the ability to subscribe to initial public offerings of bank stock at par, even though the stock traded for a substantial premium.[16] The Regency's hold on bank chartering came to an end when the state legislature was forced to change the state's voting laws in 1826, finally allowing universal manhood suffrage. Within a decade, the Regency lost its control of the state legislature, and in 1837 the now dominant Whig Party enacted America's first free banking law. By 1841, New Yorkers had established 43 free banks, with a total capital of $10.7 million. By 1849, the number of free banks mushroomed to 111 (with $16.8 million in paid capital). By 1859 there were 274 free banks with paid-in capital of $100.6 million.[17] Other states soon followed New York's lead. By the early 1860s, twenty-one states adopted some variant of the New York law, and as they did so, they encouraged bank entry and increased competition.[18]

Free banking did not, however, eliminate all supply constraints on the number of banks. The free banking laws of most states precluded the chartering of branch banks. Virtually all banks in the nineteenth-century United States, except those in some Southern states, were unit (single-branch) banks. This unusual organization of the banking system was the outcome of an unlikely political coalition: populists who feared bank monopolies at the state level allied with bankers who wanted to create local monopolies.

From the federal government's point of view, allowing the states to charter banks had a major drawback: it did not provide the federal government with a source of finance. This problem came to the fore during the Civil War, when the financial needs of the federal government skyrocketed. The federal government therefore passed laws in 1863, 1864, and 1865 that were designed to eliminate the state-chartered banks and replace them with a system of national banks that would finance the government's war effort. Federally chartered banks had to invest one-third of their capital in federal government bonds, which were then held as reserves by the comptroller of the currency against note issues. That is, banks had to make a loan to the federal government in exchange for the right to issue notes. Consistent with the goal of maximizing credit to the federal government, the National Banking Act made the granting of a charter an administrative procedure: as long as minimum capital and reserve requirements were met, the charter was granted. It was free banking on a national scale.

The federal government could neither abrogate the right of states to charter banks nor prevent state-chartered banks from issuing banknotes. It could, however, impose a 10% tax on banknotes and then exempt federally chartered banks from the tax, thereby giving state banks strong incentives to obtain new, federal charters. In the short run, the response of private banks was as the federal government expected: the number of state-chartered banks declined from 1,579 in 1860 to 349 by 1865. Federal banks grew dramatically: from zero in 1860 to 1,294 in 1865. They continued growing, reaching 7,518 by 1914, controlling $11.5 billion in assets in that year.[19]

In the long run, however, the political institutions of the United States frustrated the federal government's goal of a single, federally chartered banking system. They also undermined the barriers to entry in banking that had been created by the National Banking System. The federal government had effectively nationalized the right to issue banknotes by creating a 10% tax on the notes of state-chartered banks in 1865. The 1865 law did not, however, say anything about checks drawn on accounts in state-chartered banks. State banks therefore aggressively pursued deposit banking, and checks drawn on those accounts became an increasingly common means of exchange in business transactions.[20] The result was that state-chartered banks actually outgrew federally chartered banks during the period from 1865 to 1914. In 1865, state banks accounted for only 21% of all banks and 13% of total bank assets. By 1890 there were more state banks than national banks, and state banks controlled the majority of assets. Circa 1914, 73% of all banks were state banks, and state banks controlled 58% of assets.

Competition between states and the federal government, as well as competition between states, to provide attractive regulatory environments gave rise to a banking system unlike that of any other country. In the first place, in 1914 there were 27,349 banks in the United States. In the second place, almost none of these banks had branches. Most states had laws that prevented branch banking, even by nationally chartered banks. Even those states that did not explicitly forbid branch banking had no provision in their laws for branches. Hence, 95% of banks were unit banks, and the banks that did have branches tended to be small: the average number of branches operated by these banks was less than five.[21] The reason for these laws was a feature of American politics that by now should be familiar to readers of this essay: bankers seeking local monopolies allied themselves with populist politicians who opposed the centralization of economic power represented by large banks. This banking structure was not without its disadvantages. Large numbers of small unit banks exacerbated banking crises; made it difficult for banks to capture scale economies; and allowed bankers to earn rents from local monopolies.[22] Unit banking with free entry did, however, mean that all markets in the United States were contestable: any market that generated rents for a monopolist was subject to entry by a competitor seeking those rents.

Consider, now, how different the evolution of America's political institutions and banking system was from those of Brazil. Indeed, Brazil is a prime example of a country in which the most powerful interest groups—planters, merchants, and financiers—structured institutions so as to limit political access to the broad mass of the population. They also forged a coalition with Brazil's political elites, most particularly the Portuguese royalty that served as the country's monarchs, which allowed for a financial system based on rent sharing among the two groups. These arrangements came under threat only once, when the monarchy was overthrown in 1889 and the new government allowed virtually unlimited access to bank charters. Nevertheless, within a few years of the creation of the republic, the old set of arrangements was re-created and Brazil went back to a system in which the government limited the number of banks, and, in exchange, the banks extended credit to the government. Indeed, Brazil ultimately created a banking system that was dominated by a single super-bank that had a monopoly on the right to branch across state lines—and that bank also served as the banker to the central government. Indeed, the government was a major stockholder in the bank.

Brazil's first bank, the Banco do Brasil, was founded in 1808 when King Dom João VI was transported to Brazil by the British

Navy following Napoleon's invasion of Portugal. From Dom João's point of view, the purpose of the Banco do Brasil was clear: finance the expenses of his government. In order to get Brazil's merchants and landowners to buy stock in the bank, Dom João granted it a number of lucrative privileges: a monopoly on the issuance of paper money, a monopoly on the export of luxury goods, a monopoly on the handling of government financial operations, the right to have debts to the bank treated as having the same legal standing as debts owed to the royal treasury, and the right to collect new taxes imposed by the king—and then to hold those taxes as interest-free deposits for a period of ten years.[23]

There was nothing to stop the king, however, from reneging on his promises and expropriating the bank. The merchants and landowners whom the government needed to buy the bank's shares remained so wary that the Banco do Brasil was unable to achieve its original capitalization goals until 1817, eleven years after it was founded. Their wariness was not unfounded: most of the bank's business consisted of printing banknotes that were then used to buy bonds issued by the imperial government. As the amount of banknotes increased, so too did inflation. In effect, the bank was the government's agent in creating an inflation tax, and that inflation tax hit everybody, including the bank's shareholders, who likely did not receive an inflation-adjusted rate of return adequate to compensate them for the opportunity cost of their capital: the nominal rate of return on owner's equity in the Banco do Brasil from 1810 to 1820 averaged 10% per year, which probably did not exceed the rate of inflation by a wide margin.[24] Worse, in 1820, Dom João reneged on the arrangement by which the bank could hold the proceeds from the new taxes that he had created. The following year, he returned to Portugal and took with him all of the metals that he and his court had deposited in the bank, exchanging them for whatever banknotes they had in their possession. The Banco do Brasil then continued to function through the rest of the 1820s and was used by Dom João's son, the Emperor Dom Pedro I, in much the same way as it had been used previously—to finance government budget deficits through note issues.[25]

In 1822 Dom Pedro, at the urging of local elites and with the consent of his father, declared Brazil independent. Independence, however, occasioned a major change in Brazil's political institutions. The merchants and landowners who drafted the Constitution of 1824 gave parliament, and not the emperor, the ultimate responsibility to tax, spend, and borrow. They also specified an elected lower house of parliament and restricted the vote on the basis of wealth so that the lower house represented their interests. As Summerhill has pointed out, this change had two consequences: the emperor could not default on loans that he had contracted from landowners and merchants; and members of those elite groups could use their control of parliament to make sure that competing economic groups could not obtain bank charters. In point of fact, from the closing of the Banco do Brasil by parliament in 1829 to the mid-1850s, parliament permitted only seven new banks to be formed—all of which had limited provincial charters that created local banking monopolies.[26]

This set of arrangements worked well for the incumbent bankers, but it came at a cost to the emperor: after 1829 the imperial government did not have a bank that it could use to finance budget deficits. Finding a solution was difficult because creating a national bank large enough to finance the government required aligning the incentives of all the incumbent bankers some of whom were able to use their influence in parliament to undo whatever deals the emperor struck. Thus, parliament authorized a second Banco do Brasil in 1853 but then removed its right to issue banknotes just four years later.[27]

A compromise was not reached until the 1860s when a coalition was formed between the bankers and the imperial government. An 1860 law specified that corporate charters, including those for banks, not only needed the approval of parliament and the emperor's cabinet, but also required approval from the emperor's Council of State, whose members enjoyed life tenure. In 1863, the Second Banco do Brasil merged with two other Rio de Janeiro banks, the Banco Comercial e Agrícola and the Banco Rural e Hipotecario, which transferred to the Banco do Brasil their rights of note issue, thereby creating something that the emperor had been seeking for a decade: a note-issuing bank that acted as the government's fiscal agent.[28] The government got its bank, and the economic elite got their banks, but no one else could get a bank charter—and no one from outside the small group of "barons" who sat on a bank board was eligible for a loan.[29]

Some sense of how restricted the banking industry in Brazil was can be gleaned from the following data. As late as 1888, Brazil had only twenty-six banks, whose combined capital totaled only U.S. $48 million. Fifteen of these twenty-six banks were located in Rio de Janeiro—and the largest of them, the Banco do Brasil, controlled more than 40% of all bank assets. Another ten banks were located in the state of Sao Paulo; half of these were, in fact, affiliates of Rio de Janeiro banks. Across the other eighteen states in Brazil, there were only six banks.[30] Putting this into comparative perspective, we see that in 1888, bank assets per capita in Brazil totaled $2.40 U.S., and in Mexico in 1897, they were nearly three times this level, at $6.74. In the United States, in 1890, they were $85.

This set of arrangements—a coalition between the political elites who ran the government and a small number of merchant-financiers who created a narrowly based banking system—came under threat only once, when the monarchy was overthrown and a federal republic was created. Space constraints prevent us from exploring how and why the coalition that had supported the emperor fell apart, but one crucial piece of the story was the abolition of slavery in 1888. Abolition drove a wedge between Brazil's planter class and the imperial government. In an effort to placate the planters by making credit more easily available, the imperial government awarded concessions to twelve banks of issue and provided seventeen banks with interest-free loans. The easy credit policies of 1888 were not enough, however, to stem the tide of Brazil's republican movement. In November 1889,

Dom Pedro II was overthrown in a military coup and a federal republic was created.

For a time, the creation of a federal republic undermined the arrangements that had supported a small and concentrated banking industry. The 1891 Constitution gave each of Brazil's twenty states considerable sovereignty, ending the central government's monopoly on the chartering of banks. This put the federal republic's first finance minister, Rui Barbosa, under considerable pressure: if he did not grant additional charters to new banks in order to satisfy the demand for credit from Brazil's growing regional economic elites—most particularly planters and manufacturers—those elites would get their own state governments to do so. As a result, Rui Barbosa quickly pushed through a series of financial reforms, one of whose features was that the federal government allocated bank charters to virtually all comers through a general incorporation law, and another of whose features was that banks could engage in whatever kind of financial transactions they wished. These reforms produced dramatic results. Recall that in 1888 there were only twenty-six banks in the entire country; in 1891 there were sixty-eight.[31]

The problem was that Brazil's political institutions did not create any mechanisms that allowed the country's farmers, artisans, and small-scale manufacturers to pressure public officials to create competitively structured banking markets. In the first place, less than 5% of the population had the right to vote. In the second place, power was concentrated in a strong presidency: congress was more a consultative forum than a legislative body.[32] In the third place, congress selected the president, which allowed the political elites of the two largest states, Minas Gerais and São Paulo, to form a coalition and trade the presidency between them.

Brazil's central government soon found itself in a difficult position. The 1891 Constitution denied it access to a crucial source of tax income, revenues from export taxes, which were now collected directly by states. The government therefore contracted gold-denominated foreign loans to make up for the budget shortfall. The government also allocated the right to issue banknotes to a number of banks, each of which aggressively printed and lent currency. Their note issues, in addition to driving a speculative boom in the stock market, also drove up inflation. The result was a currency mismatch: a hard-currency-denominated debt, a domestic-currency-denominated source of income (import taxes paid in Brazilian milreis), and an inflation that drove down the international value of the domestic currency. The central government had three options: spend less, raise taxes, or curtail the growth of the money supply. It chose options two and three. In 1896 the government decided once again to restrict the right to issue currency to a single bank—the Banco da República, which was a private commercial bank that had a special charter making it the agent of the treasury. Two years later, the government increased taxes and restructured its foreign debt. These moves, coupled with the already shaky financial situation of many of the banks, produced a massive contraction of the banking sector, taking down, among other banks, the Banco da República. In 1891 there were sixty-eight banks operating in Brazil.[33] By 1899 there were fifty-four, and the numbers kept falling. By 1906 there were only nineteen, and their combined capital was, in real terms, less than half that of the banks in 1899.[34]

That contraction occasioned yet another round of reforms, which in 1906 produced a fourth Banco do Brasil. Like its predecessors, the fourth Banco do Brasil was a private commercial bank. It differed from the others, however, in that the central government was a major stockholder, subscribing to almost one-third of its shares, and the president of the republic had the right to name the president of the bank, along with one of its four directors.[35] For the better part of the next six decades, the Brazilian banking system was dominated by the Fourth Banco do Brasil, which acted both as a commercial bank and as the treasury's financial agent. The charter that created the bank included a number of lucrative privileges, not the least of which was that it was the only bank allowed to branch across state lines.[36] The implication of this feature of the Banco do Brasil's concession cannot be overstated: The Banco do Brasil soon came to control one-quarter of total bank deposits; those deposits were directed to the purchase of bonds issued by the treasury of the central government.[37] Private commercial banks, which were chartered by state governments, existed as well, but there were few of them and they were typically the treasury arms of large conglomerates. They were designed to mobilize capital for firms affiliated with the owners of the bank, not to extend credit broadly. As late as 1930, when the First Republic was overthrown in a coup, Brazil had fewer banks than it had in 1899.[38]

In short, the political economy of Brazilian banking was not very complex: regardless of which particular political elite was in power, that elite forged a coalition with incumbent financiers. The arrangements they created provided bankers with oligopoly rents and the central government with a bank to fund its budget deficits. In the years following World War I, state governments began to copy the model of the Banco do Brasil, establishing state-owned banks whose purpose was to finance their budget deficits. That is, the banks took deposits from private individuals and then invested the proceeds in the bonds of state governments. The disadvantage of this system, however, was that it allocated credit very narrowly: to state governments, the federal government, and large business enterprises whose owners were tied to the banks.[39]

Mexico provides an even more dramatic case of a country in which the lack of effective political competition gave rise to constraints on competition in banking. In Mexico, the institutional constraints on the government were so weak that the only way that bankers would deploy their capital in a chartered bank was if they could form a coalition with the political elites that ran the states and the federal government. During most of the nineteenth century, Mexico was so politically unstable that forging such coalitions was impossible—and hence there were no chartered banks. To the degree that any credit intermediation existed, it was through private financial houses, but these lacked the advantages conferred by a charter: limited liability for shareholders, primacy as a creditor in the event of borrower bankruptcy, and the ability to issue banknotes that had the status of legal tender. These private banking houses were thus necessarily limited in scale. In the last decades of the nineteenth century, one political-military leader, Porfirio Díaz, created a durable dictatorship, one of whose outcomes was a stable but highly uncompetitive banking system that provided credit only to the government and to the enterprises owned by the bankers.

Mexico achieved independence from Spain in 1821, but Mexico's post-independence elites did not agree on the institutions that should govern the new country. Some sought to create a constitutional monarchy and to maintain all of the other political and economic institutions of the colony, including the centralization of political power and exemptions from trial in civil courts for the army and clergy. Others wanted a federal republic—though one in which suffrage would be restricted on the basis of literacy, in a society where few were literate.

These two groups, one conservative and centralist, the other liberal and federalist, engaged in a series of coups, countercoups, and civil wars from independence to the 1870s. All sides in these conflicts preyed on the property rights of their opponents. Every government that came to power also inherited a depleted treasury and no ready source of income. To meet their need for large infusions of cash, Mexico's nineteenth-century governments borrowed from the country's wealthy merchant-financiers. When governments changed or when governments faced sufficient threat, they reneged on these debts.[40]

Given this environment, the country's merchant-financiers had no incentive to obtain bank charters. The severity of this problem is made evident by one of the Mexican government's most desperate moves. Precisely because there was so little bank credit, in 1830 the country's manufacturers pressured the government into founding a government-owned industrial development bank (the Banco de Avío). In 1842, desperate for cash, the government ransacked the vaults of its own bank.[41] Not surprisingly, Mexico had no private, chartered banks at all until 1863—and that charter was granted to a foreign bank (the British Bank of London, Mexico, and South America) by the puppet government of a foreign power (the Emperor Maximilian, who had been installed by the French).

The unstable nature of Mexican politics, and the underdeveloped state of Mexico's banking system, changed dramatically during the thirty-five-year dictatorship of Porfirio Díaz (1876–1911). Díaz confronted the same problem as every government before him. He lacked sufficient tax revenues to finance a government capable of unifying the country and putting an end to internecine warfare. Borrowing his way out of this situation was difficult because Mexico had a long history of defaulting on its debts to its international and domestic creditors. In fact, Díaz himself had reneged on debts to some of the banks that had been founded in Mexico City during the early years of his rule.[42]

Díaz did, however, have an advantage over earlier Mexican presidents. Because of the dramatic growth of the U.S. economy, Díaz could attract foreign direct investment in mining, petroleum, and export agriculture that would create a tax base. The problem for Díaz was how to start the virtuous cycle of foreign direct investment, state capacity, economic growth, and political stability.

The solution that Díaz hit upon to jump-start this process was to create a banking system that could finance the government. He did this by engineering the merger of the two largest banks in Mexico City, thereby establishing a monopoly bank of issue—the Banco Nacional de México (Banamex). The deal was simple: Banamex got a charter from the government that gave it a set of extremely lucrative privileges and, in return, Banamex extended a credit line to the government. These privileges included the rights to issue banknotes up to three times the amount of its reserves, to act as the treasury's fiscal agent, to tax farm customs receipts, and to run the mint. In addition, the government established a 5% tax on all banknotes, and then it exempted Banamex notes from the tax. Díaz simultaneously got congress to pass a commercial code that removed the authority of state governments to issue bank charters. Any bank that wanted to compete with Banamex had to obtain a charter from Díaz's secretary of the treasury—and he could say no with impunity.[43]

Mexico's already existing banks, some of which were owned by powerful provincial politicians, realized that the commercial code and Banamex's special privileges put them at a serious disadvantage. They therefore obtained an injunction against the 1884 Commercial Code, citing the 1857 Constitution's antimonopoly clause. The ensuing legal and political battle ground on for thirteen years, until Secretary of Finance José Yves Limantour finally hammered out a compromise in 1897. Under this agreement, Banamex shared many (though not all) of its special privileges with the Banco de Londres y México, state governors chose which business group in the state would receive a bank charter from the federal government, and that state bank would effectively be granted a local monopoly. The arrangement held together because the federal government monopolized bank chartering. Legal barriers to entry into banking could not be eroded by competition between states, or between states and the federal government, because states did not have the right to charter banks.

Mexico's 1897 banking law was deliberately crafted to limit the number of banks that could compete in any market. First, the law specified that the secretary of the treasury *and* the federal congress had to approve bank charters (and additions to capital), which by that time had become a rubber stamp for the dictator.[44] Second, the law created high minimum capital requirements—more than twice the amount for a national bank in the United States.[45] Third, the law established a 2% annual tax on paid-in capital. The first bank granted a charter in each state, however, was granted an exemption from the tax. Fourth, banks with territorial charters were not allowed to branch outside of their concession territories, preventing banks chartered in one state from challenging the monopoly of a bank in an adjoining state. In short, the only threat to the monopoly of a state bank could come from a branch of Banamex or the Banco de Londres y México.[46]

These segmented monopolies were made incentive compatible with the interests of Mexico's political elite, who received seats on the boards of the major banks (and thus were entitled to director's fees and stock distributions). The board of directors of Banamex, for example, was populated by members of Díaz's coterie, including the president of congress, the under-secretary of the treasury, the senator for the Federal District, the president's chief of staff, and the brother of the secretary of the treasury. Banks with limited territorial concessions were similarly populated with powerful politicians, the only difference being that state governors, rather than cabinet ministers, sat on their boards.[47]

The resulting banking system had one major advantage and one major disadvantage. The advantage was that the construction of Banamex created, for the first time in Mexican history, a stable banking system. Moreover, by the standards of developing economies today, Mexico's banking system was quite sizable: in 1910, bank assets were 32% of GDP—about the same ratio that Mexico has today.[48] Moreover, this banking system provided the government with a stable source of public finance, which allowed Díaz the financial breathing room he needed to slowly redraft tax codes and increase federal tax revenues to the point that he ran balanced budgets. It also allowed Díaz, with the help of Banamex's directors, to renegotiate Mexico's foreign debt—which had been in default for several decades. State governors obtained a similar advantage: the banks within their borders were a steady source of loans to the state government.[49]

The disadvantage was that Mexico had a concentrated banking system. In 1911, there were only thirty-four incorporated banks in the entire country. Half of all assets were held in just two banks: Banamex and Banco de Londres y México.[50] The vast majority of markets had, at most, three banks: a branch of Banamex, a branch of the BLM, and a branch of the bank that held that state's territorial concession. The banking industry's high level of concentration had a variety of negative effects on the rest of the economy. Banamex and the Banco de Londres y México acted like inefficient monopolists, driving up their rates of return by holding excess liquidity.[51] In addition, the concentrated nature of the banking industry gave rise to concentration in the rest of the economy. Mexico's banks tended only to allocate credit to firms owned by their own board members. The logical implication of a small number of banks and insider lending was that there was a reduced number of firms in finance-dependent, downstream industries.[52]

The coalition that supported the Díaz dictatorship fell apart after three decades. The same set of institutions that underpinned growth in banking—an alliance between economic elites and politicians to create and share rents—also existed in other sectors of the economy. Indeed, restrictions on bank charters were a fundamental weapon in the arsenal of tactics employed by the country's largest industrialists to constrain competition in manufacturing.[53] As was the case in banking, the resulting growth in those sectors tended to heighten inequality and in time produced organized resistance to the dictatorship. That resistance took up armed force in 1910, removing Díaz from power in 1911 and opening up a decade-long period of coups, rebellions, and civil wars.

Every side in the Mexican Revolution preyed upon the banking system. The lack of political stability meant that it was not possible for Mexico's bankers to forge durable coalitions with the country's political elites. By 1916 the financial system had become a shell: stripped of its liquid assets, it existed in a moribund state.[54]

Space constraints prevent us from exploring in detail how Mexico's postrevolutionary political institutions conditioned the development of the banking sector. Suffice to say, however, that the party-based dictatorship that came to rule Mexico after the revolution created a new coalition with Mexico's financiers. One basic element of that coalition was the creation of a banking system that was remarkably similar to the one that had existed under Díaz: the number of banks was limited, bankers tended to make loans to enterprises that they controlled, and everyone else was starved for credit. These features of the Mexican banking system have been loosened only in recent years, as a result of the country's transition to democracy.

Are there any general lessons that we might draw from these three cases? Do they help explain why democratic political institutions and broad-based banking systems go together? One of the primary themes that emerges from the history of the three cases is that bankers and public officials have strong incentives to create regulatory structures that generate sources of finance for the government and positive returns for bankers, but do so by limiting competition among banks, thereby driving up the cost of credit for everyone else. Bankers need the government to grant them the privileges necessary to carry out the business of banking, such as limited liability, the right to issue banknotes, or priority as a creditor in the event their borrowers declare bankruptcy. From the banker's point of view, the fewer such concessions the government grants the better because limiting the number of chartered banks raises their rates of return on capital. From the government's point of view, there is no obvious reason it should not accede to this demand from the bankers: it can trade limits on the number of bank charters for agreements from the banks to make it loans at favorable terms. In point of fact, as the Mexican case demonstrates, bankers may have reasons to refuse to deploy their capital at all unless the government constrains competition so as to raise rates of return: the government's power to regulate also grants it the power to expropriate bank wealth; and there may be no way for the government to credibly promise not to do so. All the government can do is create a regulatory environment that dampens competition to the point that bankers are compensated for the risk that the government can expropriate them.

The history of Brazil suggests that simply establishing an elected parliament is not a sufficient solution to the problem created by coalitions between politicians and bankers. Brazil successfully limited the government's ability to expropriate the bankers by creating an elected parliament in which bankers and other government debt holders were represented. However, there was nothing to keep the same bankers who sat in parliament from blocking charters for new banks. The private users of credit—farmers, artisans, and small-scale manufacturers—did not have the right to vote. From their point of view, the result was little different from that obtained under the Díaz dictatorship in Mexico: the amount of credit available to them was tightly constrained. The evidence also suggests that simply shifting the political system from a constitutional monarchy to a federal republic, but one in which the suffrage was tightly constrained, did not have much effect. Federalism promised to open up the banking system, but within a few years the central government had effectively re-created the same constraints on new bank charters that existed under the monarchy.

The history of the United States indicates that a broadly distributed suffrage, when coupled to federalism and a system of checks and balances in the central government that reflected the federal structure of the polity, produced a very different long-run outcome in terms of the structure of the banking system and the distribution of credit. It was not just that farmers, artisans, and manufacturers could vote their preferences; rather, it was that they could do so at both state and national levels, and that state legislatures were under pressure to offer attractive regulatory environments so as to attract capital and labor. It was the combination of these political institutions that created incentives for legislators to undermine the initial organization of American banking, giving rise to a competitive structure that existed no where else in the world.

The implication should be clear: the only conditions under which one observes large and competitively structured banking systems are those in which the authority and discretion of public officials are institutionally limited, and part of those limits are imposed by effective suffrage. This conclusion is consistent with the cross-sectional regression results of both economists and political scientists. It is also consistent with the history of the three cases analyzed here. One obvious question is whether it is consistent with the history of cases beyond those we have studied in this essay. Assessing whether the pattern holds is a task in which historians have an obvious advantage, but which will require that they be willing to address questions that come from outside their own field of study, learn the language and techniques of those fields, and think in an explicitly comparative framework.

## NOTES

The author would like to acknowledge the helpful comments on an earlier draft made by Aaron Berg, Jared Diamond, Ross Levine, Noel Maurer, James Robinson, and Hamilton Ulmer. An earlier version of some of this material appeared in "Political Institutions and Financial Development: Evidence from the Political Economy of Bank Regulation in Mexico and the United States," in Stephen Haber, Douglass C. North, and Barry R. Weingast, eds., *Political Institutions and Financial Development* (Stanford, CA, 2008), pp. 10–59.

1. Raghuram G. Rajan and Luigi Zingales, "Financial Dependence and Growth," *American Economic Review* 88 (1998): 559–586; Ross Levine, "The Legal Environment, Banks, and Long Run Economic Growth," *Journal of Money, Credit, and Banking* 30 (1998): 596–620; Levine, "Finance and Growth: Theory and Evidence," in Philippe Aghion and Steven Durlauf, eds., *Handbook of Economic Growth* (Amsterdam, 2005), pp. 251–278.

2. Thorsten Beck, Asli Demirguc-Kunt, and Ross Levine, "A New Database on Financial Development and Structure," www.go.worldbank.org (accessed February 12, 2008).

3. James R. Barth, Gerard Caprio Jr., and Ross Levine, *Rethinking Bank Regulation: Till Angels Govern* (New York, 2006), chapter 5; Michael D. Bordo and Peter Rousseau, "Legal-Political Factors and the Historical Evolution of the Finance-Growth Link," National Bureau of Economic Research Working Paper 12035 (Cambridge, MA, 2006); Philip Keefer, "Beyond Legal Origin and Checks and Balances: Political Credibility, Citizen Information,

and Financial Sector Development," in Stephen Haber, Douglass C. North, and Barry R. Weingast, eds., *Political Institutions and Financial Development* (Stanford, CA, 2008), pp. 125–155.

4. The reasons for the larger size of the U.S. banking system have been linked by economic historians to England's political institutions. See Laurence J. Broz and Richard S. Grossman, "Paying for Privilege: The Political Economy of Bank of England Charters, 1694–1844," *Explorations in Economic History* 41 (2004): 48–72; P. L. Cottrell and Lucy Newton, "Banking Liberalization in England and Wales, 1826–1844," in Richard Sylla, Richard Tilly, and Gabriel Tortella, eds., *The State, the Financial System, and Economic Modernization* (Cambridge, 1999), pp. 75–117. On the relative sizes of the U.S. and British banking systems, see Peter Rousseau and Richard Sylla, "Emerging Financial Markets and Early U.S. Growth," *Explorations in Economic History* 42 (2004): 1–26.

5. Alexander Keyssar, *The Right to Vote: The Contested History of Democracy in the United States* (New York, 2000), p. 8.

6. Richard Sylla, John B. Legler, and John Wallis, "Banks and State Public Finance in the New Republic: The United States, 1790–1860," *Journal of Economic History* 47 (1987): 391–403; John Wallis, Richard E. Sylla, and John B. Legler, "The Interaction of Taxation and Regulation in Nineteenth Century U.S. Banking," in Claudia Goldin and Gary D. Libecap, eds., *The Regulated Economy: A Historical Approach to Political Economy* (Chicago: University of Chicago Press, 1994), pp. 122–144.

7. Howard Bodenhorn, *State Banking in Early America: A New Economic History* (New York, 2003), pp. 17, 244.

8. Wallis, Sylla, and Legler, "The Interaction of Taxation and Regulation," pp. 135–139; Bodenhorn, *State Banking in Early America*, p. 142; John Majewski, "Jeffersonian Political Economy and Pennsylvania's Financial Revolution from Below, 1800–1820" (mimeo, University of California, Santa Barbara, 2004).

9. Carl Lane, "For a 'Positive Profit': The Federal Investment in the First Bank of the United States, 1792–1802," *William and Mary Quarterly* 54 (1997): 601–612; James O. Wettereau, "The Branches of the First Bank of the United States," *Journal of Economic History* 2 (1942): 66–100; Richard Sylla, "Experimental Federalism: The Economics of American Government, 1789–1914," in Stanley Engerman and Robert Gallman, eds., *The Cambridge Economic History of the United States*, vol. 2: *The Long Nineteenth Century* (New York, 2000), pp. 483–542; Hugh Rockoff, "Banking and Finance,

1789–1914," in Engerman and Gallman, eds., *The Cambridge Economic History of the United States*, vol. 2, pp. 643–684.

10. Bray Hammond, "Jackson, Biddle, and the Bank of the United States," *Journal of Economic History* 7 (1947): 1–23; Peter Temin, "The Economic Consequences of the Bank War," *Journal of Political Economy* 76 (1968): 257–274; Stanley L. Engerman, "A Note on the Economic Consequences of the Second Bank of the United States," *Journal of Political Economy* 78 (1970): 725–728; Rockoff, "Banking and Finance," pp. 643–684.

11. Arthur Grinith III, John Joseph Wallis, and Richard E. Sylla, "Debt, Default, and Revenue Structure: The American State Debt Crisis in the Early 1840s," National Bureau of Economic Research, Historical Working Paper (Cambridge, MA, 1997); Sylla, "Experimental Federalism"; Bodenhorn, *State Banking in Early America*, pp. 86, 148, 152, 228–234.

12. Stanley L. Engerman and Kenneth L. Sokoloff, "The Evolution of Suffrage Institutions in the New World," National Bureau of Economic Research Working Paper 8512 (2001); Keyssar, *The Right to Vote*, p. 29.

13. Bodenhorn, *State Banking in Early America*, p. 12.

14. Rousseau and Sylla, "Emerging Financial Markets and Early U.S. Growth," pp. 1–26.

15. Ta-Chen Wang, "Courts, Banks, and Credit Markets in Early American Development" (PhD diss., Stanford University, 2006), p. 83.

16. Bodenhorn, *State Banking in Early America*, pp. 134, 186–188; Howard Bodenhorn, "Bank Chartering and Political Corruption in Antebellum New York: Free Banking as Reform," in Edward Glaeser and Claudia Goldin, eds., *Corruption and Reform: Lessons from America's Economic History* (Chicago: University of Chicago Press, 2008), pp. 231–258; Frank Otto Gatell, "Sober Second Thoughts on Van Buren, the Albany Regency, and the Wall Street Conspiracy," *Journal of American History* 53 (1966): 26; David Moss and Sarah Brennan, "Regulation and Reaction: The Other Side of Free Banking in Antebellum New York," Harvard Business School Working Paper 04-038 (2004), p. 7.

17. Bodenhorn, *State Banking in Early America*, pp. 186–192; Wallis, Sylla, and Legler, "The Interaction of Taxation and Regulation," pp. 122–144; Moss and Brennan, "Regulation and Reaction."

18. Howard Bodenhorn, "Entry, Rivalry, and Free Banking in Antebellum America," *Review of Economics and Statistics* 72 (1990): 682–686; Howard Bodenhorn, "The Business Cycle and Entry into Early American Banking," *Review of Economics and Statistics* 75 (1993): 531–535; Andrew

Economopoulos and Heather O'Neill, "Bank Entry during the Antebellum Period," *Journal of Money, Credit, and Banking* 27 (1995): 1071–1085; Kenneth Ng, "Free Banking Laws and Barriers to Entry in Banking, 1838–1860," *Journal of Economic History* 48 (1988): 877–889; Hugh Rockoff, "The Free Banking Era: A Reexamination," *Journal of Money, Credit, and Banking* 6 (1974): 141–167; Hugh Rockoff, "New Evidence on Free Banking in the United States," *American Economic Review* 75 (1985): 886–889.

19. Charles W. Calomiris and Eugene N. White, "The Origins of Federal Deposit Insurance," in Claudia Goldin and Gary D. Libecap, eds., *The Regulated Economy: A Historical Approach to Political Economy* (Chicago, 1994), p. 151; Lance E. Davis and Robert E. Gallman, *Evolving Financial Markets and International Capital Flows: Britain, the Americas, and Australia, 1865–1914* (New York, 2001), p. 268; Richard Sylla, *The American Capital Market, 1846–1914: A Study of the Effects of Economic Development on Public Policy* (New York, 1975), pp. 249–252.

20. Moss and Brennan, "Regulation and Reaction"; Sylla, *The American Capital Market*, pp. 62–73; Davis and Gallman, *Evolving Financial Markets*, p. 272.

21. Calomiris and White, "The Origins of Federal Deposit Insurance," pp. 145–188; Davis and Gallman, *Evolving Financial Markets*, p. 272.

22. Michael D. Bordo, Hugh Rockoff, and Angela Redish, "The U.S. Banking System from a Northern Exposure: Stability versus Efficiency," *Journal of Economic History* 54 (1994): 325–341.

23. Carlos Manuel Peláez, "The Establishment of Banking Institutions in a Backward Economy: Brazil, 1800–1851," *Business History Review* 49 (1975): 460–461.

24. Author's estimates, based on data in Peláez, "The Establishment of Banking Institutions," pp. 459, 462.

25. Peláez, "The Establishment of Banking Institutions," pp. 456–463.

26. William Summerhill, *Inglorious Revolution: Political Institutions, Sovereign Debt, and Financial Underdevelopment in Imperial Brazil* (New Haven, CT, forthcoming).

27. Carlos Manuel Peláez and Wilson Suzigan, *Historia Monetária do Brasil: Análise da Política, Comportamento e Instituiçoes Monetárias* (Brasília, 1976), pp. 82–87.

28. Ibid., p. 103.

29. Summerhill, *Inglorious Revolution*; Anne G. Hanley, *Native Capital: Financial Institutions and Economic Development in Sao Paulo, Brazil, 1850–1905* (Stanford, CA, 2005), p. 38.

30. Peláez and Suzigan, *Historia Monetária do Brasil,* chapter 4; Hanley, *Native Capital,* p. 123; Steven Topik, *The Political Economy of the Brazilian State, 1889–1930* (Austin, TX, 1987), pp. 28–29.

31. Paolo Neuhaus, *História Monetária do Brasil, 1900–45* (Rio de Janeiro, 1975), p. 22; Gail D. Triner, *Banking and Economic Development: Brazil, 1889–1930* (New York, 2000), p. 47.

32. Triner, *Banking and Economic Development,* p. 18.

33. Neuhaus, *História Monetária do Brasil,* p. 22; Triner, *Banking and Economic Development,* p. 47.

34. Calculated from data in *Jornal do Commercio,* various issues.

35. Steven Topik, "State Enterprise in a Liberal Regime: The Banco do Brasil, 1905–1930," *Journal of Interamerican Studies and World Affairs* 22 (1980): 402, 413.

36. Gail D. Triner, "Banks, Regions, and Nation in Brazil, 1889–1930," *Latin American Perspectives* 26 (1999): 135.

37. Topik, "State Enterprise in a Liberal Regime," pp. 402–417.

38. Calculated from data in *Jornal do Commercio,* various issues.

39. Morris Bornstein, "Banking Policy and Economic Development: A Brazilian Case Study," *Journal of Finance* 9 (1954): 312–313.

40. David W. Walker, *Business, Kinship, and Politics: The Martinez del Rio Family in Mexico, 1824–1867* (Austin, TX, 1987), chapters 7 and 8; Barbara Tennenbaum, *The Politics of Penury: Debt and Taxes in Mexico, 1821–1856* (Albuquerque, NM, 1986).

41. Robert Potash, *The Mexican Government and Industrial Development in the Early Republic: The Banco de Avío* (Amherst, MA, 1983), p. 118.

42. Noel Maurer and Andrei Gomberg, "When the State Is Untrustworthy: Public Finance and Private Banking in Porfirian Mexico," *Journal of Economic History* 64 (2004): 1087–1107; Carlos Marichal, "The Construction of Credibility: Financial Market Reform and the Renegotiation of Mexico's External Debt in the 1880's," in Jeffrey L. Bortz and Stephen H. Haber, eds., *The Mexican Economy, 1870–1930: Essays on the Economic History of Institutions, Revolution, and Growth* (Stanford, CA, 2002), pp. 93–119.

43. Maurer and Gomberg, "When the State Is Untrustworthy," pp. 1087–1107; Noel Maurer, *The Power and the Money: The Mexican Financial System, 1876–1932* (Stanford, CA, 2002), pp. 34–40; Stephen Haber, Armando Razo, and Noel Maurer, *The Politics of Property Rights: Political Instability, Credible Commitments, and Economic Growth in Mexico, 1876–1929* (New York, 2003), chapter 4.

44. Armando Razo, *Social Foundations of Limited Dictatorship: Networks and Private Protection during Mexico's Early Industrialization* (Stanford, CA, 2008), p. 78.

45. Stephen Haber, "Industrial Concentration and the Capital Markets: A Comparative Study of Brazil, Mexico, and the United States, 1830–1930," *Journal of Economic History* 51 (1991): 559–580; Noel Maurer and Stephen Haber, "Related Lending and Economic Performance: Evidence from Mexico," *Journal of Economic History* 67 (2007): 551–581.

46. Maurer and Haber, "Related Lending and Economic Performance," pp. 551–581.

47. Haber, Razo, and Maurer, *The Politics of Property Rights*, pp. 88–90; Razo, *Social Foundations of Limited Dictatorship*, pp. 101–165.

48. Stephen Haber, "Banking with and without Deposit Insurance: Mexico's Banking Experiments, 1884–2004," in Asli Demirguc-Kunt, Edward Kane, and Luc Laeven, eds., *Deposit Insurance around the World: Issues of Design and Implementation* (Cambridge, MA, 2008), pp. 219–252.

49. Marichal, "The Construction of Credibility," pp. 93–119; Maurer, *The Power and the Money*, pp. 16–18; Gustavo Aguilar, "El sistema bancario en Sinaloa (1889–1926): Su influencia en el crecimiento económico," in Mario Cerutti and Carlos Marichal, eds., *La banca regional en México, 1870–1930* (Mexico City, 2003), pp. 47–100; Mario Cerutti, "Empresariado y banca en el norte de México, 1879–1910: La fundación del Banco Refaccionario de la Laguna," in Cerutti and Marichal, eds., *La banca regional en México, 1870–1930*, pp. 168–215; Leticia Gamboa Ojeda, "El Banco Oriental de Mexico y la formación de un sistema de banca, 1900–1911," in Cerutti and Marichal, eds., *La banca regional en México, 1870–1930*, pp. 101–133; Leonor Ludlow, "El Banco Mercantil de Veracruz, 1898–1906," in Cerutti and Marichal, eds., *La banca regional en México, 1870–1930*, pp. 134–167; María Guadalupe Rodríguez López, "La banca porfiriana en Durango," in Mario Cerruti, ed., *Durango (1840–1915): Banca, transportes, tierra e industria* (Monterrey, Nuevo León, 1995), pp. 7–34; María Guadalupe Rodríguez López, "Paz y bancos en Durango durante el Porfiriato," in Cerutti and Marichal, eds., *La banca regional en México, 1870–1930*, pp. 254–290; Maria Eugenia Romero Ibarra, "El Banco del Estado de México, 1897–1914," in Cerutti and Marichal, eds., *La banca regional en México, 1870–1930*, pp. 216–251; Jaime Olveda, "Bancos y banqueros en Guadalajara," in Cerutti and Marichal, eds., *La banca regional en México, 1870–1930*, pp. 291–320.

50. Mexico, Secretaria de Hacienda, *Anuario de Estadística Fiscal, 1911–12* (Mexico City, 1912), pp. 236, 255.

51. Maurer, *The Power and the Money*, pp. 85–87.
52. Haber, "Industrial Concentration," pp. 559–580; Maurer and Haber, "Related Lending and Economic Performance," pp. 551–581.
53. Haber, Razo, and Maurer, *The Politics of Property Rights*, chapter 5.
54. Maurer, *The Power and the Money*, pp. 134–159; Haber, Razo, and Maurer, *The Politics of Property Rights*, chapter 4.

# 4

## Intra-Island and Inter-Island Comparisons

JARED DIAMOND

This chapter presents two comparative studies, both dealing with islands but lying at opposite extremes of comparative history with regard to number of societies compared, quantitation, and use of statistics. My first study is a narrative, nonquantitative, nonstatistical historical comparison of the two nations that divide the modest-sized Caribbean island of Hispaniola, in order to address the question: why did living conditions gradually become so much poorer and more desperate in the island's western half (now Haiti) than in the eastern half (now the Dominican Republic), even though the western half was formerly far richer and more powerful than the eastern half? My second comparison is a quantitative, statistical one of eighty-one Pacific island societies, in order to understand why Polynesian Easter Island, famous for erecting gigantic stone statues, also became famous for suffering one of the most extreme cases of deforestation and resulting social conflict in the Pacific.

My comparison of Haiti and the Dominican Republic belongs to the field of studies termed *natural experiments of borders*. These studies seek to identify the effects of human institutions on history by studying the creation or removal of a border drawn arbitrarily across a landscape (i.e., not coinciding with a major environmental boundary). In one form of the "experiment," one examines the effect of drawing a border where previously there was none, thereby causing two formerly similar societies to diverge: for example, the creation of the border between East and West Germany in 1945, between North and South Korea in 1945, and between the Baltic Republics and Russia in 1991. Conversely, the opposite "experiment" examines the effect of removing a border where previously there was one: as illustrated by the reunification of East and West Germany in 1989,[1] and the recent entry of Slovenia into the European Union. These comparisons can shed light on the effects of differing institutions and histories. They reduce the effects of other variables, either by comparison of the same geographic area before and after the creation or removal of the border, or by simultaneous comparison of two neighboring and geographically similar areas.

Haiti is the poorest country in the Americas and one of the poorest countries in the world.[2] It is more than 99% deforested, with massive soil erosion. Its government is unable to provide most of its citizens with even the most basic services, such as water, electricity, sewage disposal, and education. In contrast, the Dominican Republic, though still a developing nation, now has an average per capita income six times that of Haiti, remains 28% forested, and maintains the most comprehensive natural reserve system of the New World. It is the world's third leading exporter of avocados and the leading exporter of great baseball players, as every admirer of Pedro Martinez and Sammy Sosa knows. It is a functioning democracy in which in recent elections the incumbent presidents have lost and have peacefully retired. With a population nearly equal to that of the Dominican Republic, Haiti has only one-fifth of the Dominican Republic's number of employed workers, one-fifth of its number of cars and trucks, one-sixth of its miles of paved roads, one-seventh of its number of people with higher education, one-eighth of its number of physicians, one-eleventh of its annual quantity of oil imported and consumed, one-seventeenth of its per capita medical spending, one-twenty-fourth of its quantity of electricity generated, one-twenty-seventh of its annual exports, and one-thirty-third of its number of television sets. At the same time, Haiti has a population density 72% higher than the Dominican Republic's, 2.5 times the Dominican Republic's infant mortality rate, five times the number of malnourished children under the age of 5, seven times the number of cases of malaria, and eleven times the number of cases of AIDS.

Yet those two nations share the same island. Modern Haiti's desperate condition becomes even more striking when one reflects on the fact that in colonial times western Hispaniola, then known by its French name of St. Domingue, was by far the richest colony in the Americas and possibly in the world, accounting for almost two-thirds of France's worldwide foreign investments.[3] Even after the economic and social devastation and population decline associated with western Hispaniola's long wars of independence, Haiti remained much richer and more powerful than the Dominican Republic, which it conquered and annexed during the years 1822–1844. Not until the first few decades of the twentieth century did the Dominican economy overtake Haiti's.[4] How can we account for this stunning reversal of fortune?

From the air, anyone who has flown from Miami to Santo Domingo will have seen the obvious border standing out on the landscape 30,000 feet below, as if the island had been cut by a sharp knife. To the west of the knife line, the land is brown and treeless; to the east of the line, it is green and forested. If one actually stands on the border facing north and turns to one's left, one sees the muddy bare fields of Haiti, while a few dozen yards away to the right of the line begin the pine forests of the Dominican Republic. This sight makes clear that it is impossible to understand Haiti without understanding the Dominican Republic.

I shall now give a brief and oversimplified narrative comparison of their historical trajectories. To anyone who would complain that the story is more complicated than my description of it, I would answer: yes, of course it is much more complicated; be grateful that length limits for my chapter oblige me to reduce this section on Hispaniola to just a few pages and to describe three major sets of factors, and prevent me from asking you to read 793 pages setting out seventy-three other factors. My interpretation of the differences between Haitian and Dominican societies involves climatic and environmental differences independent of humans; cultural (including linguistic), economic, and political differences that arose in the course of human history, and that played out differently in the colonial era and in the postindependence era; and individual differences between the two countries' long-entrenched twentieth-century dictators, but those individual differences may not have been as separate a factor as might at first appear.

The first set of differences involves the different environments of the western and eastern parts of Hispaniola. Because the wind-bearing rains come mostly from the east, rainfall decreases from east to west, and the western (Haitian) side of the island is drier. It is also steeper, with thinner and less fertile soils, and without the broad Cibao Valley in the Dominican Republic's center, which contains the island's most fertile soils and most productive land for agriculture. Those environmental differences made the Haitian side more prone to deforestation (because of lower rainfall and hence slower tree regrowth) and more prone to soil erosion (because of the greater steepness and shallower soils).

In Haiti, as elsewhere in the world, the consequences of deforestation have included not only soil erosion but also decreased soil fertility, loss of timber and other forest-derived building materials, increased sediment loads in rivers, decreased watershed protection and hence decreased hydroelectric power potential, and the loss of wood for making charcoal, Haiti's principal fuel for cooking. Because forests themselves generate rain as a result of water transpiration through trees, deforestation tends to create a vicious cycle as the felling of trees reduces rainfall, thereby making the landscape more prone to further deforestation, which in turn further reduces rainfall. Thus, even if the human societies of Haiti and the Dominican Republic had been culturally, economically, and politically identical (which they have not been), the Haitian part of Hispaniola would still have faced more serious environmental problems.

The second set of differences between Haiti and the Dominican Republic involves different colonial histories. Spain, the first European nation to colonize Hispaniola, established its capital in the east, at Santo Domingo near the mouth of the Ozama River. Founded in A.D. 1496 by Christopher Columbus's brother Bartolomeo, Santo Domingo served for several decades as the capital of all of Spain's New World possessions, until its importance was diminished by Spanish conquests in Mexico and Peru. Hence French, British, and Dutch pirates seeking to intercept Spanish galleons sailing home to Spain from Santo Domingo established themselves in the western part of Hispaniola, on the same island as Santo Domingo but as far as possible from the center of Spanish government. In the 1600s, France gained control of the western part of Hispaniola, as recognized by the Treaty of Ryswick in 1697, with borders definitively drawn by the Treaty of Aranjuez in 1777.

By that time, however, France was richer than Spain, could afford to buy and import many slaves, and had few other New World colonies competing for investment and attention. The French colony of western Hispaniola that would later become Haiti ended up with a population composed 85% of slaves. By the 1600s, however, Spain had much more profitable New World colonies (especially Mexico and Peru) and could not afford to buy (or did not buy) many slaves to bring to the eastern part that became the Dominican Republic, whose slave population became only 10–15% of the total population. As of 1785, the slave population was about 500,000 in the French part of Hispaniola but only between 15,000 and 30,000 in the Spanish part.[5]

The much greater wealth (gross product) of western (later Haitian) than eastern (later Dominican) Hispaniola in colonial times resulted from facts or events of human history rather than from environmental considerations. That is, colonial Haiti was richer not *because* of its environmental advantages, but *despite* its environmental disadvantages of lower rainfall, steeper slopes, thinner and less fertile soils, and lack of a broad central valley. In short, the historical facts or events that led to colonial Haiti becoming richer included Spain's capital being established at the convenient port site of Santo Domingo in eastern Hispaniola, for reasons that had nothing to do with the environmental advantages of eastern Hispaniola for agriculture (in Columbus's time the Spaniards were bent on extracting gold from the Indians rather than on developing plantations); French pirates consequently establishing themselves in the west; France being richer than Spain (hence better able to afford slaves), for reasons that had nothing to do with Hispaniola; and Spain having more attractive New World investment opportunities than Hispaniola.

The historical developments that left Spain in the east and France in the west brought three sets of heavy consequences for the differences between Haiti and the Dominican Republic that we observe today. First, Haiti ended up with considerably higher human population density, despite its agricultural disadvantages. Second, rather than return to France empty, the many French ships bringing slaves to Haiti from Africa carried back wood from Haiti's forests, and those timber exports plus Haiti's denser human population and drier climate commenced Haiti's deforestation. Finally, Haitian slaves, who came from many different original African-language groups, developed for communication a Creole language of their own, just as did many other slave societies.[6] Today, about 90% of Haiti's population still speaks only Haitian Creole (a language spoken by virtually no one else in the world except emigrant Haitians), and only about 10% of the population speaks French. That is, Haitians are linguistically isolated from the rest of the world.[7] In the Dominican Republic, however, the overwhelmingly dominant language is Spanish; there was never a huge slave population, so that a strictly indigenous Creole language comparable to Haitian Creole never developed. The minor Dominican languages are major world languages spoken by emigrant communities (English, Chinese, Arabic, Catalan, and Japanese).[8]

Thus, cultural differences between a densely populated, Creole-speaking, slave society in the west and a more sparsely populated,

Spanish-speaking, nonslave society in the east were already pronounced by the late 1700s, on the eve of Haitian and Dominican independence. Those differences were reinforced by the different speeds and violence of the achievement of independence, and by different developments after independence, in the two parts of Hispaniola. Haiti's slaves achieved freedom and independence in 1804, after ferocious struggles against French armies beginning in 1791, the return of a Napoleonic French army in 1801 to restore French rule, France's treacherous capture of the slave leader Toussaint-L'Ouverture at a parley, and the French evacuation of Haiti beginning in 1803. Those events led Haitians correctly to distrust Europeans and to fear that a return of Europeans could mean yet another attempt to reimpose slavery. Hence independent Haiti killed the remaining whites, and divided and destroyed their plantations. Thereafter, the last thing that most Haitians wanted was European immigration and investment. Conversely, the last thing that many slave-owning Europeans and Americans wanted was to see a slave revolt succeed, so they refused opportunities to invest in or help Haiti, and that became a major factor behind Haiti's increasing poverty.[9] A further obstacle to relations between Haitians and Europe or the United States was the language barrier: Europeans and Americans did not understand Haitian Creole, and few Haitians spoke French. This language barrier was already in place at the time of Haitian independence. However, the lack of European and American involvement in Haiti during the postindependence period contributed to the language barrier's persistence, by ensuring that Haitian Creole would not be extensively replaced by a European language.

In the Dominican part of Hispaniola, the "struggle" for independence unfolded very differently. The Spanish settlers of eastern Hispaniola were so little interested in independence that, after the departure in 1809 of French troops and then of British naval forces that had controlled the Spanish colony during the Napoleonic Wars, the settlers requested that the Spanish motherland maintain their status as a colony.[10] Not until 1821 did the settlers declare independence, whereupon they were promptly conquered and annexed by the much stronger and more numerous Haitians, who were not expelled until 1844. In 1861, at the request of the Dominican leader, Spain reannexed Dominican territory until 1865, when (after an increasingly fierce Dominican rebellion beginning in 1863) the queen of Spain finally annulled the annexation of "a territory Spain did not really want."[11] Throughout the nineteenth century, aided by the settlers' speaking a European language (Spanish) and spared Haiti's legacy of being founded by a successful slave revolt, the Dominican Republic developed exports and attracted increasing European investment and emigration from a wide variety of European immigrant groups, including not only Spaniards but also Germans, Italians, Lebanese, and Austrians, whose economic significance was out of proportion to their modest numbers.[12]

By 1930, then, Haiti and the Dominican Republic had diverged to a minor extent because of (and initially despite) environmental differences, and to a major extent because of cultural, economic, and political differences that had already existed before the independence era of 1791–1821, only to become amplified after independence. The remaining factor promoting the divergence of Haiti and the Dominican Republic was the difference between their two dictators, both of them with long tenures in power (especially Rafael Trujillo's thirty-one years), equally evil, but very different in their foreign and economic policies. Trujillo, dictator of the Dominican Republic from 1930 until 1961, sought personal wealth. To that end, he converted the Dominican state virtually into his private business. In order to enrich himself, he developed many Dominican export industries that he personally owned or controlled: exports of beef, cement, chocolate, cigarettes, coffee, rice, salt, sugar, tobacco, wood, and other products. He also developed and owned or controlled airlines, banks, gambling casinos, hotels, insurance companies, land, shipping lines, and textile mills. He invited a Puerto Rican scientist and Swedish foresters to survey the forests of the Dominican Republic, which he then rigorously protected from being cut by others, in order that he personally could profit from them by well-managed logging operations. He pocketed 10% of the salaries of Dominican state employees. He even took a personal cut of the earnings of prostitutes. Thus, the Dominican economy and export industries grew under the evil Trujillo and continued to grow under his long-serving successor Joaquín Balaguer and under other presidents who followed. In Haiti, however, the dictator "Papa Doc" Duvalier (1957–1971) had little interest in economic development, export industries, or logging for his own profit, did not bring in foreign consultants, and allowed deforestation to continue.

One might be inclined to attribute this difference in economic policy between Haiti's and the Dominican Republic's dictators merely to chance differences between individuals. Other contributing factors include nationalistic tension between these neighboring countries (fostered by Trujillo's order to kill 15,000 Haitians and by Duvalier's threat to support anti-Trujillo Dominican exiles), occasional cooperation between the two dictators (e.g., Trujillo paying Duvalier in cash for Haitian workers to cut cane for Dominican sugar mills), and episodes of American military intervention in both countries. Both Trujillo and Duvalier were distinctive individuals, and no one would claim that Trujillo was a typical Dominican or that Duvalier was a typical Haitian.

However, there is more to the difference between Trujillo's and Duvalier's economic policies than just chance differences between individuals. Specifically, in his economic policies Trujillo pursued (to his private advantage) the Dominican Republic's long-standing interest in exports and foreign trade, and he was able to enlist (voluntarily or by compulsion) thousands of other Dominicans in his efforts, while Duvalier instead maintained a disinterest in or hostility to exports and foreign trade of long standing in independent Haiti's history.[13]

This qualitative comparison of Haiti with the Dominican Republic thus helps illuminate why Haiti became so poor. The role of Haiti's background as a major slave colony is of course familiar to historians.[14] But there is scope for more detailed and extensive comparisons that will ultimately increase our understanding of these neighboring countries sharing the same island. One extension would be to recognize that, although Haiti and the Dominican Republic alone offer just a two-country natural experiment, more might be learned through a five-country comparison, by extending the study to include the three other political entities on the neighboring islands of the Greater Antilles (Cuba, Jamaica, and Puerto Rico). The other extension would be to carry out quantitative comparisons, at different historical times, of Haiti and the Dominican Republic, in order to trace in time how their differences with respect to measures of wealth, forest cover, population, and exports developed. In the 1700s, Haiti was far richer than what is now the Dominican Republic; today it is far poorer. When did the Dominican Republic catch up to and overtake Haiti, and how much (if any) of the Dominican Republic's lead had already developed before Trujillo?

My other case study involves an effort to understand deforestation and the resulting collapse of Polynesian society on Easter Island, one of the most famous and most discussed problems of Polynesian history.[15] For the most part, it gets studied by people who call themselves archaeologists, rather than by people who call themselves historians, because the collapse befell a preliterate society, and so we lack the archival written evidence that is a hallmark of studies by historians. Nevertheless, the Polynesian collapse on Easter Island is still a problem of human history. This study illustrates the ubiquitous challenge that historians face in identifying the most significant causes of multidetermined or multicausal phenomena and illustrates how this problem can be approached by means of quantitative statistical comparisons of many individual case studies.

The basic facts are that Easter Island's Polynesians chopped down or burned, and thereby exterminated, almost all of the island's dozens of tree species. That course of action sounds like a really shortsighted one for people who depended on wood and trees for their cooking fuel, heating fuel, canoes, house construction materials, rope, fertilizer, and sleds and levers for transporting and erecting statues. Not surprisingly, as a result of that deforestation, the Easter Islanders ended up in a civil war, starving, and with a collapse of population and political organization.[16]

Yet this dire result is surprising when we consider that exactly the same ancestral people, Polynesians, and two groups of related peoples, Melanesians and Micronesians, colonized hundreds of other Pacific islands that did not suffer such a catastrophic outcome.[17] Was it that Easter Islanders were uniquely improvident and became addicted to the uniquely extravagant habit of carving and erecting big stone statues? But Polynesians on other islands were given to extravagant customs of their own, such as building thousands of big wooden canoes and big stone temples, without suffering a collapse.

Seven years ago, I met the University of Hawaii archaeologist Barry Rolett, who had been doing excavations and studying modern societies on other Polynesian islands, the Marquesas, where neither massive deforestation nor societal collapse had occurred prior to European arrival. Barry and I wondered whether the differing outcomes between the Marquesas and Easter Island were due to the islands' different environments. For example, the Marquesas are wetter and warmer than Easter Island, so that one would expect chopped-down trees to be replaced more rapidly by growth of new trees on the Marquesas than on Easter. But because there are many other differences between the Marquesas and Easter Island, a comparison of just those two islands could not have justified our attributing the different outcomes to those particular differences in rainfall and temperature.

Hence Barry spent two years assembling a database of sixty-nine Pacific islands, which he coded for the degree of deforestation that resulted from Polynesian settlement by the time that Europeans first saw the island. Barry could not express degree of deforestation by a number, but he did find it possible to place it more crudely along a five-point scale: the degree of deforestation ranged from complete deforestation for Easter through various intermediate degrees of deforestation to slight or negligible deforestation for some other islands. Next, Barry and I coded nine environmental variables and four agricultural variables for each island, either numerically or by ranking them crudely along two-point, three-point, or four-point scales. For example, exact numerical values for the age of each island in years are mostly unknown, so we instead just categorized island age as "young," "medium," or "old." Then we arranged for four sets of statistical analyses of the correlations between those variables and the degree of deforestation: bivariate correlation, multivariate regression, multivariate tree models, and residual analyses.[18] For twelve of the sixty-nine islands we were able to profit from a further natural experiment within each island: different sites on the same island had different environments and ended up with different degrees of deforestation. Because neither Barry nor I possess statistical competence, we worked in collaboration with a professional statistician, who did the actual analyses.

At the outset, we wondered about the role of cultural differences, especially the well-known differences among Polynesian societies in their agricultural practices. Did inter-island variation in agricultural methods help explain why some islands ended up deforested, while others did not? We put much effort into coding and analyzing the four main types of Polynesian agricultural practices for our eighty-one islands or locations: wet-field cultivation of taro; dry-field cultivation of yams, taro, and other crops; breadfruit arboriculture; and arboriculture of Tahitian chestnut and canarium nuts. We classified each type as to whether it was absent, present but minor, important, or dominant on each island. But none of those four agricultural practices proved statistically significant in explaining inter-island variation in deforestation.

In contrast, our data set did yield statistically significant effects for all nine environmental variables on deforestation.[19] As for the first two variables (rainfall and temperature), whose effects Barry and I had already suspected when we began the study, deforestation did prove to be lower on islands with higher rainfall and warmer temperatures. That outcome is easily understandable: rainfall and temperature are the main two determinants of plant growth rates. The faster new trees grow back as people chop down mature trees, the less deforestation the island suffers in the steady state.

The next three outcomes involved island age, wind-borne ash, and wind-borne dust. Deforestation turned out to be lower on younger than on older volcanic islands, lower on islands situated near volcanoes that release wind-borne ash than on islands whose volcanoes instead release flowing lava, and lower on islands to which stratospheric winds carry lots of dust for thousands of miles eastward from the steppes of Central Asia than on islands far from that dust plume. Our climatologist and ecologist colleagues had suggested that we try these three variables, and their effects came to us as a big surprise: we had never dreamed that volcanic ash and Asian dust might somehow be related to Polynesian island deforestation. But our colleagues pointed out the connection, which on reflection proves understandable: as every gardener knows, high soil nutrient levels increase rates of plant growth. Gardeners also know that added nutrients get leached out with time, and that is why older volcanoes have more leached soils and lower tree growth rates and more extensive deforestation in the steady state than do younger volcanoes. However, leached nutrients also become replenished by nutrients in wind-borne ash or dust, so that islands receiving much ash or dust have more rapid tree regrowth and hence suffer less deforestation.[20]

Our sixth variable, makatea, refers to a sharp coral terrain resembling huge irregular piles of broken glass, full of dangerous sharp deep holes, and horrible to walk on. Not surprisingly, ancient Polynesians also did not like to walk on makatea terrain, and so islands with makatea suffered less deforestation than islands without this terrain.

Finally, the seventh, eighth, and ninth variables were island area, elevation, and isolation. Deforestation decreased with area and elevation and increased with island isolation, for multiple reasons including rain generation by clouds around the mountains of high islands, and low perimeter/area ratios of big islands.

Collectively, these nine variables accounted for most variation in deforestation among Pacific islands. In particular, our final multiple regression equation predicted Easter to suffer especially extensive deforestation because all nine environmental variables were unfavorable for Easter's inhabitants: Easter Island receives the least wind-blown ash and dust of any Pacific island; it is nearly the coldest and most isolated Polynesian island; it completely lacks makatea; and it is relatively low, small, old, and dry.

Thus Easter became deforested not because its inhabitants were especially shortsighted or did especially strange things, but because they had the bad luck to find themselves living on one of the Pacific's most environmentally fragile islands, with the lowest regrowth rates of trees. We could never have teased apart this complex multicausal problem without a quantitative statistical analysis of a big database. For example, if we had studied just one island, or even if we had compared one wet island with one dry island, the effect of rainfall alone would have been confounded or obscured by the effects of the eight other variables. Similarly, epidemiologists could never have identified the many risk factors, or even a single risk factor, for cancer just by publishing a single case study of one smoker. Easter constitutes just one piece of a massive natural experiment on Pacific islands. By comparing many islands, one can confidently extract many conclusions, whereas by studying just a single island, it would be difficult to extract even a single conclusion.

With further effort, it may prove possible to identify still other factors that made Easter Island prone to deforestation. Two more environmental variables that we have not yet coded and analyzed, but that might prove significant, are month-to-month or year-to-year variation in rainfall and variation in nutrient inputs from seabird guano. In addition, as another possible predisposing cultural variable besides agricultural practices, one might wonder whether inter-island variation in political systems could have affected the outcome. For instance, were islands with strong chiefs more or less likely to end up deforested than islands with weak chiefs? Easter Island ranked as intermediate in its political system, with neither weak chiefs nor strong kings but with so-called paramount chiefs who provided some economic and cultural integration to the island's society without being able to eliminate the power of the island's dozen individual chiefs. Kirch's (Chapter 1) comparisons of Pacific island political systems have shown that larger and more productive islands, capable of supporting larger human populations, tended to end up with stronger chiefs.[21] Hence some of the effect of island area on deforestation that Barry Rolett and I detected may have been mediated by island variation in political systems—or may have unfolded *despite* island variation in political systems tending to oppose deforestation. These are among the many questions of Easter Island history meriting further study.

## NOTES

It is a pleasure to acknowledge my debts to Richard Turits, Matt Smith, and Peter Zoll for fruitful discussions about Hispaniola; and to many members of the History Department and other departments at Duke University and at UCLA, for stimulating brainstorming. Material was drawn from Chapter 2 of *Collapse: How Societies Choose to Fail or Succeed*, copyright © 2005. Published by Viking Penguin, a division of Penguin Group (USA) Inc.

1. Axel Ockenfels and Joachim Weimann, "Types and Patterns: An Experimental East-West-German Comparison of Cooperation and Solidarity," *Journal of Public Economics* 71 (1999): 275–287.
2. Comparative studies of Haiti and the Dominican Republic include Rayford Logan, *Haiti and the Dominican Republic* (New York, 1968); Rafael Emilio Yunén Z., *La Isla Como Es* (Santiago, Republica Dominicana, 1985); Bernardo Vega, *Trujillo y Haiti* (Santo Domingo, 1988 and 1995); Brenda Gayle Plummer, *Haiti and the United States: The Psychological Moment* (Athens, GA, 1992), chapter 8; and Michele Wecker, *Why the Cocks Fight: Dominicans, Haitians, and the Struggle for Hispaniola* (New York, 1999). Introductions to the literature on Haiti include C. L. R. James, *The Black*

*Jacobins*, 2nd ed. (London, 1963); Mats Lundahl, *Peasants and Poverty: A Study of Haiti* (London, 1979); Lundahl, *The Haitian Economy: Man, Land, and Markets* (London, 1983); Lundahl, *Politics or Markets? Essays on Haitian Underdevelopment* (London, 1992); Michael Dash, *Culture and Customs of Haiti* (Westport, CT, 2001); Lauren T. Dubois, *Avengers of the New World* (Cambridge, MA, 2004); John Garrigus, *Before Haiti* (New York, 2006); David Nicholls, *From Dessalines to Duvalier: Race, Colour, and National Independence in Haiti* (Cambridge, 1992); and Brenda Gayle Plummer's above-cited *Haiti and the United States*. Standard histories of the Dominican Republic are Frank Moya Pons, *The Dominican Republic: A National History* (Princeton, NJ, 1998); Moya Pons, *Manual de Historia Dominicana*, 9th ed. (Santiago, Republica Dominicana, 1999); and Roberto Cassá, *Historia, Social y Económica de la Republica Dominicana*, 2 vols. (Santo Domingo, Republica Dominicana, 1998 and 2001). More specific studies of the Dominican Republic include Martin Clausner, *Rural Santo Domingo: Settled, Unsettled, Resettled* (Philadelphia, 1973), and Harry Hoetink, *The Dominican People, 1850–1900: Notes for a Historical Sociology* (Baltimore, MD, 1982). Accounts of the Trujillo era in the Dominican Republic include Howard Wiarda, *Dictatorship and Development: The Methods of Control in Trujillo's Dominican Republic* (Gainesville, FL, 1968); Claudio Vedovato, *Politics, Foreign Trade and Economic Development: A Study of the Dominican Republic* (London, 1986); and Richard Lee Turits, *Foundations of Despotism: Peasants, the Trujillo Regime, and Modernity in Dominican History* (Palo Alto, CA, 2002). Accounts of the Duvalier era in Haiti include David Nicholls's above-cited *From Dessalines to Duvalier* and Michel-Rolph Trouillot, *Haiti, State against Nation: The Origins and Legacy of Duvalierism* (New York, 1990). I previously compared Haiti and the Dominican Republic in chapter 11 of my book *Collapse* (New York, 2005).

3. Here, I use the phrase "richest colony" in the sense of "with the highest gross national product." "Rich" and "poor" are commonly used either in that sense of "with high or low gross national product," or else in the sense of "with high or low average per capita income." In the previous text paragraph where I referred to Haiti as the poorest country in the Americas today, my measure was average per capita income. Haiti's modern population of around 8 million means that, multiplying that average per capita income times population, Haiti's gross national income (related but not identical to product) is higher than that of two mainland South American nations

(Guyana and Suriname) with populations ten or twenty times lower than Haiti's, though with per capita incomes nearly three times higher.

Naturally, labeling colonial St. Domingue/Haiti as rich does not mean that most individual Haitians were rich. Instead, in colonial times most Haitians were desperately poor slaves of African origin, dying in huge numbers from overwork and undernutrition; Haiti's immense wealth was controlled by its small minority of French planters, with a significant role also played by about 30,000 free people of color. Today as well, 95% of Haiti's population is identified as black; the remaining small minority is identified as mulattoes (mostly) or whites (a few); a mulatto elite dominated political power until 1946; and French is still the language of the elite. See Nicholls, *From Dessalines to Duvalier.*

While average differences in population makeup between the two halves of Hispaniola are real, they are often exaggerated in the public mystique. Dominicans tend to emphasize their supposed homogeneity, whiteness, and number of European immigrants, which they contrast with a Haitian population viewed (and viewing itself) as black and with a smaller number of European immigrants.

4. The wealth of French St. Domingue was derived mainly from large sugar plantations. After the Haitian revolution, Haitian agriculture eventually became based on small peasant landholdings, and the principal cash crop became coffee, to which Haiti's mountainous terrain is well suited. Coffee exports increased greatly in the last decades of the French colonial era and permitted export agriculture (and consequent deforestation) to expand from Haiti's coastal plains (suitable for sugar plantations) into its mountainous interior. Spain also developed large sugar plantations in its Hispaniola colony in the 1500s, but these plantations went into decline toward the end of that century for debated reasons. Large sugar plantations were reestablished in the Dominican Republic in the twentieth century.

5. Extended discussions of the debated reasons why the French part of Hispaniola ended up with many more slaves than the Spanish part will be found in Turits, *Foundations of Despotism,* chapter 1; Moya Pons, *The Dominican Republic,* chapter 2; and Cassá, *Historia Social y Económica de la Republica Dominicana,* chapters 7–9. Slaves were purchased not by the French or Spanish governments themselves but by private individuals. Prices of slaves came to be higher and less affordable in Spanish than in French colonies, due at least in part to higher Spanish government taxes on slaves as a policy. The role of this factor is apparent from the boom in slave

imports into Spanish Cuba when the Spanish government dropped slave taxes in 1790. The question discussed in my text could thus be rephrased to ask why the Spanish government but not the French government lacked the interest and incentive to help private individuals purchase slaves. For further discussion, see David Eltis, *Economic Growth and the Ending of the Transatlantic Slave Trade* (New York, 1987).

6. Many different so-called Creole languages have arisen independently around the world. Linguists distinguish between two types of languages that arise in contact situations: so-called pidgin languages, which arise spontaneously between groups (such as colonists and workers, or visiting traders and local residents) who speak different native languages but need to communicate with each other; and Creole languages, which arise when a generation of children of parents speaking pidgin as a second language begins to adopt, and to develop further, that pidgin as their primary language. Among discussions of creolization are Robert A. Hall Jr., *Pidgin and Creole Languages* (Ithaca, NY, 1966); Derek Bickerton, *Roots of Language* (Ann Arbor, MI, 1981); and Bickerton, *Language and Species* (Chicago, 1990).

7. The role of language as a contributor to Haiti's current poverty is debated. Most historians rate other factors, such as Haiti's political instability and overpopulation and underdeveloped communications infrastructure, as more significant factors. Haitians migrate in large numbers across linguistic barriers to the Dominican Republic, other Caribbean nations, and the United States. Haitian Creole is comprehensible to speakers of other French Creoles in some other small Caribbean nations, commonwealths, or French departments that formerly were French colonies (Martinique, Guadeloupe, Dominica, and St. Lucia). Creole has not prevented foreign intervention in Haiti, nor some European and North American and Arabic immigration into Haiti. The segment of Haiti's population most connected by business and diplomatic ties to other countries is Haiti's elite, which speaks French (and often English and Spanish as well). But the fact remains that most Haitians speak only Haitian Creole with which they cannot communicate outside the Caribbean, whereas virtually all Dominicans speak Spanish, a language spoken by 400 million other people in the world. The consequences of this fact warrant further study.

8. Barbara F. Grimes, ed., *Ethnologue: Languages of the World*, vol. 1 (Dallas, TX, 2000), summarizes the number of speakers of each language in the Dominican Republic and in Haiti on pp. 301 and 311, respectively.

9. It was not until the years 1825–1838, several decades after Haitian independence, that France, Britain, the Netherlands, Denmark, and Sweden extended diplomatic recognition to Haiti. The Vatican and the United States did not do so until 1860 and 1862, respectively. But the effects of this foreign diplomatic ostracism of Haiti and of Haitian distrust of foreigners, though undoubtedly significant, should not be exaggerated and did not constitute an impervious cordon. British traders were already trading with Haiti by 1807, and the United States was the leading source of imports into Haiti even during the era of diplomatic nonrecognition. Lebanese immigrants to Haiti in the 1890s, numbering about 2,000 by 1895, played an important role in commerce until many were expelled in 1905.

10. Dominicans now scornfully apply the term *España Boba* (Silly Spain) to this period of their history (Moya Pons, *The Dominican Republic*, p. 117).

11. Moya Pons, *The Dominican Republic*, p. 218.

12. Another factor relevant in this connection has been the much higher population density of Haiti than of the Dominican Republic, a difference that translated itself into much more unoccupied or unutilized land in the Dominican Republic than in Haiti. Through the nineteenth century, much Dominican land was only sparsely inhabited and was utilized mainly for hunting wild pigs and cattle. That land was potentially available for foreign settlers, foreign investors, and twentieth-century development of large sugar plantations. Some historians consider the effect of the Dominican Republic's lower population density as a more important factor in its surpassing Haiti, developing exports, and attracting European investment and immigration than the language difference between the two halves of the island, Haitian fear of foreigners, and foreign refusal to acknowledge Haiti's legitimacy.

13. Interpretations of Trujillo and Duvalier, and of the differences between them, are controversial among historians. Neither Trujillo nor Duvalier would have been as successful in retaining power without the nationalism generated by tension with the other half of Hispaniola. Another important consideration is the different years and different international contexts in which Duvalier and Trujillo came to power. Trujillo began his rise to power in the 1920s, when U.S. Marines were still occupying the Dominican Republic, and he initially worked closely with those occupation forces. In contrast, Duvalier attained power in 1957 after two decades of pro-American presidents of Haiti, and Duvalier's rejection of that cooperation with the United States (reminiscent of Trujillo's cooperation in the 1920s) gained popular legitimacy for Duvalier despite his cruelty.

14. Space limitations prevent me from exploring many other factors significant in understanding the different developments of Haiti and the Dominican Republic. For example, twentieth-century Haiti and the Dominican Republic, like most other Caribbean nations, both repeatedly attempted to develop a tourist industry to contribute to their economies. These efforts have achieved mixed success, but they have been more successful in the Dominican Republic. Brenda Gayle Plummer, "The Golden Age of Haitian Tourism," discusses how the tourist industry failed to live up to its promise in Haiti. In the twentieth century the United States occupied both parts of Hispaniola, with some intention of improving conditions for the inhabitants, though with different effects; for example, American land surveyors encountered more peasant resistance in Haiti than in the Dominican Republic. The governing elite and the peasants reached different compromises or standoffs in Haiti and in the Dominican Republic. One way to characterize the different outcomes is that the Haitian elite obtained money by taxing imports and exports, otherwise largely ignored the peasants, and failed to provide transportation and infrastructure that might have improved the prosperity of Haitian small farms, whereas a compromise was reached in the Dominican Republic under which the peasants were provided with some support or infrastructure that allowed them to produce cash crops, balanced by terrorist governmental control.

15. Jo Anne Van Tilburg, *Easter Island: Archaeology, Ecology and Culture* (Washington, DC, 1994); John Flenley and Paul Bahn, *The Enigmas of Easter Island* (New York, 2002); John Loret and John T. Tanacredi, eds., *Easter Island: Scientific Exploration into the World's Environmental Problems in Microcosm* (New York, 2003); Diamond, *Collapse,* chapter 2.

16. A recent dissenting view proposes that Easter Island society collapsed only after European arrival and due to European impacts, rather than before European arrival and due to Polynesian impacts; and that the deforestation was caused by rats rather than by people; see Terry Hunt, "Rethinking the Fall of Easter Island," *American Scientist* 94 (2006): 412–419. However, abundant archaeological, palynological, and paleontological evidence from the five or more centuries before European arrival demonstrates serious pre-European impacts, including the extinction of all of the island's land-bird species and most of its seabird species originally exploited for food, extinction of almost all of the island's tree species, soil erosion from that removal of the forest, decrease in exploitation of dolphins and tuna as meat sources (because of the loss of trees with which to build canoes for fishing),

replacement of wood by agricultural scraps as fuel in ovens (because of the loss of trees), loss of palm sap and nuts as major food sources, abandonment of upland plantations, resort to living in caves as defensive retreats when fighting became widespread, and an end to carving statues (because of the loss of wood necessary to transport and erect them); see Jared Diamond, "Easter Island Revisited," *Science* 317 (2007): 1692–1694. Palm stumps chopped off at ground level, and burned stumps and nuts, demonstrate deforestation by people rather than by rats (Andreas Mieth and Hans-Rudolf Bork, "History, Origin and Extent of Soil Erosion on Easter Island [Rapa Nui]," *Catena* 63 [2005]: 244–260).

17. Peter Bellwood, *The Polynesians: Prehistory of an Island People,* revised ed. (London, 1987); Patrick Vinton Kirch, *The Lapita Peoples: Ancestors of the Oceanic World* (Cambridge, MA, 1997); Matthew Spriggs, *The Island Melanesians* (Cambridge, MA, 1997).

18. Here is a short crash course in these widely used statistical methods. Briefly, bivariate correlation examines whether two variables tend to occur in significant association with each other, but it examines only the two particular variables selected. Also, it does not ask whether their association could actually be mediated by some third variable rather than represent a true cause/effect relation between the two variables first selected. For instance, ownership of a Rolls Royce car is associated with long lifespan, not because Rolls Royce ownership directly promotes longevity, but because of the mediating effect of wealth: Rolls Royce ownership requires wealth, which permits good medical care and diet, which are what directly promote longevity. Multivariate regression seeks to mitigate these limitations of bivariate correlation by simultaneously testing for an association of one dependent variable (the variable whose variation is to be explained) with two or more independent variables (the variables that might explain that variation), ranking those associations in strength, and weeding out bivariate associations that are weak or actually mediated by another variable. Multivariate tree models seek to identify one or more clusters of several independent variables acting together on a dependent variable and to rank those clusters in strength. Residual analysis examines the remaining variation (the so-called residual variation) in one's dependent variable that still remains unexplained after some statistical analysis (e.g., after a multiple regression analysis). One then attempts to explain that residual variation, and thus to extract even more conclusions than were extracted by the first stage of this statistical analysis. In effect, residual analysis looks at "outlying data points":

that is, points whose values are still higher or lower than predicted by the first stage of statistical analysis.

19. Tables of the bivariate and multivariate regression coefficients, sequences in which predictive variables enter multivariate tree analyses, explained variances, and details of the statistical analyses are presented by Barry Rolett and Jared Diamond, "Environmental Predictors of Pre-European Deforestation on Pacific Islands," *Nature* 431 (2004): 443–446.

20. Amy Austin and Peter Vitousek, "Nutrient Dynamics on a Precipitation Gradient in Hawaii," *Oecologia* 113 (1998): 519–529; O. A. Chadwick, L. A. Derry, P. M. Vitousek, B. J. Huebert, and L. O. Hedin, "Changing Sources of Nutrients during Four Million Years of Ecosystem Development," *Nature* 397 (1999): 491–497; P. Ginoux et al., "Sources and Distributions of Dust Aerosols Simulated with the GOCART Model," *Journal of Geophysical Research* 106 (2001): 20255–20273.

21. Patrick Vinton Kirch, *The Evolution of the Polynesian Chiefdoms* (Cambridge, 1984); Kirch, *On the Road of the Winds: An Archaeological History of the Pacific Islands before European Contact* (Berkeley, CA, 2000).

# 5

## Shackled to the Past: The Causes and Consequences of Africa's Slave Trades

NATHAN NUNN

Africa's history is intimately connected with slavery. The continent has experienced four large slave trades, all of which date back at least to the mid-fifteenth century. The oldest of the slave trades, the trans-Saharan, Red Sea, and Indian Ocean slave trades, all date back to at least A.D. 800. During these trades, slaves were taken from land south of the Saharan desert, inland of the Red Sea, and inland of the coast of Eastern Africa, and were shipped to Northern Africa and the Middle East. The largest and most studied of the slave trades is the trans-Atlantic slave trade, where beginning in the fifteenth century, slaves were shipped from West Africa, West Central Africa, and Eastern Africa to the European colonies in the New World. Although the trans-Atlantic slave trade was the shortest in duration, it was the largest and most penetrating of the four. Between the fifteenth and eighteenth centuries, upwards of 12 million slaves were taken from the continent of Africa. The total number of slaves shipped during this same time period in the other three slave trades is somewhere around 6 million. In total, nearly 18 million slaves were shipped in the four slave trades over this 400-year period.[1]

Given the sheer magnitude of the slave trades, it is natural to ask what effect, if any, they had on African societies. This is an old and much debated question in the African history literature. A number of authors, dating back to at least the writings of Basil Davidson and

Walter Rodney, argue that the slave trades had a significant adverse impact on the political, social, and economic development of Africa.[2] For example, in his book *Slavery and African Life*, Patrick Manning argues that "slavery was corruption: it involved theft, bribery, and exercise of brute force as well as ruses. Slavery thus may be seen as one source of precolonial origins for modern corruption."[3] Along similar lines, Joseph Inikori argues that the long-term consequence of Africa's slave trades was to "alter the direction of the economic process in Africa away from development and towards underdevelopment and dependence."[4]

Recent research has examined the impact of the slave trades on specific ethnic groups. These studies have begun to uncover and document the detrimental effects of the slave trades on the institutional and social structures of African societies. They show how the external demand for slaves caused political instability, weakened states, promoted political and social fragmentation, and resulted in a deterioration of domestic legal institutions.[5]

The view of others, such as John Fage and David Northrup, is that the slave trades had little effect on the subsequent socioeconomic development of Africa.[6] David Northrup, examining the effects of the slave trade in southeastern Nigeria, concludes that "while it is true that the slave trade was cruel and produced a climate of fear and suspicion, its social and economic effects which can be measured were surprisingly benign."[7] These differences in opinion are not surprising. Even direct observers of the slave trades had very different views of the effects that the slave trades were having on African societies at the time. For example, while the English slave trader, Archibald Dalzel, felt that African societies were unaffected by the slave trade, the explorer and missionary, David Livingstone, argued that the slave trade had a devastating impact on African societies.[8]

This chapter attempts to shed light on this issue by using statistical analysis to examine the relationship between the severity of the slave trades and subsequent economic performance for different parts of Africa. This analysis is done by first constructing estimates of the number of slaves taken from each region of Africa between 1400 and 1900. The estimates are constructed by combining data of the number of slaves shipped from each African port or coastal region with data from historical documents reporting the ethnic identities of slaves shipped from Africa. Construction of the slave export estimates builds on the vast empirical literature that has evolved from the research of African historians over the past four decades. Because data on current economic performance, such as per capita gross domestic product (GDP), are only available at the national level, the statistical tests performed in the chapter use current countries as the unit of observation. As a result, when estimates of the number of slaves taken from different parts of Africa are constructed, a "part" is defined as the portion of the continent that today is a country. Although current political boundaries are completely arbitrary, particularly from a historical perspective, the limited availability of current economic data necessitates use of the modern nation-state as the unit of analysis.

An issue that arises when using modern countries as the unit of analysis is that they are different sizes. Therefore, variation in the number of slaves taken from different countries will reflect, at least to some degree, differences in country size. Therefore, the constructed country-level slave export measures are "normalized" to take into account differences in country size.

The logic of the statistical tests is as follows. If the slave trades are partly responsible for Africa's current underdevelopment, then one should observe that the parts of the continent from which the largest number of slaves were taken in the past are also the parts of the continent that are the poorest today. The tests performed in this chapter examine whether this pattern is observed in the data. The results confirm that the areas from which the most slaves were taken are indeed the parts of Africa that are the poorest today. As will be shown, this relationship is extremely strong, and it remains even when other important determinants of economic development, such as climate, geography, natural resource endowments, and past colonial experience are taken into account. Although these statistical correlations provide evidence that the slave trades adversely affected Africa's economic development, this evidence is still not conclusive. The reason is that it may have been the case that the parts of Africa from which the largest number of slaves were taken were initially the most underdeveloped. Because these characteristics persist today, these parts of Africa continue to be relatively underdeveloped. Therefore, one would observe that the parts of Africa that exported many slaves in the past are also poor today, even if the slave trades did not *cause* these areas to become underdeveloped. This alternative explanation is tested in the data by examining whether it was in fact the initially least developed parts of Africa that engaged most heavily in the slave trades. Consistent with the historical evidence, the data suggest that the parts of Africa that were initially the most developed, not the least developed, supplied the largest number of slaves.

Although this line of inquiry is different from previous historical research that examines the impacts of Africa's slave trades, the results presented here complement the evidence from these previous studies. For example, the macro-statistical perspective of this study complements more micro-level historical case studies, such as Walter Hawthorne's analysis of the impact of the slave trade on the Balanta, or Andrew Hubbell's study of the effects of the slave trade in the region of Souroudougou.[9] If the slave trades were detrimental to subsequent social and economic development, then these effects should be observed both at the micro level, when looking at specific ethnic groups during specific time periods, and at the macro level, when looking at broad patterns across the whole African continent over a longer time horizon. It may be that the slave trades had very specific impacts in some places during certain periods of time, but that these are not general effects present across a wide cross-section of societies. Evidence from the broader, more macro perspective presented here can shed light on how generalizable specific examples are. The use of macro-statistical analysis also complements broad historical studies that also take a macro perspective and examine the larger impacts of the slave trades within Africa. Examples of studies of this type include Paul Lovejoy's *Transformations in Slavery* and Patrick Manning's *Slavery and Occidental Life*.[10] This study can be seen as an extension of this line of research that simply applies more formal statistical techniques to examine the economic impacts of Africa's slave trades.

## ESTIMATES OF THE NUMBER OF SLAVES FROM AFRICAN COUNTRIES

### Construction Procedure

The analysis of this chapter builds on a long empirical tradition in the African history literature. The seminal work is Philip Curtin's (1969) *The Atlantic Slave Trade: A Census*, which used data available at the time to provide a detailed description and comprehensive analysis of the origins and destinations of slaves shipped during the trans-Atlantic slave trade.[11] Since Curtin's publication in 1969, a very impressive amount of additional information has been collected and analyzed by African historians. The most recent and most extensive efforts are the *Trans-Atlantic Slave Trade Database*, which was developed by David Eltis, Stephen Behrendt, David Richardson, and Herbert Klein (1999), as well as the *Louisiana Slave Database* and the *Louisiana Free Database*, constructed by Gwendolyn Midlo Hall (2005).[12] Another notable contribution to this literature is Patrick Manning's work with computer models to generate simulations of the estimated demographic impacts of Africa's slave trades. The results were presented in a series of journal articles and in his book *Slavery and African Life*, which was published in 1990.[13]

The present analysis extends this line of research by using the wealth of available data to construct estimates of the number of slaves taken from the different parts of Africa. Then, the statistical relationship between the number of slaves taken in the past and current economic performance is examined.

The data used to construct the slave export estimates can be grouped into two categories. The first category includes data that report the total number of slaves exported from each port or region in Africa. For the trans-Atlantic slave trade, the data are from the updated version of the *Trans-Atlantic Slave Trade Database,* which records 34,584 voyages from 1514 to 1866. These data are gathered from documents and records located around the world. In most European ports, merchants were required to register their ships, declare the volume and value of goods transported, pay duties, and obtain formal permission to leave the port. Therefore, for each ship and voyage, typically, there exists a number of different registers and documents. In the database, 77% of the trans-Atlantic slave voyages after 1700 have shipping information from more than one source. Specific voyages are documented in as many as sixteen different sources. The average number of sources of data for each voyage is six. According to the authors' estimates, the database contains 82% of all trans-Atlantic slaving voyages ever attempted.[14] The first purchase of slaves recorded in the *Trans-Atlantic Slave Trade Database* is in 1526, decades after the beginning of the trans-Atlantic slave trade. For this reason, Ivana Elbl's estimates of the number and locations of slaves shipped during the early period of the Atlantic slave trade are also used. Elbl's estimates, which cover the period from 1450 to 1521, are based primarily on volume estimates recorded by observers at the time, as well as direct numerical data from surviving records.[15] For the Indian Ocean, Red Sea, and trans-Saharan slave trades, estimates published by Ralph Austen are used. The estimates are constructed using all available documents, records, and accounts by observers and government officials on the location and volume of slave exports.[16]

Using these data alone, one could construct estimates of the number of slaves that were shipped from the ports of each coastal country. However, the data do not provide information on where the slaves were originally captured. Slaves shipped from the ports of a coastal country may have come from a country located further inland. To construct estimates of the proportion of slaves shipped from the coast that came from inland countries, a second source of data that reports the ethnic identity of slaves shipped from Africa is also used. This information comes from a wide variety of different sources, including records of sale, plantation inventories, slave registers, slave runaway notices, court records, prison records, marriage records, death certificates, baptismal records, parish records, notarial records, and slave interviews.

Data on the ethnic identity of slaves shipped during the trans-Atlantic slave trade come from fifty-four samples, all from secondary sources. The sources report a total of 80,656 slaves for which their ethnic identity could be identified and a total of 229 distinct ethnic designations. Of the 200 plus ethnic designations, the most commonly observed are the Kongo, Fon, Yoruba, Malinke, Wolof, Bambara, and Hausa. Table 5.1 summarizes information about the ethnicity samples from the trans-Atlantic slave trade. Some of the largest samples are from British Caribbean slave censuses taken in the early nineteenth century. These data have been collected and published by Barry Higman in his book *Slave Populations of the British Caribbean, 1807–1834*. The data from this source include the samples from Anguilla, Berbice, Trinidad, St. Lucia, and St. Kitts listed in Table 5.1.[17] Another large sample is from Mary Karasch's book *Slave Life in Rio de Janeiro,* which provides information on a number of samples of slaves from Rio de Janeiro. The samples are from prison records, death certificates, and Free Africans' records.[18] One of the largest samples of slaves comes from Gwendolyn Midlo Hall's *Louisiana Slave Database* and *Louisiana Free Database.* For the early period of the trans-Atlantic slave trade, the largest sample, which is from Peru, is taken from Frederick Bowser's *The African Slave in Colonial Peru.*[19]

An important concern that arises from the sample of slaves reported in Table 5.1 is whether the sample is representative of the overall population of slaves shipped during the trans-Atlantic slave trade. A quick look at the table suggests that the answer is clearly no. For example, there are many more samples (and slaves) from the nineteenth century than from the eighteenth century, even though the height of the slave trade was reached in the eighteenth century. The nonrepresentativeness of the sample is a concern. However, as described below, the slave ethnicity data are so constructed as to minimize the measurement error caused because the ethnicity sample is not representative of the full population of slaves.

Data on the ethnic origins of slaves are much less plentiful for the Indian Ocean, trans-Saharan, and Red Sea slave trades. For the Indian Ocean slave trade, only one article, by Abdul Sheriff, published in *Slavery & Abolition* in 1988, has information on the ethnic origins of a significant sample of slaves shipped during this slave trade.[20] In this article, Sheriff reports the ethnic origins of 1,620 slaves emancipated in Zanzibar in 1860 and 1861. However, when reporting the data, Sheriff only lists the number of slaves of the six largest ethnic groups, Yao, Nyasa, Ngindo, Sagara, Mrima, and Nyamwezi, with all other slaves grouped under the heading "Others." Because of this shortcoming, the primary documents, which are housed in the Zanzibar National Archives, were examined. Two additional slave lists were also discovered at the archives. These were lists of slaves that were emancipated in 1884–1885 and in 1874–1908. The list recorded the slave's name, age, ethnic identity, date freed, and former master's name.[21] Together, the three samples include 9,774 slaves with eighty different ethnicities. Two additional samples of slaves shipped to Mauritius in the nineteenth century are also available. However, these samples only distinguish between slaves that were originally from the island of Madagascar and slaves from mainland Africa.[22] The data from the Mauritius samples are used to distinguish between slaves who were originally from mainland Africa and those from Madagascar. The number of slaves from mainland Africa are then disaggregated using the sample of slaves from the Zanzibar National Archive documents, as well as a small sample of nine slaves from Harris's *The*

**Table 5.1**  Slave ethnicity data for the trans-Atlantic slave trade

| Location | Time period | No. of ethnic groups | No. of slaves | Type of document |
|---|---|---|---|---|
| Valencia, Spain | 1482–1516 | 77 | 2,675 | Crown records |
| Puebla, Mexico | 1540–1556 | 14 | 115 | Notarial records |
| Dominican Republic | 1547–1591 | 26 | 22 | Records of sale |
| Peru | 1548–1560 | 16 | 202 | Records of sale |
| Mexico | 1549 | 12 | 80 | Plantation accounts |
| Peru | 1560–1650 | 30 | 6,754 | Notarial records |
| Lima, Peru | 1583–1589 | 15 | 288 | Baptism records |
| Colombia | 1589–1607 | 9 | 19 | Various records |
| Mexico | 1600–1699 | 28 | 102 | Records of sale |
| Dominican Republic | 1610–1696 | 33 | 55 | Government records |
| Chile | 1615 | 6 | 141 | Records of sale |
| Lima, Peru | 1630–1702 | 33 | 409 | Parish records |
| Rural Peru | 1632 | 25 | 307 | Parish records |
| Lima, Peru | 1640–1680 | 33 | 936 | Marriage records |
| Colombia | 1635–1695 | 6 | 17 | Slave inventories |
| Guyana | 1690 | 12 | 69 | Plantation records |
| Colombia | 1716–1725 | 33 | 59 | Government records |
| French Louisiana | 1717–1769 | 23 | 223 | Notarial records |
| Dominican Republic | 1717–1827 | 11 | 15 | Government records |
| South Carolina | 1732–1775 | 35 | 681 | Runaway notices |
| Colombia | 1738–1778 | 11 | 100 | Various records |
| Spanish Louisiana | 1770–1803 | 79 | 6,615 | Notarial records |
| St. Dominique | 1771–1791 | 25 | 5,413 | Sugar plantations |
| Bahia, Brazil | 1775–1815 | 14 | 581 | Slave lists |
| St. Dominique | 1778–1791 | 36 | 1,280 | Coffee plantations |

| Location | Year | | | Source |
|---|---|---|---|---|
| Guadeloupe | 1788 | 8 | 45 | Newspaper reports |
| St. Dominique | 1788–1790 | 21 | 1,297 | Fugitive slave lists |
| Cuba | 1791–1840 | 59 | 3,093 | Slave registers |
| St. Dominique | 1796–1797 | 56 | 5,632 | Plantation inventories |
| American Louisiana | 1804–1820 | 62 | 223 | Notarial records |
| Salvador, Brazil | 1808–1842 | 6 | 456 | Records of manumission |
| Trinidad | 1813 | 100 | 12,460 | Slave registers |
| St. Lucia | 1815 | 62 | 2,333 | Slave registers |
| Bahia, Brazil | 1816–1850 | 27 | 2,666 | Slave lists |
| St. Kitts | 1817 | 48 | 2,887 | Slave registers |
| Senegal | 1818 | 17 | 80 | Captured slave ship |
| Berbice | 1819 | 66 | 1,127 | Slave registers |
| Salvador, Brazil | 1819–1836 | 12 | 871 | Manumission certificates |
| Salvador, Brazil | 1820–1835 | 11 | 1,106 | Probate records |
| Sierra Leone | 1821–1824 | 68 | 605 | Child registers |
| Rio de Janeiro, Brazil | 1826–1837 | 31 | 772 | Prison records |
| Anguilla | 1827 | 7 | 51 | Slave registers |
| Rio de Janeiro, Brazil | 1830–1852 | 190 | 2,921 | Free Africans' records |
| Rio de Janeiro, Brazil | 1833–1849 | 35 | 476 | Death certificates |
| Salvador, Brazil | 1835 | 13 | 275 | Court records |
| Salvador, Brazil | 1838–1848 | 7 | 202 | Slave registers |
| St. Louis/Goree, Senegal | 1843–1848 | 21 | 189 | Emancipated slaves |
| Bakel, Senegal | 1846 | 16 | 73 | Sales records |
| d'Agoué, Benin | 1846–1885 | 11 | 70 | Church records |
| Sierra Leone | 1848 | 132 | 12,425 | Linguistic and British census |
| Salvador, Brazil | 1851–1884 | 8 | 363 | Records of manumission |
| Salvador, Brazil | 1852–1888 | 7 | 269 | Slave registers |
| Cape Verde | 1856 | 32 | 314 | Slave census |
| Kikoneh Island, Sierra Leone | 1896–1897 | 11 | 185 | Fugitive slave records |

*African Presence in Asia.* In total, the Indian Ocean ethnicity data include 21,048 slaves with eighty different ethnicities.

Ethnicity data for the Red Sea and the trans-Saharan slave trades are much less abundant. The Red Sea data are from two samples: a sample of five slaves from Bombay, India, and a sample of sixty-two slaves from Jedda, Saudi Arabia. The sample from India is from Harris's *The African Presence in Asia,* and the sample from Saudi Arabia is from two British reports submitted to the League of Nations and published in the League of Nations' *Council Documents* in 1936 and 1937.[23] In total, the samples provide information for sixty-seven slaves, with thirty-two different ethnicities recorded. For the trans-Saharan slave trade, two samples are available: one from Central Sudan and the other from Western Sudan. The samples provide information on the origins of 5,385 slaves, with twenty-three different ethnicities recorded.[24] The main shortcoming of the Saharan ethnicity data is that they do not provide samples from all regions from which slaves were taken during the Saharan slave trade. However, the shipping data from Ralph Austen provide information not only on the volume of trade, but also on which caravan slaves were shipped, the city or town in which the caravan originated, the destination of the caravan, and in some cases, the ethnic identity of the slaves being shipped. Because only six main trade routes crossed the desert, the information on the volume, origins, and destinations of the slave caravans allows one to produce rough estimates of the origins of slaves shipped during this trade. Admittedly, the final estimates for the Saharan slave trade are very poor. This is also true for the Red Sea slave trade. However, it will be shown that all of the statistical results are completely robust with or without the estimates of slaves shipped during these two slave trades. That is, the statistical findings remain even if the Red Sea and Saharan slave trades are completely ignored because of the poor quality of their data.

Combining the ethnicity data with the shipping data, estimates of the number of slaves taken from each country in Africa are constructed.[25] The construction procedure follows the following logic.

Using the shipping data, one first calculates the number of slaves shipped from each coastal country in Africa. As mentioned, the problem with these numbers is that slaves shipped from the ports of a coastal country may not have come from that country, but from inland countries that lie landlocked behind the coastal country. To estimate the number of slaves shipped from the coast that would have come from these inland countries, the sample of slaves from the ethnicity data is used. Each ethnicity is first mapped to modern country boundaries. This step relies on a great amount of past research by African historians. The authors of the secondary sources, from which the data were taken, generally also provide a detailed analysis of the meaning and locations of the ethnicities appearing in the historical records. In many of the publications, the authors created maps showing the locations of the ethnic groups recorded in the documents. For example, detailed maps are provided in Higman's samples from the British Caribbean, Koelle's linguistic inventory of free slaves in Sierra Leone, Mary Karasch's samples from Rio de Janeiro, Aguirre Beltran's sample from plantation and sales records from Mexico, Adam Jones's sample of liberated child slaves from Sierra Leone, and David Pavy's sample of slaves from Colombia.[26] Other sources also provide excellent summaries of the most common ethnic designations used during the slave trades. These include Philip Curtin's *The Atlantic Slave Trade: A Census,* ethnographer George Peter Murdock's *Africa: Its Peoples and Their Cultural History,* and Gwendolyn Midlo Hall's *Slavery and African Ethnicities in the Americas: Restoring the Links.*[27]

Many of the ethnic groups in the ethnicity sample do not map cleanly into one country. The quantitatively most important ethnic groups that fall into this category include the Ana, Ewe, Fon, Kabre, and Popo, who occupied land in modern Benin and Togo; the Kongo, who resided in what is now the Democratic Republic of Congo and Angola; the Makonde, localized within Mozambique and Tanzania; the Malinke, who lived within Senegal, Gambia, Mali, Guinea, Ivory Coast, and Guinea-Bissau; the Nalu, from Guinea-

Bissau and Guinea; the Teke, living in land within Gabon, Congo, and Democratic Republic of Congo; and the Yao from Malawi, Mozambique, and Tanzania. In such cases, the total number of slaves from each ethnic group was divided between the countries using information from George Peter Murdock's *Africa: Its Peoples and Their Cultural History*. Ethnic groups were first mapped to his classification of over 800 ethnic groups in Africa. Using a digitized version of a map provided in his book and GIS software, the proportion of land area in each country occupied by the ethnic group was calculated. These proportions were then used as weights to disaggregate the total number of slaves of an ethnicity between the countries.

Using the ethnicity sample, one can calculate an estimate of the number of slaves shipped from each coastal country that would have come from each inland country. On the basis of these figures, the number of slaves that came from all countries in Africa, both coastal and inland, is then computed. Because, over time, slaves were increasingly being taken from areas further inland, the estimation procedure is performed separately for each of the following four time periods: 1400–1599, 1600–1699, 1700–1799, 1800–1900. In other words, for each time period, the shipping data and ethnicity data from that time period only are used in the calculations. In the end, the procedure yields estimates of the number of slaves taken from each country in each of the four slave trades for each of the four time periods listed above.

### Potential Issues and Concerns

Constructing estimates using both the ethnicity data and the shipping data, rather than using just the ethnicity data alone, helps to minimize measurement error that may arise because the ethnicity samples are not fully representative of the entire population of slaves shipped during the slave trades. Because the procedure only uses the ethnicity samples to disaggregate slaves between coastal and inland areas, their nonrepresentativeness will not produce biased estimates unless this somehow causes an over- or undersampling of inland or coastal ethnic groups. (This latter bias is considered explicitly below.)

Many potential sources of measurement error may be encountered in constructing the slave export estimates. One potential source arises from possible inaccuracies in the historic documents that recorded slave ethnicities. However, it is likely that a reasonable amount of care was taken when slave ethnicities were documented. Because slaves were legally defined as property, those engaged in the buying and selling of slaves had a strong incentive to correctly identify the birthplace or "nation" of slaves.[28] The ethnicity of slaves also mattered to their owners because the skills of slaves varied by their ethnicity and because of perceived differences in physical strength, frequencies of suicide, and rebelliousness.[29] Manuel Moreno Fraginals writes about the importance of slave ethnicities to slave owners and the care taken to correctly identify and record the ethnic identity of slaves: "The slave trade was the business that involved the greatest amount of capital investment in the world during the eighteenth and nineteenth centuries. And a business of this size would never have kept up a classificatory scheme had it not been meaningful (in overall general terms, in keeping with reality) in designating in a *very precise* way the merchandise that was being traded."[30] There were many ways of identifying the ethnicity or "nation" of a slave. The easiest way was often by a slave's name. Slaves were sometimes given a Christian first name and a surname that identified their ethnicity.[31] A slave's ethnicity could often be determined from ethnic markings, such as cuts, scars, the filing of teeth, and hairstyles.[32]

An important issue is whether Europeans had the knowledge and ability to correctly understand the true ethnicities of African slaves. This issue has been at the core of an important debate about the Europeans' creation of artificial ethnic designations during the slave trades. A number of studies argue that "Igbo" was not a term used by people from the Biafran interior to identify themselves, but instead was constructed by Europeans.[33] Others have argued that "Igbo" is an indigenous term that reflected a true collective identity.[34] Although this question is very important, whether ethnic designations are artificial constructs is not a concern for the data construction procedure used here. Because the recorded ethnicities are only used to link slaves to a geographic location, the origins of the terms used are not important. Whether the term *Igbo* was artificially constructed by Europeans or whether it was a term used by Africans to identify themselves does not change the constructed slave export figures. All that is important is that the term *Igbo* refers to slaves who originated from an area that today is part of Nigeria.

The most significant form of measurement error likely arises because only slaves who survived the voyage outside of Africa appear in the records. This fact results in a biased sample that underrepresents slaves from the interior. This is because the further inland a slave originated, the longer the journey was and the more likely it was that he or she died along the way. Because of the high rates of mortality during the slave trades, this form of measurement error may be significant. Estimates of cross-Atlantic mortality rates ranged from 7 to 20%, depending on the time period and the length of the voyage.[35] Death rates during the trek to the coast are known with less certainty, but estimates range from 10 to 50%.[36] Similarly, slaves from the interior will also be underrepresented in the ethnicity data if they were more likely to enter into domestic slavery than slaves captured closer to the coast. In addition, the misclassification of slave ethnicities will tend to be biased against slaves from further inland. For example, Russell Lohse finds evidence that Spanish slave masters sometimes substituted a middleman slave-trading state for the specific ethnic origins of individuals, and at other times they classified slaves based on their port of embarkation rather than their true ethnic identity.[37] The important question is how this form of measurement error affects the statistical tests of a relationship between slave exports and economic development. Doing the necessary statistical calculations, one can show that this form of measurement error causes the estimated relationship between slave exports and current income to be biased toward zero.[38] That is, the dominant form of measurement error will tend to hide any relationship that may exist in the data, and it will not cause us to observe a strong relationship if one does not really exist. Therefore, if a relationship is found in the data, then we can be reasonably certain that it is in spite of measurement error, and not because of the measurement error. In fact, because of the measurement error, the relationship found in the data is likely an underestimate of the true relationship between the slave trade and economic development today.

A final source of measurement error may arise because of the assumption that slaves shipped from the coast of a country are either from that country or from directly inland of that country. In reality, slaves from a country may have come from a neighboring coastal country or from an adjacent country. Two samples of slaves can be used to test the validity of this assumption. In the two samples, both the ethnicity of the slaves and the port from which they were shipped are known. One sample is of 886 slaves shipped from the Cameroons estuary, a sample that has been examined by David Eltis and G. Ugo Nwokeji. The second sample, of fifty-four slaves shipped from the coast of Nigeria, is examined by Paul Lovejoy.[39] Because the origin and port of shipment are known for the slaves in the samples, they can be used to test the precision and accuracy of the estimation procedure. The results of the tests show that in the Eltis and Nwokeji sample of 886 slaves, 98% are correctly identified, and in the Lovejoy sample of fifty-four slaves, 83% are correctly identified. Overall, in the two samples as a whole, 97% of the slaves are correctly identified.

The slave export estimates are reported in Table 5.2. The table shows the total number of slaves taken from different parts of Africa, defined by current nation-states, between 1400 and 1900. Totals disaggregated by slave trade are reported, as well as a total for all slave trades. The constructed estimates appear to be consistent with the general evidence of where the primary slaving areas were. During

*Table 5.2* Estimated slave exports from 1400 to 1900 by country

| Country | Trans-Atlantic | Indian Ocean | Trans-Saharan | Red Sea | Total in all slave trades |
|---|---|---|---|---|---|
| Angola | 3,607,402 | 0 | 0 | 0 | 3,607,402 |
| Nigeria | 1,410,970 | 0 | 555,796 | 59,337 | 2,026,103 |
| Ghana | 1,603,392 | 0 | 0 | 0 | 1,603,392 |
| Ethiopia | 0 | 200 | 813,899 | 633,357 | 1,447,456 |
| Mali | 524,031 | 0 | 509,950 | 0 | 1,033,981 |
| Sudan | 615 | 174 | 408,261 | 454,913 | 863,963 |
| Dem. Rep. of Congo | 759,270 | 7,047 | 0 | 0 | 766,317 |
| Mozambique | 382,378 | 243,484 | 0 | 0 | 625,862 |
| Tanzania | 10,834 | 523,992 | 0 | 0 | 534,826 |
| Chad | 823 | 0 | 409,368 | 118,673 | 528,864 |
| Benin | 454,099 | 0 | 0 | 0 | 454,099 |
| Senegal | 221,723 | 0 | 98,731 | 0 | 320,454 |
| Togo | 287,675 | 0 | 0 | 0 | 287,675 |
| Guinea | 242,529 | 0 | 0 | 0 | 242,529 |
| Burkina Faso | 183,101 | 0 | 0 | 0 | 183,101 |
| Mauritania | 419 | 0 | 164,017 | 0 | 164,436 |
| Guinea-Bissau | 156,084 | 0 | 0 | 0 | 156,084 |
| Malawi | 88,061 | 37,370 | 0 | 0 | 125,431 |
| Madagascar | 36,349 | 88,927 | 0 | 0 | 125,276 |
| Republic of Congo | 94,486 | 0 | 0 | 0 | 94,486 |
| Kenya | 303 | 12,306 | 60,351 | 13,490 | 86,450 |
| Sierra Leone | 69,377 | 0 | 0 | 0 | 69,377 |
| Cameroon | 62,405 | 0 | 0 | 0 | 62,405 |
| Algeria | 0 | 0 | 61,835 | 0 | 61,835 |
| Ivory Coast | 52,602 | 0 | 0 | 0 | 52,602 |
| Somalia | 0 | 229 | 26,194 | 5,855 | 32,278 |
| Zambia | 6,552 | 21,406 | 0 | 0 | 27,958 |
| Gabon | 27,393 | 0 | 0 | 0 | 27,393 |
| Niger | 150 | 0 | 0 | 19,779 | 19,929 |
| Gambia | 12,783 | 0 | 5,693 | 0 | 18,476 |
| Libya | 0 | 0 | 8,848 | 0 | 8,848 |
| Liberia | 6,794 | 0 | 0 | 0 | 6,794 |
| Uganda | 900 | 3,654 | 0 | 0 | 4,554 |

*Table 5.2* (continued)

| Country | Trans-Atlantic | Indian Ocean | Trans-Saharan | Red Sea | Total in all slave trades |
|---|---|---|---|---|---|
| South Africa | 1,944 | 87 | 0 | 0 | 2,031 |
| Central African Rep. | 2,010 | 0 | 0 | 0 | 2,010 |
| Egypt | 0 | 0 | 1,492 | 0 | 1,492 |
| Zimbabwe | 554 | 536 | 0 | 0 | 1,090 |
| Namibia | 194 | 0 | 0 | 0 | 194 |
| Burundi | 0 | 87 | 0 | 0 | 87 |
| Equatorial Guinea | 11 | 0 | 0 | 0 | 11 |
| Djibouti | 0 | 5 | 0 | 0 | 5 |
| Botswana | 0 | 0 | 0 | 0 | 0 |
| Seychelles | 0 | 0 | 0 | 0 | 0 |
| Comoros | 0 | 0 | 0 | 0 | 0 |
| Swaziland | 0 | 0 | 0 | 0 | 0 |
| Rwanda | 0 | 0 | 0 | 0 | 0 |
| São Tomé and Principe | 0 | 0 | 0 | 0 | 0 |
| Cape Verde Islands | 0 | 0 | 0 | 0 | 0 |
| Lesotho | 0 | 0 | 0 | 0 | 0 |
| Morocco | 0 | 0 | 0 | 0 | 0 |
| Mauritius | 0 | 0 | 0 | 0 | 0 |
| Tunisia | 0 | 0 | 0 | 0 | 0 |

the trans-Atlantic slave trade, slaves were taken in the greatest numbers from the Slave Coast (Togo, Benin, and Nigeria), West Central Africa (Democratic Republic of Congo and Angola), and the Gold Coast (Ghana). All of the countries that today are located in these parts of Africa appear among the top exporting countries on the list. Ethiopia and Sudan, which were the primary sources of slaves shipped during the Red Sea and Saharan slave trades, also appear among the top exporting countries. The low number of slave exports from South Africa and Namibia is consistent with the general view that these areas exported "virtually no slaves." Even the finer differences between geographically close countries are consistent with the qualitative evidence from the African history literature. Patrick Manning writes that "some adjoining regions were quite dissimilar: Togo exported few slaves and the Gold Coast many; Gabon exported few slaves, and the Congo exported many." The estimates are consistent with Manning's observation. Exports from Togo are far less than from Ghana, and exports from Gabon are less than from the Republic of Congo.[40]

Overall, the slave export estimates appear to provide a reasonable measure of the true number of slaves taken from the different parts of Africa. Because the dominant form of measurement error present in the data will cause a statistical bias against a relationship being found, if a relationship is found, then we can be reasonably certain that the relationship is in spite of the measurement error and not because of it.

## THE RELATIONSHIP BETWEEN HISTORIC SLAVE EXPORTS AND INCOME TODAY

If the slave trades are part of the explanation for why Africa is significantly poorer than the rest of the world today, then by looking within Africa, one should observe a pattern of development today that mirrors the past intensity of the slave trades. The poorest African countries should be the countries that had the greatest number of slaves taken during the slave trades. A way of examining whether this relationship exists is to look at a graph that shows the relationship between each country's current level of income per capita and its past slave exports. The first issue that arises is that one needs to account for differences in country size. Some countries may have had more slaves exported because they are large. For this reason, the number of slaves exported is divided (i.e., normalized) by the size of the country measured by its land area. One could also use other measures of country size. The results shown below are essentially identical when the current population or the average estimated population between 1400 and 1900 or the current arable land is used instead. The advantage of using land area is that it is much more accurately measured than historic population and arable land, and it is not endogenously affected by the slave trades like current population.

Figure 5.1 shows the relationship between current income and slave exports normalized by land area. In the graph, the horizontal axis measures the normalized number of slaves exported, whereas the vertical axis measures the average income per person in 2000.[41] Each country is represented by a point on the graph, and each point is also labeled with the country name. The graph shows an interesting pattern. If a country has a high value of slave exports (it is located on the eastern portion of the graph), then it also tends to have a low value of income (it is located on the southern portion of the graph). Countries that had *more* slaves taken in the past have *lower* incomes in 2000. Or, equivalently, countries that had *fewer* slaves taken in the past have *higher* incomes today. Another way of expressing the relationship between the two variables is to say that there is a *negative relationship* between slave exports and income. The figure also reports a straight line showing the line that best fits the data. The line is calculated using a statistical technique called *ordinary least squares* or *OLS* for short.[42] As shown, the best fitting line slopes downward, confirming statistically the negative relationship between income and slave exports that is apparent in the scatter of country observations.

Although the relationship shown in Figure 5.1 is suggestive, this evidence presents a number of concerns. First, many of the countries that have the lowest slave exports are either small islands or North African countries, both of which tend to be richer than the other countries in Africa. If these countries are rich for reasons unrelated to the slave trades, then the relationship in Figure 5.1 is potentially misleading. One strategy to account for the potential problem posed

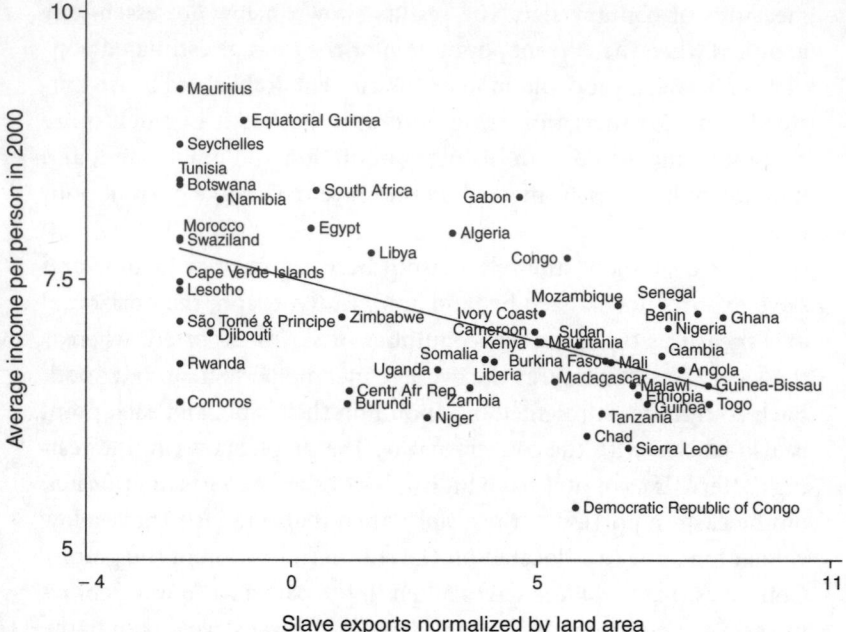

Figure 5.1   The relationship between slave exports (normalized by land area) and income per capita in 2000.

by islands and North African countries is to remove these countries from the sample. Doing this does not change the results. If one removes the ten North African and island countries in the sample, there remains a strong negative relationship between slave exports and income.[43]

A second strategy is to try and take into account the differences between these countries and the rest of Africa. Using a statistical technique called *multivariate regression analysis,* one can take any measurable difference between countries into account. Important country characteristics include their location, which can be measured by the latitude and longitude of the country's centroid; their climate, which can be measured by rainfall, humidity, and temperature; and the natural openness of the country, which can be captured by the total amount of coastline of each country relative to its land area. This last characteristic accounts for the main difference between islands and mainland countries. To account for the specific characteristics of North African countries, one can use measures of the fraction of each country's population that is Islamic and the origin of each country's legal system.[44] Other factors that may be important determinants of income are the countries' endowments of natural resources, such as oil, gold, and diamonds. The final factor, which like the slave trades is also a historic factor, is a country's history of colonial rule, particularly the identity of its colonizer. Using multivariate regression analysis, one finds that even after taking all of these factors into account, a strong negative relationship between slave exports and current income remains. Remarkably, the strength of the relationship barely diminishes even when all of these other factors are taken into account.[45] Figure 5.2 is analogous to Figure 5.1 except that it plots the values of slave exports, after the impact of the other factors on slave exports has been taken into account, and the values of income after the impact of the other factors on income has been controlled for.[46] Like Figure 5.1, Figure 5.2 also shows a clear negative relationship between slave exports and income.

An additional concern with the estimated relationship between slave exports and income arises because of inaccuracies and mismeasurements in the constructed slave export estimates. Certainly, the data are measured with error. The issue is whether this error is causing the negative relationship between slave exports and income observed in Figures 5.1 and 5.2. As discussed earlier, the effect of the dominant form of measurement error in the data is that even if a relationship exists, it will be less likely to be observed. It is very unlikely that measurement error alone would induce a relationship between slave exports and income when one does not exist. There are also strategies that can be employed to check how the measurement errors present in the data affect the statistical results. The lowest

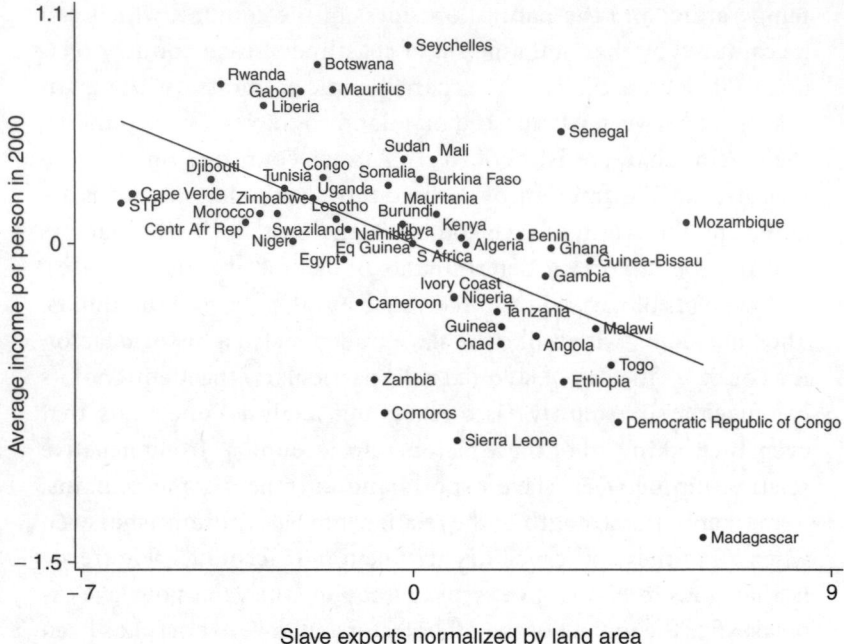

Figure 5.2   The relationship between slave exports (normalized by land area) and income per capita in 2000, after taking into account other country characteristics.

quality ethnicity and shipping data are from the earlier time periods, and from the Red Sea and trans-Saharan slave trades. One can exclude the Red Sea and trans-Saharan slave trades, or exclude the early time periods from the total slave export figures. Looking at only total slave exports from the trans-Atlantic and Indian Ocean slave trades, a strong negative relationship between slave exports and contemporary income is still found. This is true even if the slave export totals are restricted to include only the trans-Atlantic slave trade, which has the best quality data.[47] Similarly, restricting the total slave exports to include only slaves shipped during the eighteenth and nineteenth centuries, the centuries for which data are most abundant, also yields a strong negative relationship between slave exports and income.[48]

## THE CAUSES OF THE SLAVE TRADES

### Initial Prosperity

Despite the robustness of the negative relationship between slave exports and current income, the interpretation of the relationship remains uncertain. This is because the statistical results reported to this point do not *prove* that the slave trades *caused* lower levels of income today. An alternative explanation for the relationship is that societies that were initially underdeveloped may have been more likely to engage in the slave trades, and these same societies are still relatively underdeveloped today. To assess which explanation is most likely, it is important to test whether initially less developed societies tended to export more slaves. Examining the historical evidence, one does not find any evidence that less advanced societies exported more slaves during the slave trades. To the contrary, the evidence suggests that if any differences existed, it may have been the more advanced societies from which more slaves were taken.

Initial trade between Africans and Europeans was primarily in legitimate commodities, not slaves. During this time, only societies that were sufficiently developed were able to facilitate trade with the Europeans. As an example, consider the early Portuguese trade in West Central Africa. Between 1472 and 1483, the Portuguese sailed south along the west coast of Central Africa, testing various points of entry to look for trading partners. They were unable to find any societies north of the Zaire River that could support trade. Jan Vansina writes that "the local coastal societies were just too small in terms of people and territory; their economic and social institutions were too undifferentiated to facilitate foreign trade."[49] Sustained trade did not occur until the Portuguese found the Kongo Kingdom, located just south of the Zaire River. Because the kingdom had a centralized government, national currency, and well-developed markets and trading networks, it was able to support trade with the Europeans. When European demand later turned to slaves, the established preference to trade with the most developed parts of Africa continued. Because the more prosperous areas were also the most densely populated, large numbers of slaves could be efficiently obtained if civil wars or conflicts could be instigated.[50]

Using data on initial population densities, one can test statistically whether it was the more prosperous or less prosperous areas that selected into the slave trades. Estimates of the initial populations of the different parts of Africa are available from Colin McEvedy and Richard Jones's *Atlas of World Population History*.[51] Although the data are estimates, they can be used to construct rough measures of the average population density of different parts of Africa prior to the slave trade. Since the societies at the time were in a Malthusian state, any material advances manifested themselves as increased populations rather than increased incomes, and therefore population density can be used as an indicator of pre–slave trade economic prosperity. Figure 5.3 shows the relationship between initial prosperity, measured by population density in 1400, and slave exports normalized by land area. The figure shows that there is a *positive relationship* between initial population density and slave exports.[52] Countries that were initially the most prosperous and most densely populated tend to be the countries that subsequently exported the largest number of slaves. According to the figure, many parts of Africa that were more developed in 1400, such as the parts of Africa that today include Ghana, Nigeria, Democratic Republic of Congo, Togo, Benin, and Gambia, exported very large numbers of slaves. Conversely, many parts of Africa that were comparatively less developed in 1400, such as Namibia, Botswana, and South Africa, exported few slaves.

One concern with the statistical evidence reported in Figure 5.3 is the quality of the historic population data used in calculating population density. The concern here with the measurement error is whether

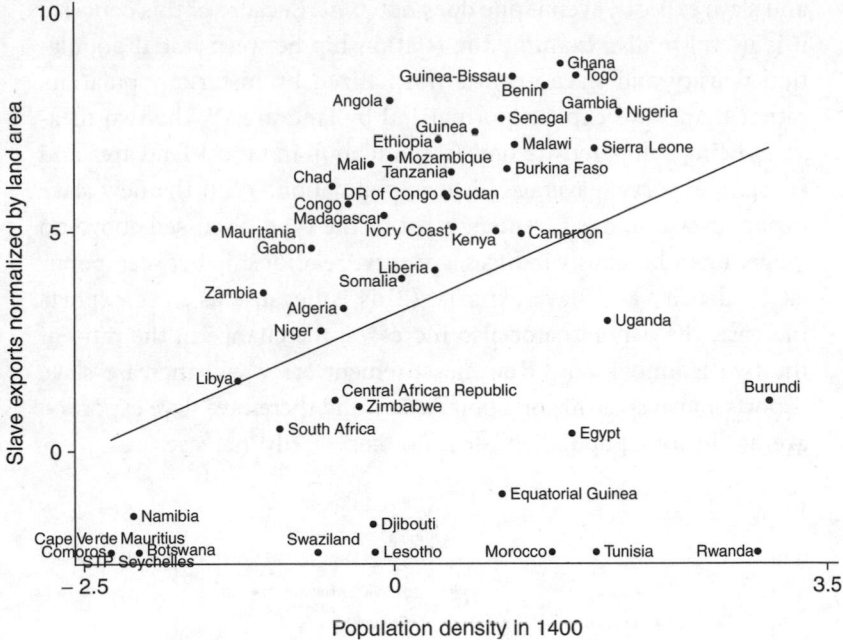

Figure 5.3   The relationship between population density in 1400 and slave exports (normalized by land area).

it may be causing the positive relationship shown in the figure. This effect would occur if past population estimates were overestimated in the parts of Africa from which large numbers of slaves were taken. To see this more clearly, consider the two variables being compared in Figure 5.3: population density and slave exports. Both measures are fractions in which the denominator is land area: (1) population in 1400 ÷ land area and (2) slave exports ÷ land area. If the construction of historic population estimates was influenced by a general under- standing of which parts of Africa the most slaves were taken from, then the estimated historic population figures will be artificially higher in areas where larger numbers of slaves were taken. This would then induce a positive relationship between initial population density and slave exports, even if one does not exist. Because of this concern, it is useful to also examine the relationship between initial population density and slave exports normalized by historic population, rather than slave exports normalized by land area.[53] The two measures being compared are now (1) population in 1400 ÷ land area and (2) slave exports ÷ average historic population. With the new slave export measure, measurement error of the type discussed above no longer unambiguously induces a positive relationship between population density and slave exports. (This is because as slave exports increase, the denominator also increases; the change in the ratio of the two is ambiguous.) The measurement error will increase slave exports and average historic population, and therefore "slave exports ÷ average historic population" does not necessarily increase.

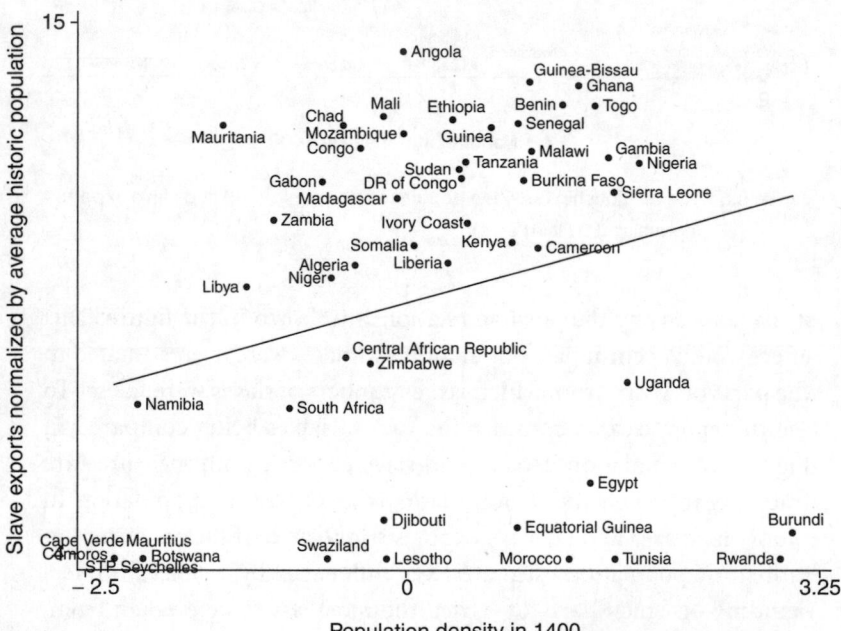

Figure 5.4   The relationship between population density in 1400 and slave exports (normalized by average historic population from 1400 to 1900).

The relationship between initial population density and total slave exports normalized by historic population is shown in Figure 5.4. As shown by the figure, even with slave exports normalized by historic population, one still observes a positive relationship between initial population density and subsequent slave exports.[54] Overall, the historic and statistical evidence does not support the notion that it was the initially least developed parts of the African continent that exported the largest numbers of slaves. Instead the data suggest the reverse. The parts of Africa that were more developed exported the largest numbers of slaves.

### The Distance from External Slave Markets

A second important determinant of the number of slaves taken was the distance from the location of the external slave markets. During the Indian Ocean slave trades, large numbers of slaves were taken from what today is Madagascar and Mozambique, partly because these areas were close to the Mascarene Islands of the Indian Ocean. Similarly, many slaves were taken from West and West Central Africa during the Atlantic slave trade, partly because of their proximity to the plantations in the Americas. This relationship can be examined statistically by calculating the overland and sailing distance from the center of each country to the closest external market for slaves. Not surprisingly, one finds a strong statistical relationship between a country's slave exports and its distance to the external slave markets. All else being equal, the further a country is from the locations of demand, the fewer slaves were taken during the slave trades.[55]

From a historic point of view, this finding may not be particularly surprising or even interesting, but from a statistical point of view, the finding is actually very useful. It can be used as an additional test of whether the slave trades really *caused* subsequent economic underdevelopment. To see how this is accomplished, consider the following thought experiment. Assume that the variation in the number of slaves taken from different parts of Africa can be explained by two factors: (1) variation in the willingness of societies to supply slaves, which was determined by various characteristics of different societies, such as initial prosperity, and (2) variation in the distance from the external demand for slaves. The first factor, the initial characteristics of societies, is the problematic factor when trying to establish whether the slave trades *caused* subsequent economic underdevelopment. As discussed, this is because these characteristics may have affected whether societies engaged in the slave trades, and these characteristics may also persist and affect income today. The concern is that these initial characteristics could be inducing a negative relationship between slave exports and current income even if the slave trades did not have an adverse effect on subsequent economic development.

The second cause of the variation in slave exports, the distance from the demand for slaves, is not affected by the initial characteristics of the African societies. Unlike the first cause, which is related to factors internal to Africa, the second cause is driven by factors outside of Africa. If the variability in slave exports that is caused by the second factor can be isolated, then this can be used to test for a causal relationship between slave exports and income today. This can be done using a statistical technique called *instrumental variables,* or *IV* for short. The technique allows one to isolate the variation in slave exports that is *unrelated* or *exogenous* to the characteristics of African societies. This is the variation in slave exports that is not being caused by the initial characteristics of societies in different parts of Africa. Because the *exogenous* variation in slave exports is unaffected by the characteristics of African societies, it can be used to generate a better estimate of the causal effect of the slave trades on economic development. The results of the *instrumental variables* technique confirm our previous findings. It shows that the negative relationship between the slave trades and subsequent economic development found in Figures 5.1 and 5.2 is in fact causal. The evidence therefore confirms that the slave trades are partly responsible for Africa's current underdevelopment.[56]

## THE CONSEQUENCES OF THE SLAVE TRADES

Given the evidence presented to this point, the natural next step is to examine the specific channels of causality underlying the relationship between the slave trades and current economic development. For this reason it is important to examine the precise manner in which slaves were captured. Based on the best available information, the most common way that slaves were taken was in wars and raids.[57] Because raids often involved villages raiding other villages, this form of slave procurement often caused relations between villages to turn hostile, even if these villages had previously formed federations, trading relations, or other ties.[58] Numerous historical accounts provide evidence of this detrimental effect of the slave trade.[59]

Slaves were not only taken through conflict between communities, during raids and wars, but they were also taken in large numbers as a result of conflict within communities, where individuals were kidnapped or sold into slavery by acquaintances, friends, or family. Sigismund Koelle reports numerous accounts of individuals being sold into slavery by family members, relatives, and "supposed friends." One of the more notable accounts is of a slave who was sold into slavery after being "enticed on board of a Portuguese vessel" by "a treacherous friend."[60] The most extreme example of this manner of enslavement is probably the Kabre of northern Togo, who during the nineteenth century developed the custom of selling their own kin into slavery.[61]

One explanation for why individuals turned on others within their own communities is that it was a consequence of the environment of insecurity that arose from increased conflict between communities. Because of this insecurity, individuals acquired weapons from Europeans to defend themselves. The slaves needed to trade with the Europeans were often obtained through local kidnappings and violence.[62] Europeans and slave traders also played a role in promoting internal conflict. Slave merchants and raiders formed strategic alliances with key groups inside villages and states in order to extract slaves. Typically, the alliances were with the younger men of the community who were frustrated by the control of power by their male elders.[63]

In many cases, the consequence of internal conflict was political instability and the collapse of preexisting forms of government.[64] Preexisting governance structures were often replaced by small bands of slave raiders, controlled by an established ruler or warlord. However, these bands were unable to develop into large, stable states. The states that were able to emerge during this period tended to be military aristocracies characterized by small size and instability.

One of the few large states that was able to emerge during this time was Asante, which began its expansion in the 1670s and grew to span an area that was four degrees in longitude and four degrees in latitude.[65] However, the timing of events suggests that the development of Asante, as well as the other states of the Gold Coast, occurred in spite of the slave trade and not because of it. Political expansion, which began in the 1670s, occurred much earlier than the slave trade and did not become important in the area until after 1700. This has led African historians, such as A. A. Boahen, to conclude that in the Gold Coast, the slave trade was the consequence and not the cause of the state-building process.[66] The other large state in Western Africa, the Oyo Empire, began its ascension in the 1650s. However, the empire was short lived. Beginning in 1780, the empire began to weaken and disintegrate, before eventually collapsing.[67]

If, as the historic evidence suggests, the external demand for slaves weakened preexisting ties between villages and discouraged the formation of larger communities, then this is a potentially important channel through which the slave trades may have affected subsequent economic development. The limited formation of larger communities and states during the slave trades may explain the high levels of ethnic fragmentation in Africa today. For economists, Africa's ethnic diversity has been a leading explanation for Africa's poor economic performance. The explanation and supporting statistical evidence were first proposed in a 1997 article published in the *Quarterly Journal of Economics* by William Easterly and Ross Levine.[68] The authors argue that ethnically diverse societies are less likely to agree on the specific public goods and policies the government should implement. Because of these disagreements, there will be less provision of public goods, such as schooling, health, and infrastructure. Easterly and Levine show that across countries, higher ethnic diversity is associated with lower levels of education, infrastructure, financial development, and with less political stability.[69]

It is possible that part of the adverse effects of the slave trades stems from the fact that they impeded the formation of larger ethnic groups and therefore resulted in more ethnic diversity today. Using the constructed slave export data, one can examine whether the data are consistent with this theory by testing whether countries that had more slaves taken in the past are more ethnically diverse today. Figure 5.5 tests for this relationship. It shows the relationship between the number of slaves exported and an updated version of Easterly and Levine's original ethnic diversity measure.[70]

Figure 5.5 shows a clear positive relationship between the two measures. The more slaves a country exported during the slave trades, the more ethnically diverse the country is today. The statistical estimates of the relationship show that as much as 50% of the differences in countries' ethnic diversity within Africa can be explained by the number of slaves exported during the slave trades.[71]

Overall, the statistical evidence does support the possibility that the slave trades, by impeding the formation of large stable communities and states, resulted in countries that today are ethnically diverse. This may explain the persistent adverse effect that the slave trades have had on economic development.

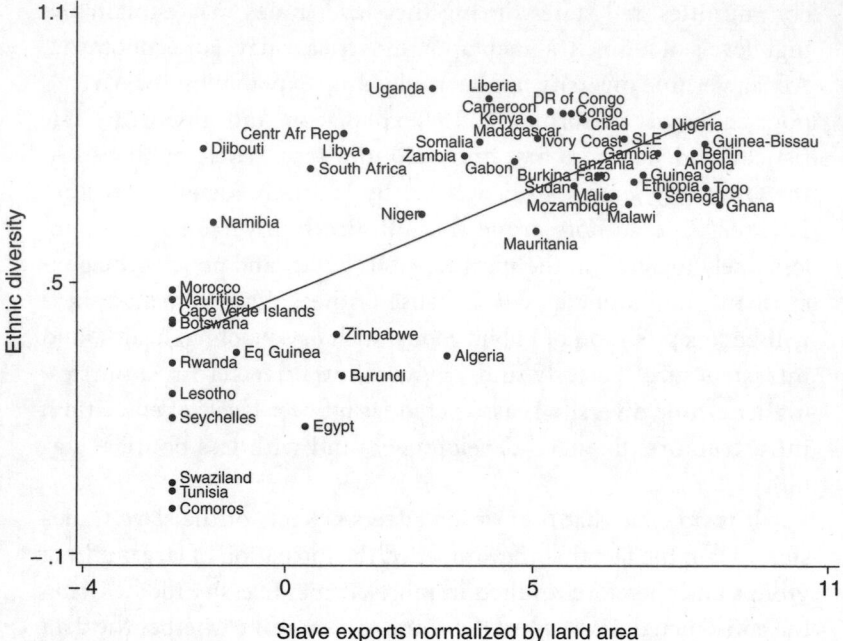

Figure 5.5   The relationship between slave exports (normalized by land area) and current ethnic fractionalization.

## QUANTIFYING THE EFFECTS OF THE SLAVE TRADES

To this point, the focus has been on examining whether there is a statistical relationship between slave exports and current income, and whether this relationship is causal. The statistical estimates allow one to also assess the magnitude of the estimated impact of the slave trades on economic development. Specifically, they can be used to provide an answer to the following question: how much better off would Africa be if the slave trades had not taken place?

To answer this question, one must first consider the average level of per capita income of African countries. Measured in the year 2000, the annual income of the typical person in Africa is $1,834.

This is significantly lower than the average per capita income in the rest of the world, which is $8,809. It is even much lower than the average per capita income for the rest of the developing world, which is $4,868.[72] Thus, not only is Africa much poorer than the rest of the world, but it is even much poorer than the rest of the developing world.[73] In this study, each country's predicted income had the slave trade not occurred is calculated. These "counterfactual" income levels are calculated by adding to each country's actual income the absolute value of the estimated relationship between slave exports and income multiplied by the estimated number of slaves exported from the country.[74] Because many different statistical estimates have been performed in this study, the highest and lowest estimates are used to provide a range of the estimated effects.

According to the calculations, if the slave trades had not occurred, then the average annual income per capita of African countries would be between $2,679 and $5,158. From these numbers it follows that between 28 and 100% of the income gap between Africa and the developing world would not exist if the slave trades had not occurred. Similarly, between 12 and 47% of the income gap between Africa and the rest of the world would not exist in the absence of the trades. The magnitudes of these estimates are striking. The largest estimated effect suggests that if the slave trades had not taken place, today's Africa would not look any different from any other developing country in the world. This is a remarkable finding. Africa's poor economic performance is one of the largest puzzles facing academics and policy makers in the world today. Even according to the lowest estimated effect, the slave trades explain almost 30% of the income gap between Africa and other developing countries. Even the lowest bound estimate produces a large effect. Although these results may not be the final and definitive explanation for the origins of Africa's severe underdevelopment, they do provide very strong evidence that a significant portion of Africa's poor performance can be explained by the legacy of its slave trades.

## CONCLUSIONS

Taken together, the evidence presented in this chapter shows that the slave trades had an adverse effect on the subsequent economic development of Africa. Using estimates of the number of slaves taken from different parts of Africa between 1400 and 1900, it was shown that the parts of the continent from which the largest number of slaves were taken are the poorest today. The estimated magnitudes of the effects of the slave trade are remarkably large. According to the largest estimate, if Africa's slave trades had not occurred, then the countries in Africa would, on average, have the same level of income as other developing countries in the world. In other words, Africa would not have become the poorest region in the world as it is today. Overall, the results presented here suggest that over four centuries of intense slaving are responsible for much of Africa's current underdevelopment.

## NOTES

I am grateful to a number of African historians who were kind enough to respond to questions as I navigated my way through the quantitative literature on Africa's slave trades. I thank Ralph Austen, David Eltis, Joseph Inikori, David Geggus, Mary Karasch, Martin Klein, Patrick Manning, G. Ugo Nwokeji, and Abdul Sheriff. This chapter has been greatly improved thanks to comments from Jared Diamond, Eva Ng, Jim Robinson, and Robert Schneider. The title of this chapter draws from the title of an April 20, 2008 *Boston Globe* story written by Francie Latour. The article discusses the research described in this chapter.

1. See, for example, Paul E. Lovejoy, *Transformations in Slavery: A History of Slavery in Africa,* 2nd ed. (Cambridge: Cambridge University Press, 2000).
2. Walter Rodney, *How Europe Underdeveloped Africa* (London: Bogle-L'Ouverture Publications, 1972); Basil Davidson, *Black Mother: The Years of the African Slave Trade* (Boston: Little, Brown and Company, 1961).
3. Patrick Manning, *Slavery and African Life* (Cambridge: Cambridge University Press, 1990), p. 124.

4. Joseph Inikori, "Africa in World History: The Export Slave Trade from Africa and the Emergence of the Atlantic Economic Order," in B. A. Ogot, ed., *General History of Africa*, vol. 5: *Africa from the Sixteenth to the Eighteenth Century* (Berkeley: University of California Press, 1992), p. 108. See also Joseph C. Miller, *Way of Death: Merchant Capitalism and the Angolan Slave Trade, 1730–1830* (Madison: University of Wisconsin Press, 1988).

5. On the impact of the slave trades on state formation and political stability see Mario Azevedo, "Power and Slavery in Central Africa: Chad (1890–1925)," *Journal of Negro History* 67 (1982): 198–211; Boubacar Barry, *Senegambia and the Atlantic Slave Trade* (Cambridge: Cambridge University Press, 1998), pp. 36–59. On the impact of the slave trades on political and social fragmentation see Andrew Hubbell, "A View of the Slave Trade from the Margin: Souroudougou in the Late Nineteenth-Century Slave Trade of the Niger Bend," *Journal of African History* 42 (2001): 25–47. For studies that examine the impact of the slave trade on judicial institutions see Martin Klein, "The Slave Trade and Decentralized Societies," *Journal of African History* 42 (2001): 49–65; Walter Hawthorne, "The Production of Slaves Where There Was No State: The Guinea-Bissau Region, 1450–1815," *Slavery & Abolition* 20 (1999): 97–124; Walter Hawthorne, *Planting Rice and Harvesting Slaves: Transformations along the Guinea-Bissau Coast, 1400–1900* (Portsmouth, NH: Heinemann, 2003).

6. See John D. Fage, "Slavery and the Slave Trade in the Context of West African History," *Journal of African History* 10 (1969): 393–404; David Northrup, *Trade without Rulers: Pre-colonial Economic Development in South-eastern Nigeria* (Oxford: Clarendon Press, 1978).

7. Northrup, *Trade without Rulers*, p. 174.

8. Patrick Manning, "Contours of Slavery and Social Change in Africa," *American Historical Review* 83 (1988): 835–857.

9. Hawthorne, *Planting Rice and Harvesting Slaves;* Hubbell, "A View of the Slave Trade from the Margin."

10. Lovejoy, *Transformations in Slavery;* Patrick Manning, *Slavery and African Life* (Cambridge: Cambridge University Press, 1990).

11. Philip D. Curtin, *The Atlantic Slave Trade: A Census* (Madison: University of Wisconsin Press, 1969).

12. See David Eltis, Stephen D. Behrendt, David Richardson, and Herbert S. Klein, *The Trans-Atlantic Slave Trade: A Database on CD-ROM* (New York: Cambridge University Press, 1999); Gwendolyn Midlo Hall, *Slavery and*

*African Ethnicities in the Americas: Restoring the Links* (Chapel Hill: University of North Carolina Press, 2005).

13. Manning, *Slavery and African Life*; Patrick Manning, "The Slave Trade: The Formal Demography of a Global System," in Joseph E. Inikori and Stanley L. Engerman, eds., *The Atlantic Slave Trade: Effects on Economies, Societies, and Peoples in Africa, the Americas, and Europe* (London: Duke University Press, 1992), pp. 117–128; Patrick Manning and W.S. Griffiths, "Divining the Unprovable: Simulating the Demography of African Slavery," *Journal of Interdisciplinary History* 19 (1988): 177–201.

14. For documentation of the database see Eltis et al., *The Trans-Atlantic Slave Trade*; David Eltis and David Richardson, "Missing Pieces and the Larger Picture: Some Implications of the New Database" (mimeo, 2006).

15. Ivana Elbl, "Volume of the Early Atlantic Slave Trade, 1450–1521," *Journal of African History* 38 (1997): 31–75.

16. Ralph A. Austen, "The Trans-Saharan Slave Trade: A Tentative Census," in Henry A. Gemery and Jan S. Hogendorn, eds., *The Uncommon Market: Essays in the Economic History of the Atlantic Slave Trade* (New York: Academic Press, 1979), pp. 23–75; Ralph A. Austen, "The 19th Century Islamic Slave Trade from East Africa (Swahili and Red Sea Coasts): A Tentative Census," *Slavery & Abolition* 9 (1988): 21–44; Ralph A. Austen, "The Mediterranean Islamic Slave Trade out of Africa: A Tentative Census," *Slavery & Abolition* 13 (1992): 214–248.

17. Barry W. Higman, *Slave Populations of the British Caribbean, 1807–1834* (Kingston, Jamaica: The Press, University of the West Indies, 1995).

18. Mary C. Karasch, *Slave Life in Rio de Janeiro* (Princeton, NJ: Princeton University Press, 1987).

19. Frederick P. Bowser, *The African Slave in Colonial Peru* (Stanford, CA: Stanford University Press, 1974).

20. Abdul Sheriff, "Localisation and Social Composition of the East African Slave Trade, 1858–1873," *Slavery & Abolition* 9 (1988): 131–145. There is also a small sample of nine slaves shipped to Bombay, India, which is available from Joseph E. Harris, *The African Presence in Asia* (Evanston, IL: Northwestern University Press, 1971). As described below, these data are also included in the ethnicity sample for the Indian Ocean slave trade.

21. The list previously examined by Abdul Sheriff is from document AA 12/3 in the Zanzibar National Archives. The two additional lists are from document AA 12/9 and document AB 71/9.

22. The two samples are from Georges Dionne, Pascal St-Amour, and Désiré Vencatachellum, "Adverse Selection in the Market for Slaves in Mauritius, 1825–1835" (mimeo, 2005), and from Barbara Valentine, "The Dark Soul of the People: Slaves in Mauritius, 2000," Data 0102, South African Data Archive, 2000.

23. League of Nations, "U.K. Government Reports to the League," *Council Documents*, C. 187 (I). M. 145. VI. B (1936): 36–39; League of Nations, "U.K. Government Reports to the League," *Council Documents*, C. 188. M. 173. VI. B (1937): 19–20.

24. The samples are from Jay Spaulding, "The Business of Slavery in the Central Anglo Egyptian Sudan, 1910–1930," *African Economic History* 17 (1988): 23–44; Martin A. Klein, "The Slave Trade in the Western Sudan during the Nineteenth Century," *Slavery & Abolition* 13 (1992): 39–60.

25. The construction of the slave export estimates is briefly sketched out here. All of the details of the calculations are documented in previous research. See Nathan Nunn, "The Long-Term Effects of Africa's Slave Trades," *Quarterly Journal of Economics* 122, no. 2 (2008): 569–600.

26. Higman, *Slave Populations of the British Caribbean, 1807–1834;* Sigismund Wilhelm Koelle, *Polyglotta Africana; or A Comparative Vocabulary of Nearly Three Hundred Words and Phrases, in More than One Hundred Distinct African Languages* (London: Church Missionary House, 1854); Mary C. Karasch, *Slave Life in Rio de Janeiro;* Gonzalo Aguirre Beltran, *La Poblacion Negra de Mexico, 1519–1810* (Mexico City: Fondo de Cultura Economica, 1940); Adam Jones, "Recaptive Nations: Evidence Concerning the Demographic Impact of the Atlantic Slave Trade in the Early Nineteenth Century," *Slavery & Abolition* 11 (1990): 42–57; David Pavy, "The Provenience of Colombian Negroes," *Journal of Negro History* 52 (1967): 35–58.

27. Curtin, *The Atlantic Slave Trade;* George Peter Murdock, *Africa: Its Peoples and Their Cultural History* (New York: McGraw-Hill Book Company, 1959); Hall, *Slavery and African Ethnicities in the Americas.*

28. See Harold D. Wax, "Preferences for Slaves in Colonial America," *Journal of Negro History* 58 (1973): 371–401.

29. See Paul E. Lovejoy, "Ethnic Designations of the Slave Trade and the Reconstruction of the History of Trans-Atlantic Slavery," in Paul E. Lovejoy and David V. Trotman, eds., *Trans-Atlantic Dimensions of Ethnicity in the African Diaspora* (New York: Continuum, 2003), p. 32.

30. Manuel Moreno Fraginals, "Africa in Cuba: A Quantitative Analysis of the African Population in the Island of Cuba," in Vera Rubin and Arthur

Truden, eds., *Comparative Perspectives on Slavery in New World Plantation Societies* (New York: New York Academy of Sciences, 1977), p. 190. The emphasis is in the original.

31. See, for example, Jean-Pierre Tardieu, "Origins of the Slaves in the Lima Region in Peru (Sixteenth and Seventeenth Centuries)," in Doudou Diene, ed., *From Chains to Bonds: The Slave Trade Revisited* (New York: Berghahn Books, 2001), pp. 43–55.

32. See the description in Karasch, *Slave Life in Rio de Janeiro*, pp. 4–9, and in Christian Georg Andreas Oldendorp, *C. G. A. Oldendorp's History of the Mission of the Evangelical Brethren on the Caribbean Islands of St. Thomas, St. Croix, and St. John* (1777; reprint, Ann Arbor, MI: Karoma Publishers, 1987), p. 169.

33. See, for example, David Northrup, "Igbo and Myth Igbo: Culture and Ethnicity in the Atlantic World, 1600–1850," *Slavery & Abolition* 21 (2000): 1–20.

34. See Douglas B. Chambers, "'My Own Nation': Igbo Exiles in the Diaspora," *Slavery & Abolition* 18 (1997): 73–77; Douglas B. Chambers, "The Significance of Igbo in the Bight of Biafra Slave-Trade: A Rejoinder to Northrup's 'Myth Igbo,'" *Slavery & Abolition* 23 (2002): 101–120.

35. Curtin, *The Atlantic Slave Trade*, p. 63.

36. See, for example, Lovejoy, *Transformations in Slavery*, pp. 63–64; Jan Vansina, *Paths in the Rainforests* (Madison: University of Wisconsin Press, 1990), p. 218.

37. See Russell Lohse, "Slave-Trade Nomenclature and African Ethnicities in the Americas: Evidence from Early Eighteenth-Century Costa Rica," *Slavery & Abolition* 23 (2002): 73–92.

38. The statistical proofs are given in Nunn, "The Long-Term Effects of Africa's Slave Trades."

39. See G. Ugo Nwokeji and David Eltis, "Characteristics of Captives Leaving the Cameroons for the Americas, 1822–37," *Journal of African History* 43 (2002): 191–210; Paul E. Lovejoy, "Background to Rebellion: The Origins of Muslim Slaves in Bahia," *Slavery & Abolition* 15 (1994): 151–180.

40. Patrick Manning, "Contours of Slavery and Social Change in Africa," *American Historical Review* 88 (1983): 839.

41. The income measures used throughout this chapter are from Angus Maddison, *The World Economy: Historical Statistics* (Paris: Organisation for Economic Co-operation and Development, 2003). The natural log of both measures is taken. Therefore, the graph reports logarithmic scales.

42. The line shows the OLS estimate of the following estimating equation: $\ln$ $\text{income}_i = \beta_0 + \beta_1 \ln \text{slave exports}_i + \varepsilon_i$. The coefficient and standard error for $\beta_0$ are 7.52 and 0.123, respectively. The coefficient and standard error for $\beta_1$ are $-0.118$ and 0.025. Both coefficients are statistically significant at the 1% level. The regression has fifty-two observations and the R-squared is 0.31.

43. As before, the estimating equation is: $\ln \text{income}_i = \beta_0 + \beta_1 \ln \text{slave exports}_i + \varepsilon_i$. The estimated coefficient and standard error for $\beta_0$ are 7.38 and 0.158, respectively. The coefficient and standard error for $\beta_1$ are $-0.100$ and 0.029, respectively. Both coefficients are statistically significant at the 1% level. The regression has forty-two observations, and the R-squared is 0.23. The omitted countries are Egypt, Tunisia, Algeria, Morocco, Libya, Comoros, Seychelles, Mauritius, Cape Verde Islands, and São Tomé and Príncipe.

44. Unlike the rest of Africa, all countries in North African have legal systems that are based on civil law. In the rest of Africa some countries have legal systems based on British common law, and others have legal systems based on civil law.

45. The estimating equation is now: $\ln \text{income}_i = \beta_0 + \beta_1 \ln \text{slave exports}_i + \mathbf{X}'\boldsymbol{\beta} + \varepsilon_i$, where $\mathbf{X}$ is a vector of control variables and $\boldsymbol{\beta}$ is a vector of coefficients. The coefficient and standard error for $\beta_1$ are $-0.093$ and 0.025, respectively; the coefficient $b_1$ is statistically significant at the 1% level. The regression has fifty-two observations, and the R-squared is 0.77.

46. In statistical terms, the figure shows the partial correlation plot between slave exports and income.

47. The estimated coefficient and standard error for $\beta_1$ in the two specifications are $-0.076$ and 0.019, and $-0.075$ and 0.026, respectively. Both coefficients are statistically significant at the 1% level.

48. The estimated coefficient and standard error for $b_1$ is $-0.088$ and 0.020, respectively. The coefficient is statistically significant at the 1% level.

49. Vansina, *Paths in the Rainforests,* p. 200.

50. See Joseph E. Inikori, "The Struggle against the Trans-Atlantic Slave Trade," in A. Diouf, ed., *Fighting the Slave Trade: West African Strategies* (Athens: Ohio University Press, 2003), p. 182.

51. Colin McEvedy and Richard Jones, *Atlas of World Population History* (Harmondsworth, UK: Penguin Books, 1978).

52. The estimating equation is: $\ln \text{slave exports}_i = \beta_0 + \beta_1 \ln \text{population density}_i + \varepsilon_i$. The estimated coefficient for $\beta_1$ is 1.23, with a standard error of 0.374. The coefficient is statistically significant at the 1% level.

53. The specific measure of historic population that is used is the average between 1400 and 1900. This is calculated as the sum of the population in 1400, 1500, 1600, 1700, 1800 and 1900, all divided by 6.

54. The estimating equation is: ln slave exports$_i$ = $\beta_0$ + $\beta_1$ ln population density$_i$ + $\varepsilon_i$. The estimated coefficient for $\beta_1$ is 0.735, with a standard error of 0.376. The coefficient is statistically significant at the 10% level.

55. For the statistical results see Nunn, "The Long-Term Effects of Africa's Slave Trades."

56. According to the IV estimates, the coefficient $\beta_1$ is −.208 and the standard error is 0.053. The coefficient is statistically significant at the 1% level.

57. See Koelle, *Polyglotta Africana;* Lovejoy, "Background to Rebellion."

58. See, for example, Joseph E. Inikori, "Africa and the Trans-Atlantic Slave Trade," in Toyin Falola, ed., *Africa,* vol. 1: *African History before 1885* (Durham, NC: Carolina Academic Press, 2000), pp. 389–412.

59. See Hubbell, "A View of the Slave Trade from the Margin," pp. 25–47; Azevedo, "Power and Slavery in Central Africa," pp. 198–211; Klein, "The Slave Trade and Decentralized Societies," pp. 56–57.

60. Koelle, *Polyglotta Africana.*

61. Charles Piot, "Of Slaves and the Gift: Kabre Sale of Kin during the Era of the Slave Trade," *Journal of African History* 37 (1996): 31–49.

62. Abdullahi Mahadi, "The Aftermath of the Jihad in the Central Sudan as a Major Factor in the Volume of the Trans-Saharan Slave Trade in the Nineteenth Century," in Elizabeth Savage, ed., *The Uncommon Market: Essays in the Economic History of the Atlantic Slave Trade* (London: Frank Cass, 1992), pp. 111–128; Hawthorne, "The Production of Slaves Where There Was no State," pp. 108–109.

63. See, for example, the accounts in Boubacar Barry, "Senegambia from the Sixteenth to the Eighteenth Century: Evolution of the Wolof, Sereer, and 'Tukuloor,'" in Ogot, ed., *General History of Africa,* vol. 5, pp. 262–299; Inikori, "The Struggle against the Trans-Atlantic Slave Trade," pp. 170–198; Martin Klein, "Defensive Strategies: Wasulu, Masina, and the Slave Trade," in Sylviane A. Diouf, ed., *Fighting the Slave Trade: West African Strategies* (Athens: Ohio University Press, 2003), pp. 62–78.

64. Lovejoy, *Transformations in Slavery,* pp. 68–70. For specific examples see Barry, *Senegambia and the Atlantic Slave Trade,* pp. 36–59; A. A. Boahen, "The States and Cultures of the Lower Guinean Coast," in Ogot, ed., *General History of Africa,* vol. 5, p. 424; Allen F. Isaacman, "The Countries of the Zambezi Basin," in J. F. A. Ajayi, ed., *General History of Africa,* vol. 6 (Paris:

Heinemann International, 1989), pp. 179–210; I. N. Kimambo, "The East African Coast and Hinterland, 1845–1880," in Ajayi, ed., *General History of Africa*, vol. 6, p. 247; Patrick U. Mbajedwe, "Africa and the Trans-Atlantic Slave Trade," in Falola, ed., *Africa*, vol. 1, pp. 341–342; Inikori, "The Struggle against the Trans-Atlantic Slave Trade," pp. 170–198; Elizabeth Colson, "African Society at the Time of the Scramble," in L. H. Gann and Peter Duignan, eds., *Colonialism in Africa, 1870–1960*, vol. 1: *The History and Politics of Colonialism, 1870–1914* (Cambridge: Cambridge University Press, 1969), pp. 36–37.

65. William Tordoff, "The Ashanti Confederacy," *Journal of African History* 3 (1962): 399–417; A. A. Boahen, "The States and Cultures of the Lower Guinean Coast," in Ogot, ed., *General History of Africa*, vol. 5, p. 422.

66. See Boahen, "The States and Cultures of the Lower Guinean Coast," p. 424.

67. Robin Law, *The Ọyọ Empire c.1600–c.1836: A West African Imperialism in the Era of the Atlantic Slave Trade* (Oxford: Clarendon Press, 1977).

68. William Easterly and Ross Levine, "Africa's Growth Tragedy: Policies and Ethnic Divisions," *Quarterly Journal of Economics* 112 (1997): 1203–1250.

69. For more recent evidence confirming these initial findings see Alberto Alesina, Reza Baquir, and William Easterly, "Public Goods and Ethnic Divisions," *Quarterly Journal of Economics* 114 (1999): 1243–1284; Edward Miguel and Mary Kay Gugerty, "Ethnic Diversity, Social Sanctions, and Public Goods in Kenya," *Journal of Public Economics* 89 (2005): 2325–2368.

70. The measure of ethnic diversity used in Easterly and Levine's original article is the probability that two randomly selected individuals from a country belong to different ethnic groups. The updated version of this same measure is from Alberto Alesina, Arnaud Devleeschauwer, William Easterly, Sergio Kurlat, and Romain Wacziarg, "Fractionalization," *Journal of Economic Growth* 8 (2003): 155–194.

71. The estimating equation is: ethnic diversity$_i = \beta_0 + \beta_1 \ln$ exports$_i + \varepsilon_i$. The estimated coefficient for $\beta_1$ is $-0.046$, with a standard error of $0.007$. The coefficient is statistically significant at the 1% level. The proportion of the variation in ethnic diversity explained by slave exports is given by the regression's R-squared, which is 0.50. This indicates that 50% of the variation in ethnic diversity is explained by slave exports.

72. Developing countries are defined to be countries with an average per capita income in 2000 of less than $14,000. According to this definition, the poorest developed country is Portugal, and the richest developing country is Barbados.

73. The figures are based on data from the Penn World Tables, which is the most commonly used source for income data in economics.

74. In practice, because the estimating equation uses log income and log slave exports, the logs of income and slave exports are used when performing the calculations.

# Colonial Land Tenure, Electoral Competition, and Public Goods in India

ABHIJIT BANERJEE

AND LAKSHMI IYER

Social scientists have long emphasized the importance of institutions in nurturing economic growth and development. Douglass C. North defines institutions as the "rules of the game in a society" that limit the set of choices for individuals and argues that institutions, both formal ones such as laws and constitutions and informal ones such as social norms, are important in determining the transaction costs of production and exchange, and thereby have an impact on economic growth. He goes on to discuss the mostly incremental nature of institutional change and highlights the difficulties in implementing radical institutional change. This line of argument therefore suggests that the impacts of institutions are likely to be felt for a very long time, and hence points to the need for detailed historical analysis over long periods in order to quantify the impact of institutions.[1]

Two strands of analysis have dominated the recent literature in economics on the study of institutions. The first undertakes detailed analysis within a given time or place. An example is the work of Avner Greif, who uses historical documents to examine the working of a specific institution, the Maghribi traders' coalition in the eleventh century. He documents in detail the flows of information and specific institutional practices put in place to sustain economic relationships between merchants and their overseas agents. These mechanisms, based on carefully built reputations, greatly contributed to the success of Maghribi traders. Another example is North and Barry R. Weingast's analysis of the impact of England's Glorious Revolution on the security of private rights and the consequent rapid development of capital markets. Stephen Haber, Noel Maurer, and Armando Razo examine the evolution of property rights in Mexico over time, with a view to analyzing the institutions that enabled the Mexican economy to grow substantially despite considerable political instability.[2]

Although such studies are useful in understanding how institutions have evolved, they do not provide a good counterfactual: how would things have been if this institution had been set up differently? The second strand of analysis, based on comparative studies that look at differences in the quality or type of institutions across different places, can be useful in this regard. To take a specific instance, Rafael La Porta, Florencio Lopez de Silanes, Andrei Shleifer, and Robert Vishny conducted a comparative analysis across countries with different legal systems and found that countries that have common law systems provide greater protections for minority shareholders than do countries whose legal systems are based on French civil law.[3]

La Porta et al.'s study illustrates some of the benefits and costs of this methodology. A clear benefit is that it establishes a general pattern across the world, which we would not have been able to infer from studying any one case. However, it leaves open the question of causality: perhaps countries that adopted French civil law systems were inherently different in some way from those that adopted common law systems. For instance, they may have systematically different geographic characteristics or specific precolonial legal systems that were more compatible with civil law. Therefore, the observed differences may be due to these underlying factors rather than to the legal system. Another possibility is that French civil law came as part of a package deal. French colonial rule might have changed many other institutions or policies in those countries, apart from the legal system. In this case, we might mistakenly conclude that the observed differences in outcomes are caused by differences in the legal system, when in fact the key variable might be the differences in other institutions, such as the tax code or credit market conditions. In either case, although establishing the general correlation is interesting, we are not able to conclude that it is indeed the legal system that is responsible for the differences in the outcomes we observe.[4]

The problems of inherent differences across areas, and of isolating specific institutions, are pervasive in comparative analyses. How can we get around them? We can try to choose areas that are similar in all other ways except for the specific institution being studied. This is not easy, given that we are in no position to assign institutions as we see fit and that we have to depend on the historical record. We can go some way toward this goal by picking our cases carefully, and in addition by statistically controlling for all the other elements that might matter. The problem is that we often do not know what matters, and even when we do, we may not have any way of measuring these factors.

Another solution would be to find instances where institutions were imposed from outside in such a way that the adoption of a specific institution was not dependent on underlying area characteristics. This is the approach we adopt in our essay. We compare the land revenue systems put in place in different parts of India by British colonial administrators and argue that the choice of alternative systems had nothing to do with any special feature of the areas where they were imposed. Instead, the historical record suggests that the choice of these systems was driven by the prevailing ideology in England at the time that area was brought under British political control, as well as the idiosyncratic views and relative political power of individual colonial administrators. Furthermore, since we compare different areas within British India, the areas we study are similar in many other dimensions: obviously, in the identity of the colonial power, but also in the political, administrative, and legal systems both in colonial times and today.

We use the terms *land revenue systems* or *land tenure systems* to refer to the arrangements the British colonial administration made to collect the land revenue from cultivators of the land. Up to a first approximation, all cultivable land in British India fell under one of three alternative systems: landlord-based systems (also known as *zamindari* or *malguzari*), individual cultivator-based systems *(raiyatwari)*, and village-based systems *(mahalwari)*. In the landlord-based systems, the British delegated revenue-collection authority to landlords with authority over large areas. In village-based systems, the revenue collection was delegated to village bodies consisting of several people. In individual cultivator systems, the British collected land revenue directly from the cultivator. The map in Figure 6.1 illustrates the geographic distribution of these systems.

The central question of our study is: Did areas under landlord-based systems develop differently than areas that were under other land tenure systems? We answer this question by comparing outcomes in the two types of areas in the postcolonial period, which is more than a hundred years after these systems were put in place.[5] As it turns out, the land revenue system we study was actually abolished in the early 1950s, along with many other vestiges of colonial rule. In fact, agricultural income is subjected to almost no taxes in India today. Nevertheless, the differences in historical land tenure systems could have started these areas off on very different paths. This is the possibility we investigate in our chapter. Our study is therefore in the spirit of Stanley Engerman and Kenneth Sokoloff's comparative study of New World countries, where they find that initial levels of inequality caused by specific institutional arrangements caused them to have very different development paths. In particular, areas with greater initial inequality tended to have lower investments in public education and other infrastructure.[6]

Our results are also in the spirit of what Engerman and Sokoloff have found. Areas in India that were historically under the control of big landlords (and consequently had much higher levels of historical land inequality) tended to have lower levels of investment in schools,

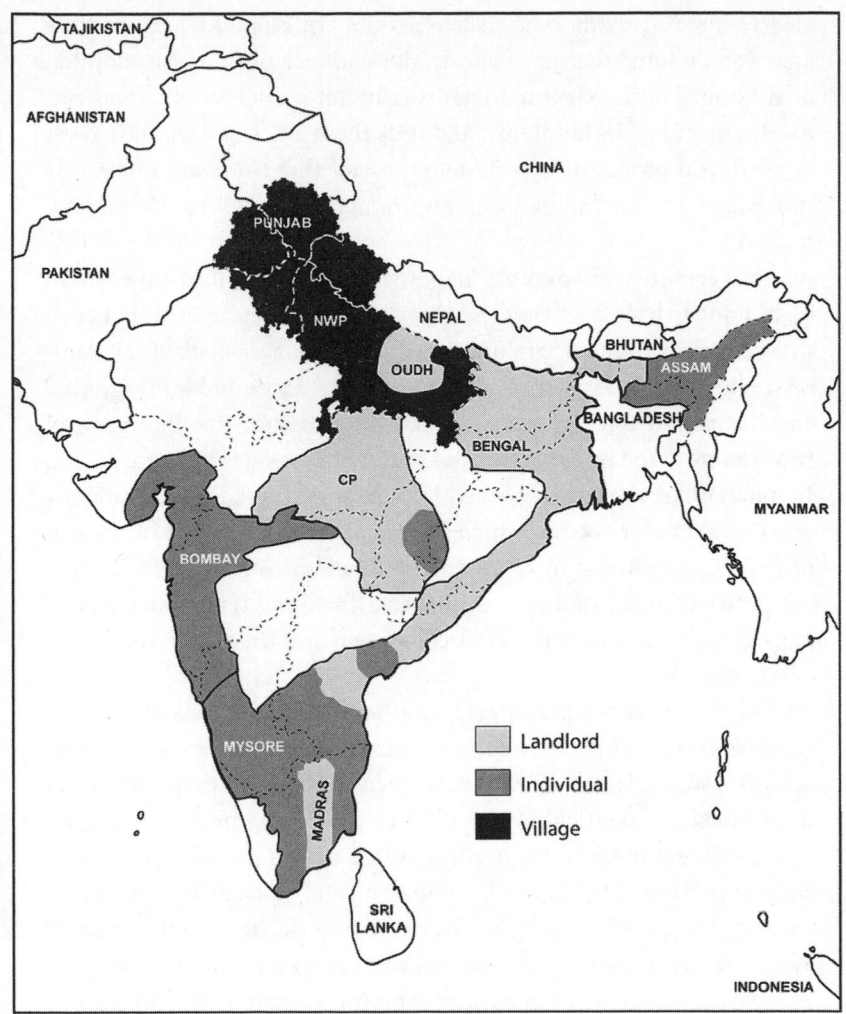

Figure 6.1   Landlord-based, individual cultivator-based, and village-based systems in British India. (Reprinted with permission of TYPEA/Peter Amirault, www.typea.com.)

electricity, and roads even as late as 1991. In related work, we have also documented that in the postindependence period, the adoption of new agricultural technologies was much slower in the areas formerly controlled by landlords, and thus these areas end up with lower agricultural productivity—despite the fact that these are inherently more fertile areas and had higher productivity levels in the colonial period.[7]

Engerman and Sokoloff suggest that this deficit in investment has to do with the fact that the elites in these areas feared that such investments might end up undermining their authority. They demonstrate that areas with higher inequality extended suffrage to a smaller proportion of their population and that the extension of the franchise to larger sections of society came later in these places. In particular, these more unequal societies typically had literacy requirements for voting, which significantly reduced the incentives of the elites to invest in large-scale public education. Thus, historical patterns of inequality continue to affect long-term outcomes by changing the nature of the political system and the pattern of democratization.[8]

In this essay, we investigate whether this hypothesis of political capture by the elites can explain our observed differences across landlord and non-landlord areas. Because the contemporary electoral rules are identical everywhere in postindependence India, we cannot expect to see any variation in this regard. It is, however, possible that those who are still the elites retain power by restricting access to the political system or by capturing the democratic process. We therefore focus on participation rates in elections as well as some standard measures of electoral competition, such as the number of candidates in elections or the winning margins, recognizing that these are outcomes of the electoral process rather than a description of the conditions under which the elections took place, which would be our ideal data. We find that non-landlord areas have slightly higher electoral participation rates than landlord areas; however, the difference in public goods provision cannot be fully explained by the differences in electoral participation. In terms of electoral competition, landlord areas look very similar to non-landlord areas in measures such as the number of people contesting the election or average vote margins.[9]

Before going into the details of our analysis, we first describe how the British came to implement different land tenure systems in different parts of India. We then explain in some detail the sense in which the land tenure institutions were "imposed" on these areas.

## COLONIAL LAND TENURE SYSTEMS IN INDIA

The British empire in India lasted nearly 200 years. The British first arrived as traders in 1613, when the English East India Company received a permit from the Mughal emperor, Jahangir, to build a factory at Surat. The East India Company won major military battles at Plassey in 1757 and Buxar in 1764, as a result of which they obtained revenue collection rights in the modern states of Bengal and Bihar (formerly Bengal Presidency) in 1765. At the same time, the British obtained four districts, known as the Northern Circars, in southern India as a grant from the Mughal emperor. Over the next century, the East India Company acquired several new territories. Large parts of the Kingdom of Mysore were annexed after the Mysore wars (1792–1801) in the south, and Bombay Presidency and parts of Gujarat in the west after conquering the Marathas in 1817–1818. Many areas of the North-West Provinces were ceded by the Nawab of Oudh for nonpayment of debts in 1801–1803, Punjab was conquered after the Sikh wars of 1846 and 1849, and Oudh itself was annexed by the British in 1856 after accusing the ruler of misrule.

In the Sepoy Mutiny of 1857, Indian troops in many parts of north India revolted against their British officers. The revolt was soon suppressed, but the British Crown decided to bring the administration of India under its direct control, and the rule of the East India Company came to an end in 1858. The British then put an end to any further annexation of territory, with the result that a large number of princely states remained in different parts of the country, all of which were under British political control but had autonomy in administrative matters. The British left India in 1947 when the Indian empire was partitioned into India and Pakistan. Large parts of former Bengal Presidency and Punjab Province are now in Bangladesh and Pakistan, respectively.[10]

Land revenue or land tax was the major source of government revenue for the British empire in India, as it had been for all previous governments. In 1841, land revenue constituted 60% of total British government revenue, though this proportion decreased over time as the British developed additional tax resources. Not surprisingly, land revenue and its collection was the most important issue in policy debates during this period.

In the early years, the British put in place a landlord-based system in most areas, largely because relying on landlords to do all the revenue collection work spared the British the effort and expense of setting up a large administrative machinery. In these areas, the revenue liability for a village or a group of villages lay with a single landlord, who was free to set the revenue terms for the peasants under his jurisdiction and to dispossess any peasants who did not pay the landlord what they owed him. The landlord could keep whatever remained after paying the British revenue demand. These revenue-collecting rights could be bequeathed, as well as bought and sold. In this sense, the landlord effectively had property rights on the land. In some of these areas, the British declared the landlords' revenue commitments to the government to be fixed in perpetuity (the Permanent Settlement of 1793). In other areas, a temporary settlement was implemented whereby the revenue was fixed for a certain number of years, after which it was subject to revision.[11]

In some cases, the presence of a landlord class before the British took over was probably one of the factors leading to the landlord system being favored. For instance, the historian Tapan Raychaudhuri states, "in terms of rights and obligations, there was a clear line of continuity in the zamindari system of Bengal between the pre- and the post-Permanent Settlement era." This was not a general feature. For instance, it was decided to have a landlord-based system in the Central Provinces, even though there was no preexisting landlord class. According to B. H. Baden-Powell, "In the Central Provinces we find an almost wholly artificial tenure, created by our revenue-system and by the policy of the Government of the day." Even in Bengal, several scholars have pointed out that these landlords were really local chieftains, and not the large farmers that the British had thought them to be.[12]

Over time, there was a shift toward establishing other types of land revenue systems. Two major changes in land revenue policy (described in detail below) set important precedents for areas conquered in later years. The trend was also supported by changing views in Britain. In the 1790s, under the shadow of the French Revolution across the Channel, the British elites were inclined to side with the landlords. In the 1820s, with peasant-power long defeated and half forgotten, British elites were more inclined to be sympathetic to the utilitarians and others who favored dealing directly with peasants.[13]

The first major shift away from landlord-based systems was in Madras Presidency, where the administrators Captain Alexander Read and Sir Thomas Munro began advocating for the establishment of an individual cultivator system in the late 1890s. Under this *raiyatwari* system, the revenue settlement would be made directly with the individual *raiyat* or cultivator. In these areas, an extensive cadastral survey[14] of the land was done and a detailed record-of-rights was prepared, which served as the legal title to the land for the cultivator. Unlike the Permanent Settlement areas, the revenue commitment was not fixed; it was usually calculated as the money value of a share of the estimated average annual output. This share typically varied from place to place, was different for different soil types, and was adjusted periodically in response to changes in the productivity of the land.

Munro strongly supported the individual cultivator system, claiming that this system would raise agricultural productivity by improving cultivator incentives, that the cultivators would be less subject to arbitrary expropriation than under a landlord, that they would have a measure of insurance (via government revenue remissions in bad times), that the government would be assured of its revenue (since small peasants are less able to resist paying their dues), and that this was the mode of land tenure prevailing in South India from ancient times. These arguments were not based on any real evidence; as Nilmani Mukherjee writes, "Making all allowance for the zeal of Munro as a champion of the ryotwari system, it cannot be denied that he was rather dogmatic in relating his favourite system to the socio-economic conditions of the Ceded Districts."[15]

Munro's views were strongly opposed by the Madras Board of Revenue, which used more or less the same arguments (in reverse, of course) for favoring landlords. The Board argued that large landlords would have the capacity to invest more and therefore productivity would be higher, the peasants' long-term relationship with the landlord would result in less expropriation than the short-term one with a government official, a large landlord would provide insurance for small farmers, a steady revenue would be assured because the landlords would be wealthy and could make up an occasional shortfall from their own resources, and this was the mode of tenure prevailing from ancient times![16]

The Board of Revenue initially overruled Munro. Starting in 1811, all the villages were put under village-level landlords with ten-year renewable leases. However, Munro traveled to London and managed to convince the Court of Directors of the East India Company of the merits of the individual-based *raiyatwari* system. The Court of Directors then ordered the Madras Board of Revenue to implement this policy all over the province after 1820 upon the expiration of the landlord leases. This important precedent influenced the system in many other places. For instance, the governor of the recently formed Bombay Presidency, Lord Elphinstone, had supported Munro during the debate in Madras and had implemented the individual cultivator system in that province in the 1820s.

At about the same time, a similar precedent was established in northern India. Landlord systems with short-term leases were initially implemented in the North-West Provinces, and considerable debate ensued as to whether or not there should be a landlord-based Permanent Settlement along the lines of that prevailing in Bengal. In 1819, Holt Mackenzie, the secretary of the Board of Revenue, wrote a famous Minute claiming that, historically, every village had had a proprietary village body, and he felt that no settlement should be declared in perpetuity that did not give proper recognition to such customary rights. This became the basis for Regulation VII of 1822, which laid the basis for village-level settlements known as the *mahalwari* system. However, the previous actions could not always be undone, and in several places the previously appointed landlords retained their positions. For instance, the Aligarh settlement officer writes, "So far indeed had the action of our first officials sanctioned the usurpations of the Talukdars, that among other cases they granted to Raja Bhagwant Singh a lease for life of the whole of the pargana Mursan for Rs.80,000 leaving the old communities entirely at his mercy." This incomplete change of regime is the reason that many districts classified as predominantly village-based nevertheless had a substantial portion of their area under landlord control. For instance, the district of Allahabad was part of the North-West Provinces, which were put under the village-based system, yet nearly two-thirds of all revenue estates were under the control of landlords.[17]

In the village-based system, village bodies that jointly owned the village were responsible for the land revenue. These bodies could be in charge of varying areas, from part of a village to several villages. The composition of the village body also varied from place to place. In some areas it was a single person or family and hence very much like the Bengal landlord system *(zamindari)*, whereas in other areas, the village bodies had a large number of members, with each person being responsible for a fixed share of the revenue. This share was either determined by ancestry (the *pattidari* system) or based on actual possession of the land (the *bhaiachara* system), the latter being very much like the individual-based *raiyatwari* system. The revenue rates in these areas were determined on fairly ad hoc grounds, based on a diverse set of factors including "an examination of rents recorded in the *jamabandis,* the rates which were actually paid by the various classes of tenants and the rates which were considered fair on each class of soil . . . These estimates are based primarily on soils, and secondly on consideration of the caste of the tenant, capabilities of irrigation, command of manure &c, all of which points received attention."[18] Except in the areas under the Permanent Settlement, the amount of revenue actually paid was often less than the stated revenue liability because remissions were granted in times of bad harvests and other hardships. Our focus here is not on the actual revenue paid or the revenue rates that prevailed at various points of time, but on the allocation of revenue and control rights in land.

There was one further change to land revenue policy, in the province of Oudh. This region was annexed by the British in 1856 and merged with the North-West Provinces to form the United Provinces (state of Uttar Pradesh today). Since the North-West Provinces had a village-based revenue system, it was proposed to extend the same to Oudh, with the Governor-General Lord Dalhousie declaring explicitly that the "desire and intention of the Government is to deal with the actual occupants of the soil, that is, with village zamindars or with the proprietary coparcenaries, which are believed to exist in Oudh, and not to suffer the interposition of middlemen as Talukdars, farmers of the revenue and such like."[19] A cadastral survey that would form the basis of this settlement was under way when the Sepoy Mutiny (which eventually turned into a full-scale war of independence in many parts of north India) broke out in 1857. After the mutiny was subdued, the British felt that having the large landlords on their side would be politically advantageous. There was thus a reversal of policy, and several landlords whose land had been taken away under the village-based settlement had the land given back to them. In 1859, the landlords were declared to have a permanent, hereditary, and transferable proprietary right. Districts that used to be part of Oudh thus came to have a larger area under landlord control than the other districts of Uttar Pradesh. No major policy changes took place after this point. Our classification of areas into different types of systems is based on the system prevailing in these areas in the 1870s and 1880s, after all of these policy changes had been implemented.

The historical record thus suggests that of the many factors that affected the choice of the land revenue system in a particular area, most were unrelated to the actual characteristics of the area itself. Places conquered by the British in earlier periods tended to get landlord systems because of the prevailing ideology in England, and the ideas of individual administrators also brought about significant changes. Places conquered later tended to follow either the ideologies of their administrators (e.g., Bombay Presidency) or the system adopted in nearby provinces, until the reversal of policy in Oudh. For instance, when Berar was ceded to the British for nonpayment of debts in 1853, it was put under an individual-based system because neighboring Bombay had been organized under this system. Punjab province was put under a village-based system because it was next to the North-West Provinces. Remarkably, none of the areas that were conquered by the British between 1820 and 1855 had a wholly landlord-based system. Areas conquered either before or after that period are much more likely to have a landlord-based system. Thus, comparing areas conquered in the period 1820–1855 with areas conquered either before or after these dates provides a particularly clean way to capture the landlord/non-landlord divide. Moreover, to the extent that the choice of the system actually responded to local conditions, the tendency was to set up non-landlord systems in the least prosperous areas. For example, the areas where landlord defaults were excessive were sometimes changed to other forms of settlement. Therefore, areas that ended up with non-landlord systems are more likely to be inherently less productive, or at least were less productive in colonial times. It has also been argued that usually landlord areas were highly fertile areas that created enough rent to support a landlord-tenant-laborer hierarchy.[20]

Many contemporary accounts support our idea that the initial choice of the land revenue system had little to do with the specific features of the area. The settlement officer of Rae Bareli district in the North-West Provinces recounts, "Nearly all the zamindars are of modern growth . . . in almost every *pargana* there were numerous villages without proprietors. All these were granted away by Government, very frequently on the most slender grounds, such as for instance to a farmer who, without a shadow of claim to proprietary right, had paid his rent to Government for 12 or 15 years regularly. The policy of the day was to get rid of such Government rights, to create *zamindars* if they could not be found." An official in Karnal district of Punjab writes, "I think there can be but little doubt that, till the English rule, individual property in land, in the sense in which we understand it, was unknown in the Tract." In Sirsa district, the British "created for the first time in each village a proprietary status, framed on the model of that in vogue in the settled districts of the North-Western Provinces, dividing off the agriculturists into proprietors and tenants in a somewhat arbitrary manner."[21]

By the 1860s, the land tenure systems were firmly in place in all parts of British India, and no major changes in the allocation of land revenue rights took place after this period. In particular, the British maintained the Permanent Settlement of Bengal, which had fixed the landlords' rents in perpetuity in 1793, even though the revenue they obtained declined significantly in real terms by the twentieth century. After Independence in 1947, almost all states passed legislation in the early 1950s, formally abolishing landlords and other intermediaries between the government and the cultivator. Several other laws were also passed, by different states at different times, regarding tenancy reform, ceilings on landholdings, and land consolidation measures.[22]

## DO LANDLORD AREAS DEVELOP DIFFERENTLY?

We examine this broad question of whether landlord areas develop differently by focusing on the availability of schools, electricity, and roads across districts of India. Such infrastructure facilities typically have a public good character, in the sense that their utilization by one person does not reduce their availability for others. Although private agents could provide such facilities, it is the case in India that these are usually provided by the government or state-owned agencies. Furthermore, the provision of such public goods is constitutionally under the purview of state governments rather than the federal government, and is therefore subject to political economy pressures arising from local conditions or local histories. These are also important infrastructure variables, which are likely to increase the welfare of the residents as well as provide a good basis for future economic growth.

We obtained data at the district level from the Indian Census of 1991 (a district is an administrative unit below the state level in India). For each district, we compute the fraction of villages that are supplied with a primary school, high school, power for domestic use, and paved roads. We thus have four measures of infrastructure for each district. These measures vary considerably across districts: eighteen districts have primary schools in less than half of their villages; on the other hand, there are thirty-seven districts where primary schools are present in more than 95% of villages. Similarly, the percentage of villages supplied with paved roads varies across districts from 10 to 100%. These differences persist despite explicit commitments by the Indian state to equalize access to infrastructure.[23]

We see striking differences in public goods provision between landlord-based areas and areas with individual cultivator systems. For instance, only 77% of villages in landlord areas were provided with primary schools in 1991, compared to 91% of villages in individual cultivator areas (Table 6.1, panel A, columns 1 and 2). The differences in other public goods are even bigger: in landlord-based areas, only 8% of villages had high schools, 31% had paved roads, and 54% had electricity. In contrast, 22% of villages in the individual cultivator areas had access to a high school, 58% had paved roads, and 86% had electricity.

**Table 6.1** Colonial land tenure and differential paths of development

| Variable | Average for landlord areas (zamindari) | Average for individual cultivator areas (raiyatwari) | Difference (2) − (1) | Percentage difference (3)/(1) | Regression difference 1 | Regression difference 2 |
|---|---|---|---|---|---|---|
| | (1) | (2) | (3) | (4) | (5) | (6) |
| | **Panel A: Fraction of villages provided with public goods, 1991** | | | | | |
| Primary schools | 0.77 | 0.91 | 0.14 | 18% | 0.11* | 0.07* |
| High schools | 0.08 | 0.22 | 0.14 | 175% | 0.13* | 0.11* |
| Power for domestic use | 0.54 | 0.86 | 0.32 | 59% | 0.34* | 0.21* |
| Paved roads | 0.31 | 0.58 | 0.27 | 87% | 0.28* | 0.25* |
| Literacy 1961 | 0.21 | 0.29 | 0.08 | 38% | 0.07* | 0.05* |

## Panel B: Electoral variables (1980s)

| | | | | | | |
|---|---|---|---|---|---|---|
| Voter turnout | 0.591 | 0.613 | 0.022 | 3.7% | 0.049* | 0.050* |
| No. of candidates | 7.520 | 6.040 | −1.480 | −19.7% | −1.279 | −0.57 |
| Winner vote share | 0.492 | 0.519 | 0.027 | 5.5% | 0.028* | 0.018+ |
| Vote margin (as share of total votes) | 0.180 | 0.200 | 0.020 | 11.1% | 0.021+ | 0.014 |
| Probability of incumbent party winning | 0.456 | 0.446 | −0.010 | −2.2% | −0.031 | −0.026 |
| No. of districts | 81 | 69 | 150 | | 233 | 233 |

*Notes:* "Regression difference 1" represents the coefficient on the non-landlord proportion obtained by running a linear regression of the dependent variable on the non-landlord proportion. This corresponds to the slope of the lines in Figures 2A–2D, 3A, 5, and 6A–6D. "Regression difference 2" represents the coefficient on the non-landlord proportion obtained by running a linear regression of the dependent variable on the non-landlord proportion, after controlling for the effects of geographic factors (rainfall, maximum and minimum temperature, being a coastal area), demographic factors (population density, percentage of Muslims, percentage of Christians, percentage of Sikhs, percentage of population belonging to the Scheduled Castes and the Scheduled Tribes, which are historically disadvantaged communities), and the total number of years of British colonial rule.

* Estimated difference is statistically significant at 5% level of significance.

+ Estimated difference is statistically significant at 10% level of significance.

Including the village-based areas in the analysis reinforces this finding. For these areas, we construct a continuous variable, which measures how much of the district was historically not under the control of landlords ("non-landlord proportion"). We illustrate here the computation for one district. The Settlement Report for Allahabad district documents the different types of land tenure prevailing in the district as follows: out of 5,679 revenue estates, 3,760 are classified as *zamindari* (i.e., under landlord control), 478 as *pattidari*, 1,216 as *imperfect pattidari,* and 225 as *bhaiyachara* (all different types of village-based systems). Hence we calculate the non-landlord proportion to be 0.34. Districts that were completely under landlord control are assigned a non-landlord proportion of zero, while districts that were wholly under the individual cultivator system are assigned a value of one.[24]

There is a strong positive relationship between the non-landlord proportion and the availability of public goods. In Figure 6.2, the y-axis shows the measure of public goods provision as the fraction of villages in the district having that public good. These are graphed against the non-landlord proportion on the x-axis. In particular, areas with intermediate levels of non-landlord control have public good levels in between those of purely landlord areas (non-landlord proportion = 0) and purely individual cultivator areas (non-landlord proportion = 1). Consistent with the lack of provision of schools, we see that landlord areas lag behind in educational attainment as well: they have significantly lower literacy levels in 1991, but also in earlier periods such as 1961 (Figure 6.3). Table 6.1 documents that, in 1961, landlord areas had an average literacy rate of 21%, while individual cultivator areas had a literacy rate of 29%. We should note that early levels of literacy might be particularly important in influencing citizens' participation in the political process, especially in preventing elite dominance through electoral institutions.

How strong are these relationships? Given the fairly wide variation in outcomes across areas, it could happen purely by chance that non-landlord areas have higher levels of access to roads than land-

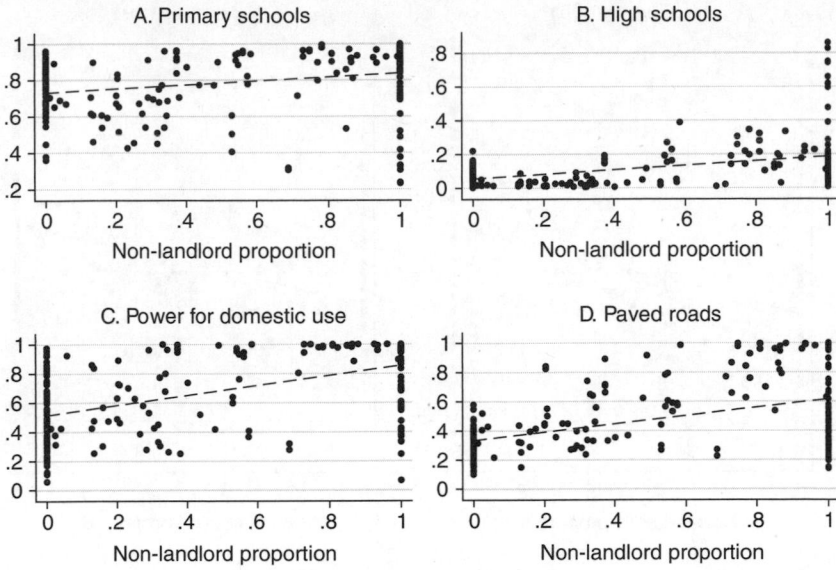

Figure 6.2    Land tenure and public goods, India districts, 1991.

lord areas. We can rule out this possibility by performing a statistical test based on the following thought experiment. Suppose we were to assign paved roads to areas in a purely random fashion, what is the probability that we would observe a slope of 0.28 when these outcomes are graphed against the non-landlord proportion? It turns out that this probability is less than 5%; in fact, it is close to zero. This is the idea behind statistical tests of significance: column 5 of Table 6.1 documents that, for each of the variables in Figure 6.2, the probability of obtaining the observed slope purely by chance is less than 5% (this is the standard threshold for tests of significance).[25]

Another way to assess the strength of the relationship with historical land tenure is to compute how much of the variation in these outcomes is explained by the non-landlord proportion. This turns out to be 7% for primary schools, 17% for high schools, 28% for power, and 21% for roads. The interpretation is that fully one-fifth of

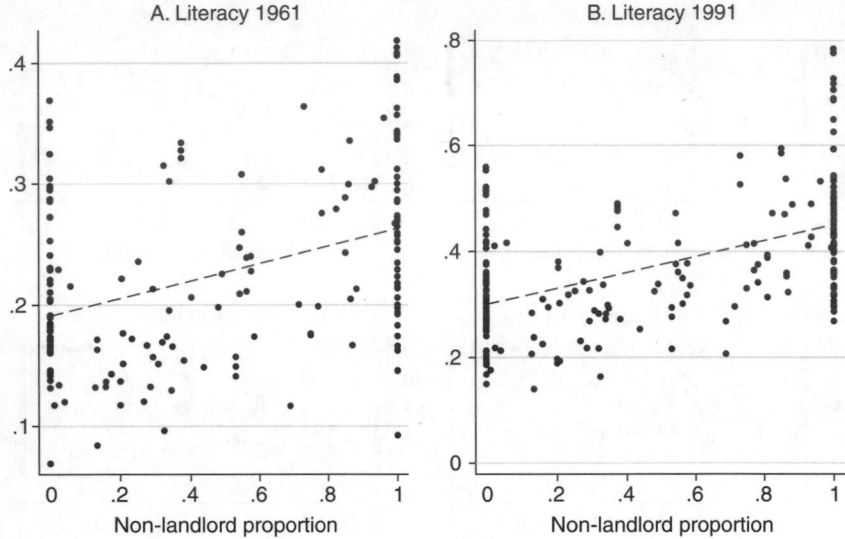

Figure 6.3    Land tenure and literacy, India districts, 1961 and 1991.

the cross-district variation observed in the provision of roads can be attributed to differences in colonial land tenure.

Are these differences really attributable to the historical land tenure system, or to other characteristics of these areas that also happen to be correlated with the land tenure system? For instance, we know that the landlord areas tend to have higher population densities. Perhaps these areas show fewer villages with schools because it is not necessary to supply schools to each village in densely populated areas. We also know that places conquered earlier are more likely to be landlord areas—do they lag behind in public goods because of a longer period of British colonial rule rather than differences in the land tenure system?

We will conduct two further analyses to establish that it is indeed the land tenure system and not these other factors that are responsible for these differences. First, we use multiple regression techniques to compute the difference between landlord and non-landlord areas after accounting for the effects of geographical variables (average rainfall levels, maximum and minimum temperatures, whether the district is on the coast), demographic characteristics (population density; percentages of Muslims, Sikhs, and Christians; percentages of Scheduled Castes and Scheduled Tribes[26] in the population) and the number of years of British rule. These differences are reported in column 6. We see that the differences between landlord and non-landlord areas are only slightly smaller than in column 5, suggesting that geographic or demographic characteristics are not driving the observed differences across different systems of land tenure. Although addition of these variables helps to explain more of the variation in public goods outcomes, colonial land tenure remains the single most important predictor. For instance, colonial land tenure explains 21% of the observed variation in provision of roads; adding geographic and demographic variables as well as the length of British rule improves this figure to 57%, which is an improvement of thirty-six percentage points. This means that variation in road provision accounted for by colonial land tenure is two-thirds of the variation accounted for by all the geographic and demographic variables together.[27]

Second, we show that the levels of public goods provision display the same nonlinear relationship with historical dates of conquest as the land tenure variable. Here we exploit the changes in British land policy discussed earlier, in particular the fact that areas conquered after 1820 and before 1856 are much more likely to have non-landlord systems than areas conquered earlier or later. The solid line in Figure 6.4 graphs the non-landlord proportion against the date of British land revenue control (which is almost always the date of British conquest). As the historical narrative indicates, there is a sharp increase in the non-landlord proportion for areas conquered after 1820 and before 1856. The dashed line in Figure 6.4 shows the fraction of villages that are provided with paved roads. This variable has a very similar and highly nonlinear relationship with the date of British land revenue control; that is, places conquered

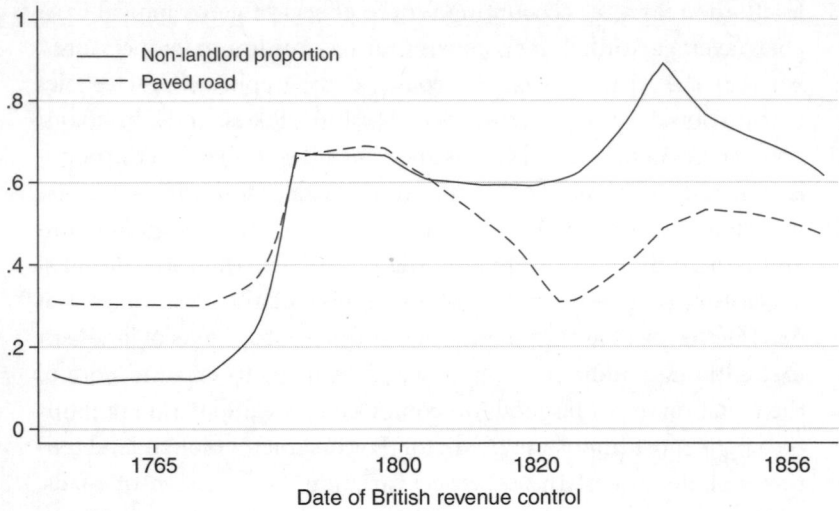

Figure 6.4   Land tenure, roads, and date of British revenue control.

after 1820 and before 1856 are better provided with roads than areas conquered just before or after these dates. This finding supports our contention that it is indeed the land tenure system that is responsible for these differences, rather than some other effect of a longer period of British rule or other steady trends over time. We do not know of any other major institutional changes that followed a similar nonlinear time path.

## DO LANDLORD AREAS LAG BEHIND BECAUSE OF POLITICAL CAPTURE?

Why do areas with different colonial land tenure systems show such different development paths many years into the future, even after the original institutions have been formally dismantled? Previous work on analyzing the impact of landlord-based land tenure systems in India has focused on the discrepancy between the owner and the cultivator of the land, or the differential incentive of the colonial state to invest in the Permanent Settlement areas because they would not obtain increased revenue as a result. These explanations are obsolete because the formal landlord systems have been dismantled, and the Indian state no longer obtains significant revenue from agriculture. However, it could be that the land distribution, and hence the income distribution, in the landlord areas continue to be more unequal than in the non-landlord areas. If the landlord areas have only very rich people and very poor people, the demand for public schooling may be lower, since the rich might send their children to private schools and the children of the poor might not go to school. By contrast, the non-landlord areas have a bigger population of those who are rich enough to want to send their children to school but too poor to afford private schooling.[28]

Two reasons explain why current economic inequality is probably not the driving mechanism here. First, the differences in land distribution and income inequality in the current period are quite small, in part because of the extensive land reforms undertaken after Independence. The Gini coefficient[29] for rural income inequality in 1987 was 0.264 for landlord areas and 0.285 for individual cultivator areas. That is, the areas formerly under landlord control had a slightly more equal income distribution than individual cultivator areas by 1987. Second, differences in public goods preferences do not explain why these areas do worse in almost every dimension of public good access. One would have expected that if residents in landlord-based areas put less weight on getting certain public goods, they would have thrown their energy into getting others. In particular, one would have thought that even if rich farmers had no incentives to lobby for schools, they would place a higher priority on roads, since they have more use for markets.[30]

The hypothesis we consider in this essay is whether the relative backwardness of these areas has something to do with how the political system operates in these areas. In particular, is it the case that elected representatives in these areas do not have sufficient incentives to deliver public goods? This could be due to the reasons suggested by Engerman and Sokoloff—that the politicians in the landlord-dominated areas do not face effective electoral competition and hence have no incentives to deliver public goods. Alternatively, it could be that the voters are less aware of their political rights in the landlord areas and therefore less able to claim what is owed to them. This explanation is quite plausible because we know that the landlord areas have lower literacy rates, and literacy and voter participation have been found to be positively related in many countries. We investigated these hypotheses by examining some standard measures of electoral participation and competition. All measures were computed using electoral data from state legislative elections of the 1980s.[31]

The evidence for this political capture hypothesis is mixed. We find that landlord areas have somewhat lower voter turnout in state elections—59% as against 61% in the individual cultivator areas—which is consistent with our hypothesis (Figure 6.5). However, elections in landlord areas do not appear to be less competitive. In fact, by some measures, they are actually more competitive. Elections in landlord areas typically have about 20% more candidates, and consequently, the vote share of the winner is smaller by three percentage points. Moreover, the vote difference between the winner and the runner-up is about two percentage points lower, and incumbent parties are 1% less likely to win in these areas. Figure 6.6 shows the graphs for these variables, and panel B of Table 6.1 provides numerical comparisons.

Are these electoral variables related to other differences noted earlier, such as the difference in literacy rates? Figure 6.7A shows that electoral turnout is positively related to literacy rates, a result consistent with results from other countries. However, the measures of electoral competition appear to be negatively related to literacy rates. Areas with higher literacy tend to have fewer candidates contesting elections, higher vote shares for the winner, and a higher probability of incumbent reelection (Figures 6.7B–6.7D).[32] We can interpret this

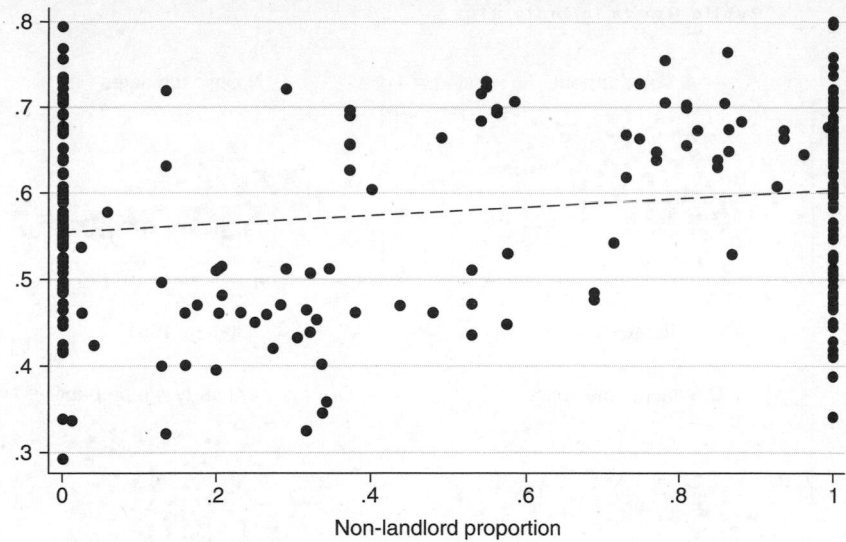

Figure 6.5   Land tenure and voter turnout, India districts, 1980s.

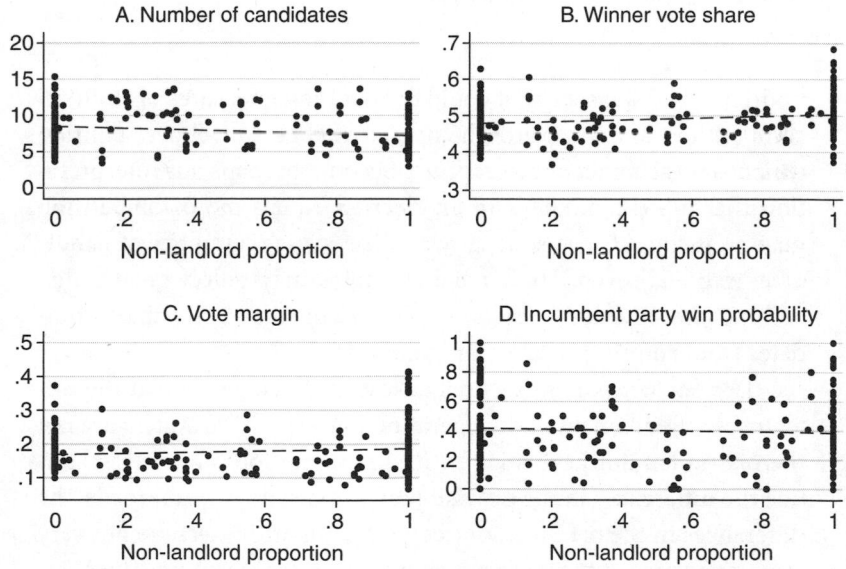

Figure 6.6   Land tenure and electoral competition, India districts, 1980s.

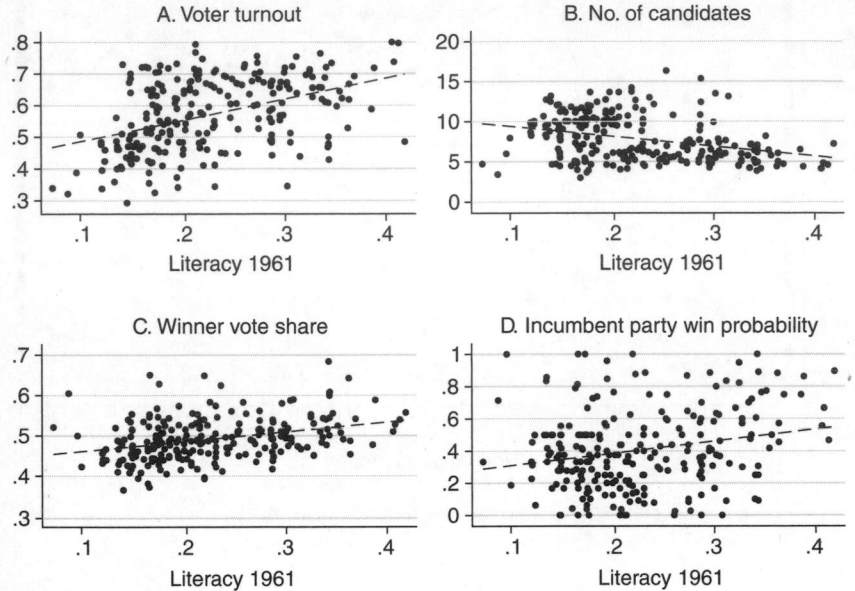

Figure 6.7 Literacy and electoral outcomes.

finding in two ways. First, it could be that these measures of electoral competition do not capture the degree of elite control over politics, which is what we set out to capture. Second, perhaps our interpretation that more candidates in an election equals more competition may be incorrect in a setting where the average number of candidates exceeds seven. Higher literacy rates may reflect greater discerning power among voters, which discourages nonviable candidates from running for election.

Two further pieces of evidence lead us to conclude that the differences we document in the operation of the political system are not the reason landlord areas lag behind non-landlord areas. First, unlike the differences in the provision of schools, power, and roads, the differences in the measures of electoral competitiveness are not very large, and some of them are not statistically significant (see the notations in column 5 of Table 6.1). This finding is reinforced when we control for the effects of geographic and demographic variables (column 6), though voter turnout remains significantly higher in non-landlord areas.

Second, although the differences in measures of political participation and competition are correlated with levels of public goods provision, they are not large enough to statistically account for the differences in public goods provision. As we might expect, districts that had higher voter turnout also have a higher provision of public goods. Figure 6.8A shows this relationship for paved roads. Less expectedly, a higher winner vote share, which typically is assumed to signify less competitive elections, also seems to be associated with better public good provision (Figure 6.8B). Figure 6.8C shows that areas with higher initial literacy also have more roads in later periods. However, we find that there continues to

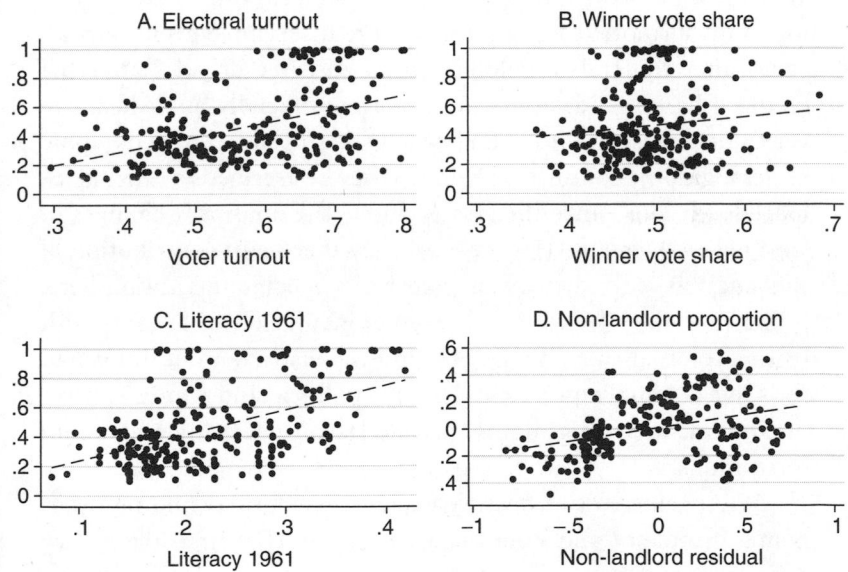

Figure 6.8   What explains provision of roads? India districts, 1991.

be a strong positive relationship between the provision of paved roads and the non-landlord proportion, after controlling for the effects of electoral turnout, vote share of the winning candidate, and literacy (Figure 6.8D). We find very similar results for the other public goods. Only for primary goods do we find that early literacy and electoral variables explain the whole of the landlord/non-landlord difference.[33]

## CONCLUSIONS

What can we conclude from this comparative analysis across districts of India? The most important result is that there are large differences in the development trajectories of areas that had different land tenure systems under British colonial rule. In particular, areas that were put under the control of landlords lag behind in the provision of public goods such as schools and roads compared to areas in which control rights in land were given to small cultivators. Furthermore, these differences are discernible even four decades after the end of colonial rule and three decades after the landlord-based land tenure systems were officially abolished. We verify that these are not simply the effects of different geographic or demographic conditions. Nor can they be ascribed to other colonial institutions, since they track closely the nonlinear changes in land policy over time (Figure 6.4). The other main contribution of this analysis is to identify the effect of a specific institution here, rather than the effect of a collection of institutions that came with British colonial rule. The fact that all the districts in our area had the same colonial power, and the same political and administrative institutions today, highlights the long-lasting effects of land tenure institutions.[34]

We considered two possible explanations for our findings: economic inequality and political participation. The first is not very different across these two types of areas today, mainly because formerly landlord-controlled areas have put considerable efforts into enacting land reforms as a means of reducing economic inequality. Political participation and literacy levels are lower in landlord areas, and this is correlated with a lower level of infrastructure provision. However, these variables cannot fully explain the public goods differences across landlord and non-landlord areas.

This result is important because it tells us that any explanation of these long-lasting effects of history has to look beyond these two obvious factors. We were unable to capture a number of other political channels in our empirical analysis. For instance, it could be the case that the more literate and politically conscious population in non-landlord areas is able to elect better-quality politicians. A more informed electorate might also lead to fewer candidates contesting elections, since weak candidates stand very little chance of winning. Better representatives might then deliver more public goods to these areas. Another possibility is that a history of elite control creates cynicism about the political system, leading to uninformed voting. A third possibility is that this lag in provision of public goods is a natural consequence of the policy priorities of the landlord areas, which were initially heavily focused on undoing the past, such as dismantling the old land tenure institutions and ensuring equality in access to land (we document some evidence of this in note 22). This priority might leave fewer resources and less political capital to devote to other development policies. It is also possible that a history of elite control creates a much more polarized electorate, whose representatives are unable to work together effectively to deliver public goods.

In conclusion, our comparative analysis highlights the impact of a specific historical institution on long-term development outcomes. Two very plausible hypotheses about the intervening mechanisms do not have the empirical weight to explain our results. We have suggested a number of other potential hypotheses, which would benefit from a new round of comparative historical research. Such detailed research could also yield new hypotheses about the long-lasting effects of historical institutions.

## NOTES

We thank Jared Diamond, James Robinson, Robert Schneider, and two anonymous referees for extremely useful suggestions. Katherine Cui provided excellent research assistance.

1. Douglass C. North, *Institutions, Institutional Change and Economic Performance* (Cambridge, 1990).
2. See Avner Greif, "Contract Enforceability and Economic Institutions in Early Trade: The Maghribi Traders' Coalition," *American Economic Review* 83 (1993): 525–548 and "Reputation and Coalitions in Medieval Trade: Evidence on the Maghribi Traders," *Journal of Economic History* 49 (1989): 857–882; Douglass C. North and Barry Weingast, "Constitutions and Commitment: The Evolution of Institutions Governing Public Choice in Seventeenth-Century England," *Journal of Economic History* 49 (1989): 803–832; Stephen Haber, Noel Maurer, and Armando Razo, *The Politics of Property Rights: Political Instability, Credible Commitments and Economic Growth in Mexico, 1876–1929* (Cambridge, MA, 2003).
3. Rafael La Porta, Florencio Lopez de Silanes, Andrei Shleifer, and Robert Vishny, "Law and Finance," *Journal of Political Economy* 106 (1998): 1113–1155.
4. The conclusions from these studies have been challenged by studies done over other time periods. Raghuram Rajan and Luigi Zingales find that common law countries are not leading in financial development in 1913 ("The Great Reversals: The Politics of Financial Development in the 20th Century," *Journal of Financial Economics* 69 [2003]: 5–50). Furthermore, the French legal system enabled much greater flexibility than the American system in the nineteenth century (Naomi R. Lamoreaux and Jean-Laurent Rosenthal, "Legal Regime and Contractual Flexibility: A Comparison of Business's Organizational Choices in France and the United States during the Era of Industrialization," *American Law and Economics Review* 7 [2005]: 28–61).
5. India became independent in 1947.
6. Stanley L. Engerman and Kenneth L. Sokoloff, "Colonialism, Inequality and the Long-Run Paths to Development," National Bureau of Economic Research Working Paper no. 11057 (Cambridge, MA, 2005).
7. Abhijit Banerjee and Lakshmi Iyer, "History, Institutions and Economic Performance: The Legacy of Colonial Land Tenure Systems in India," *American Economic Review* 95 (2005): 1190–1213.

8. Stanley L. Engerman and Kenneth L. Sokoloff, "The Evolution of Suffrage Institutions in the New World," National Bureau of Economic Research Working Paper no. 8512 (Cambridge, MA, 2001).

9. Our method is consistent with contemporary research in this area. See, for example, Daron Acemoglu, Maria Angelica Bautista, James A. Robinson, and Pablo Querubin, "Economic and Political Inequality in Development: The Case of Cundinamarca, Colombia," National Bureau of Economic Research Working Paper no. 13208 (Cambridge, MA, 2007); Abhijit Banerjee and Rohini Somanathan, "The Political Economy of Public Goods: Some Evidence from India," *Journal of Development Economics* 82 (2007): 287–314.

10. Bangladesh, formerly East Pakistan, became an independent nation in 1975. For a comparison of long-term economic outcomes between directly ruled British areas and indirectly ruled areas, see Lakshmi Iyer, "Direct versus Indirect Colonial Rule in India: Long-Term Consequences," *Review of Economics and Statistics* (forthcoming).

11. Some measures for protecting the rights of tenants and subproprietors were introduced in later years. For details on the exact delineation of rights, as well as descriptions of subtenures, see Dharma Kumar, ed., *The Cambridge Economic History of India*, vol. 2 (Cambridge, 1982), chapters I and II.

12. Tapan Raychaudhuri, "The Mid-Eighteenth-Century Background," in Kumar, ed., *The Cambridge Economic History of India*, vol. 2, p. 13; B. H. Baden-Powell, *The Land-Systems of British India*, vol. 3 (Oxford, 1892), p. 455; Ratnalekha Ray, *Change in Bengal Agrarian Society, 1760–1850* (New Delhi, 1979); Tirthankar Roy, *The Economic History of India, 1857–1947* (New Delhi, 2000), p. 38.

13. For a good discussion of the role of ideology and economic doctrines in the formation of the land revenue systems, see Ranajit Guha, *A Rule of Property for Bengal: An Essay on the Idea of Permanent Settlement* (Paris, 1963); Eric Stokes, *The English Utilitarians and India* (Oxford, 1959); Eric Stokes, "The Land Revenue Systems of the North-Western Provinces and Bombay Deccan 1830–80: Ideology and the Official Mind," in *The Peasant and the Raj: Studies in Agrarian Society and Peasant Rebellion in Colonial India* (Cambridge, 1978).

14. A cadastral survey refers to a detailed survey of the land, noting geographical features as well as ownership boundaries. This is usually carried out in order to assess ownership as well as to provide a basis for taxation. Such a survey was never carried out in many Permanent Settlement areas, since

the British, being assured of a fixed revenue from the landlords, did not need such detailed information.

15. Nilmani Mukherjee, *The Ryotwari System in Madras, 1792–1827* (Calcutta, 1962), p. 25.

16. Ibid.

17. For a detailed description of land revenue policy in northern India, see Babu Ram Misra, *Land Revenue Policy in the United Provinces, under British Rule* (Benares, 1942); W. H. Smith, *Final Report on the Revision of Settlement in the District of Aligarh* (Allahabad, 1882), p. 114. Large landlords were often referred to as *talukdars* rather than *zamindars*. In Oudh province, *talukdars* were a special class of very large landlords, who had been issued formal grants by the British which "guaranteed an indefeasible, heritable and transferable superior title in every village in their estates" (A. F. Millett, *Report on the Settlement of the Land Revenue of the Sultanpur District* [Lucknow, 1873], p. 68).

18. F. W. Porter, *Final Settlement Report of the Allahabad District* (Allahabad, 1878), p. 108.

19. Misra, *Land Revenue Policy in the United Provinces*, p. 100.

20. Roy, *The Economic History of India, 1857–1947*, p. 38.

21. J. F. Macandrew, *Report of the Settlement Operations of the Rai Bareli District* (Lucknow, 1872); Denzil Charles Jelf Ibbetson, *Report on the Revision of Settlement of the Panipat Tahsil and Karnal Parganah of the Karnal District, 1872–1880* (Allahabad, 1883), p. 96; J. Wilson, *Final Report on the Revision of Settlement of the Sirsa District in the Punjab, 1879–83* (Calcutta, 1884).

22. For a good review of these laws and their impact on state-level poverty rates, see Timothy Besley and Robin Burgess, "Land Reforms, Poverty Reduction and Growth: Evidence from India," *Quarterly Journal of Economics* 115 (2000): 341–388. This paper classifies all land reforms into four categories: abolition of intermediaries between the state and the cultivator (landlords would be one such intermediary), tenancy reforms to provide greater security of tenure to tenants, ceilings on land ownership, and land consolidation legislation. Besley and Burgess find that the first two types of reforms led to greater poverty reduction, suggesting that landlord-based systems were leading to greater poverty levels. Using their database of land reforms, we find that states dominated by landlord-based systems are much more likely to focus their efforts on passing land reform legislation: such states enacted an average of 6.5 land reform mea-

sures in the period between 1957 and 1992, while non-landlord states had an average of 3.5.

23. The Census provides information on a wider range of infrastructure provision; this information is used in Banerjee and Somanathan, "The Political Economy of Public Goods"; Abhijit Banerjee, Lakshmi Iyer, and Rohini Somanathan, "History, Social Divisions and Public Goods in Rural India," *Journal of the European Economic Association* 3 (2005): 639–647. Data on public goods provision is available for earlier periods as well. Banerjee and Iyer, "History, Institutions and Economic Performance," documents differences across landlord and non-landlord areas for 1981. In this chapter, we focus on 1991 data for two reasons. First, this emphasizes the long-lasting impact of differing historical circumstances. Second, the electoral data we use to test the specific hypothesis of political capture by elites is available on a consistent basis after 1977.

24. Revenue estates could consist of parts of villages, or more than one village. In Allahabad district, each village had 1.4 revenue estates on average. We obtained district-level Land Settlement Reports for several districts of Uttar Pradesh, Madhya Pradesh, and Punjab; these Settlement Reports were compiled by British administrators in the 1870s and 1880s. We computed the "non-landlord proportion" as the proportion of villages, estates, or land area (whichever was reported) not under the revenue liability of landlords. For Bombay Presidency, Bengal Presidency, Orissa, Berar, and districts for which we do not have district-level settlement reports, non-landlord measure is assigned as zero or one based on historical accounts of the dominant land tenure system in the district. Sources of information included Baden-Powell, *The Land-Systems of British India*; Rai M. N. Gupta, *Land System of Bengal* (Calcutta, 1940); Kumar, ed., *The Cambridge Economic History of India*, vol. 2; Misra, *Land Revenue Policy in the United Provinces*; Mukherjee, *The Ryotwari System in Madras, 1792–1827*; and Govindlal Dalsukhbhai Patel, *The Land Problem of Re-organized Bombay State* (Bombay, 1957). We obtained the non-landlord proportion for districts of Madras Presidency, as well as district-level maps for all provinces from Baden-Powell, *The Land-Systems of British India*. These maps were matched up to modern district boundaries using maps from http://www.mapsofindia.com.

25. A rigorous treatment of statistical testing of hypotheses can be found in Jeffrey R. Wooldridge, *Introductory Econometrics: A Modern Approach* (Cincinnati, 2002), chapter 4.

26. These groups have been historically disadvantaged. Scheduled Castes are communities that were traditionally at the bottom of the Hindu caste hierarchy, while Scheduled Tribes have been largely outside the Hindu caste system. The Constitution of India provides for several affirmative action programs for these groups.

27. We get similar results for the other variables. As explained earlier, colonial land tenure alone accounts for 7% of the variation in primary schools, 17% of the variation in high schools, and 28% of the variation in the provision of power. The addition of geographic and demographic variables raises the total explained variation to 26%, 43%, and 48%, respectively.

28. Stokes argues that such a discrepancy leads to lower drive and productivity in agriculture. Eric Stokes, "Dynamism and Enervation in North Indian Agriculture: The Historical Dimension," in Eric Stokes, ed., *The Peasant and the Raj: Studies in Agrarian Society and Peasant Rebellion in Colonial India* (Cambridge, 1978). Bhaduri argues that the layers of moneylenders between the landlord and the cultivator had lower incentives to invest in productive assets because that would lower their interest income from lending to peasants in the longer term. Amit Bhaduri, "The Evolution of Land Relations in Eastern India under British Rule," *Indian Economic and Social History Review* 13 (1976): 45–53. The latter view is challenged by Roy in *The Economic History of India, 1857–1947*, pp. 91–95. On the government investment view, see Amiya K. Bagchi, "Reflections on Patterns of Regional Growth in India under British Rule," *Bengal Past and Present* 95 (1976): 247–289.

29. The Gini coefficient is a widely used measure of income or asset inequality. This measure takes the value of 0 in the case of perfect equality (i.e., everybody having the same income), and 1 in the case of perfect inequality (i.e., one person in society having all the income). Higher values of the Gini coefficient represent a more unequal distribution of income or assets. The Gini coefficient can also be computed as the average difference in income for any two randomly selected individuals in the society, divided by the overall average income level. See Corrado Gini, "Measurement of Inequality and Incomes," *Economic Journal* 31 (1921): 124–126.

30. For a study documenting these differences for a very wide range of public goods, see Banerjee, Iyer, and Somanathan, "History, Social Divisions and Public Goods in Rural India."

31. For a detailed review of the evidence on literacy, income, and turnout, see Rohini Pande, "Understanding Political Corruption in Low Income Countries," in T. Paul Schultz and John Strauss, eds., *Handbook of Development*

*Economics*, vol. 4 (Amsterdam, 2008). Electoral data on post-1977 elections was obtained from the Web site of the Election Commission of India (www .eci.gov.in). The matching of state electoral constituencies to administrative districts was based on information collected from the Web sites of individual State Election Commissions. Our results exclude the states of Karnataka and Uttarakhand, for which we were not able to match up electoral constituencies to administrative districts.

32. These relationships are fairly strong, in the sense that the coefficients on literacy rates are statistically significant at the 5% level.

33. The relationships shown in Figures 6.8A and 6.8C are statistically significant, even after we control for geographic variables, demographic characteristics, and the length of British colonial rule. Similar relationships exist for the other measures of infrastructure (primary schools, high schools, and power); for these measures, the relationship with the winner's vote share is also statistically significant. In the interest of space, these results are not shown but are available from the authors upon request. The y-axis in Figure 6.8D is the residual obtained after a regression of paved roads on electoral turnout, vote share of the winning candidate, and literacy. The x-axis represents the residuals obtained from a regression of the non-landlord proportion on these same variables. The slope of the line in Figure 6.8D is 0.20, slightly less than the 0.25 obtained in column 6 of Table 6.1. Similarly, the slope is 0.01 for primary schools, 0.06 for high schools, and 0.11 for power; these compare to the earlier figures of 0.07, 0.11, and 0.21, respectively.

34. Niall Ferguson identifies several distinctive features that the British Empire tended to disseminate, which set it apart from other colonial powers. His list includes English forms of land tenure, the English language, Scottish and English banking, the common law, Protestantism, team sports, the limited state, representative assemblies, and the idea of liberty. Of this list, the English language and banking systems tend to mostly affect cities, while the other institutions in the list were not implemented differently in different parts of British India. Niall Ferguson, *Empire: The Rise and Demise of the British World Order and the Lessons for Global Power* (London, 2002), p. xxv. Several other studies in this book also document the long-lasting impact of historical institutions. Daron Acemoglu, Davide Cantoni, Simon Johnson, and James Robinson, "From Ancien Régime to Capitalism: The Spread of the French Revolution as a Natural Experiment" (Chapter 7), find that institutional reforms introduced by Napoleon's conquest of certain areas of Europe laid the foundation for the subsequent growth of capitalism

several decades later. Nathan Nunn, "Shackled to the Past: The Causes and Consequences of Africa's Slave Trades" (Chapter 5), finds that African countries that bore the brunt of the slave trade lag behind in economic outcomes even in the twentieth century.

## From Ancien Régime to Capitalism: The Spread of the French Revolution as a Natural Experiment

DARON ACEMOGLU, DAVIDE CANTONI,
SIMON JOHNSON, AND JAMES A. ROBINSON

*Am Anfang war Napoleon (In the beginning was Napoleon)*
—THOMAS NIPPERDEY

*Together with Luxemburg, Rhenish Hesse and the Palatinate,
Rhenish Prussia shares the advantage of having participated in
the French Revolution and in the social, administrative, and
legislative consolidation of its results under Napoleon. Ten
years earlier than elsewhere in Germany, corporations and
patriarchal dominance by the patricians disappeared from the
cities, having to face free competition. Rhenish Prussia has the
most developed and varied industry in Germany; an industry
whose rise can be dated back to the French domination.*
—FRIEDRICH ENGELS

One of the most important research agendas of comparative history and social science is a deeper understanding of the
causes of the world distribution of income. What can account for the
huge differences between the standards of living and life opportunities experienced in countries such as the United States and Western
Europe, and those of sub-Saharan Africa or Latin America? Historians have articulated these questions in terms of the causes of the

"Rise of the West," the "European Miracle," or the "Great Divergence."[1] These phrases refer to the process by which, starting from a situation 300 or so years ago where differences in prosperity were relatively small, a group of European countries, led by the Netherlands and Britain and subsequently followed by Germany and others, experienced sustained growth in average living standards. During the late nineteenth century, this prosperity began to disseminate to certain Neo-Europes[2] such as the United States and Australasia, and in the twentieth century it spread to a group of countries in East Asia, but much of the world—Africa, Latin America, Eastern Europe, and South Asia—remained mired in poverty.

Scholars have provided many explanations for these patterns, and a salient one emphasizes differences in institutions between countries as the main cause of patterns of comparative incomes. For example, the main institutional argument that attempts to explain economic growth within Europe in the early modern period focuses on the abolition or withering away of the institutions of the ancien régime.[3] The countries where institutions were reformed the earliest were the ones that began to grow first. This focus appears in the work of Adam Smith, who saw the economic institutions and policies of a society as being the key factor determining its economic success. Although Smith's focus was not on comparative history, the account he gives of the relative prosperity of different societies makes it clear that he thought this difference was related to the different institutions of these societies and the incentives they created. Smith argued that voluntary exchange in free markets and the resulting division of labor were key to prosperity. Such a system was obviously very different from the legacy of feudal institutions that were part of the ancien régime. Smith believed that the relative prosperity of Western Europe was closely related to the early decline of ancien régime institutions, and he argued forcefully that feudal institutions were not conducive to prosperity: "But if great improvements are seldom to be expected from great proprietors, they are least of all to be expected when they employ slaves for their workmen . . . This species of slavery still subsists in Russia, Poland, Hungary, Bohemia, Moravia, and other parts of Germany. Only in the western and southwestern provinces of Europe has it gradually been abolished altogether."[4]

When Adam Smith wrote in the late eighteenth century, significant differences in prosperity had already arisen between the west and the east of Europe. As one moved east, prosperity declined, while at the same time the prevalence of feudal institutions increased. Feudalism lingered longest in Eastern Europe, which was the most economically backward part of the Continent.[5] Contrast this with the two most dynamic economies of the early modern period, the Netherlands and England. The Netherlands was probably the European society least affected by feudal institutions such as serfdom, where the guilds were weak and where the threat of absolutism was thrown off by the Dutch Revolt of the 1570s.[6] England was the country where the institutions of the ancien régime collapsed earliest. Serfdom had vanished by 1500, guilds lost their power in the sixteenth and seventeenth centuries, the Church was expropriated and its land sold off by Henry VIII in the 1530s, the Civil War and Glorious Revolution saw the end of monopolies and royal absolutism, and strong notions of equality before the law developed at least by the early eighteenth century.[7]

Does this evidence associating the early collapse of ancien régime and feudal institutions with the rise of capitalist market economies demonstrate that these institutions indeed retarded or held back economic progress? Reaching such a conclusion presents at least two problems. First, although the decline of the ancien régime and improved economic performance may go together, this correlation could be the result of *reverse causality*. It may be that the progress of capitalism is the cause of the decline of feudalism, not the other way around. For example, an earlier generation of scholars, such as Henri Pirenne, argued precisely that it was the expansion of trade and the development of a more commercial society—what Michael M. Postan called the "Rise of the Money Economy"—that explains the dissolution of feudal institutions.[8]

Second, there is also the problem of *omitted variable bias* in which both the decline in the ancien régime and the takeoff of economic growth are the result of other events or social processes. The decision to change economic institutions or not to enforce them is a collective decision in society, which itself depends on other factors. For instance, it may be that England's geographical location or culture created a distinct economic potential for the country in the late medieval period and that these in turn determined the evolution of feudal institutions. Perhaps feudalism just became an irrelevance to a modernizing society and withered away without playing an important causal role.

An interesting illustration of omitted variable bias in exactly this context is discussed by Weber in his *Protestant Ethic and the Spirit of Capitalism*. In the early modern period, England developed both the most dynamic economy and one of the freest and least absolutist sets of political institutions in Europe. One could argue, following Douglass North and Barry Weingast,[9] that the economic performance was a direct consequence of the political innovations, yet Weber denied this, observing that "Montesquieu says (Esprit des Lois, book XX, chapter 7) of the English that they 'had progressed the farthest of all peoples of the world in three important things: in piety, in commerce, and in freedom'. Is it not possible that their commercial superiority and their adaptation to free political institutions are connected in some way with that record of piety which Montesquieu ascribes to them?"[10] Hence Max Weber directly argued that an omitted factor, here religion, explained both democracy and capitalism in England.

In investigating the relationship between the collapse of the ancien régime and the rise of capitalism, it is therefore important to recognize both the possibility of reverse causality and omitted variable bias. In the natural sciences the solution to a problem like this would be to conduct an experiment. For instance, we would ideally take a group of countries that were alike—say, all of them having a relatively backward institutional landscape—and abolish ancien régime institutions in a randomly chosen subset of these countries (the "treatment" group) while leaving unchanged the institutions of the rest (the "control" group). Then we could observe what happens to the relative prosperity of these two groups. In reality, of course, we cannot conduct such an experiment. Nevertheless, historians and social scientists can take advantage of the "natural experiments" that history sometimes offers.

By a natural experiment we mean a situation in which some historical accident or event leads economic, political, and social factors to change in some areas while remaining the same in other comparable places. If indeed the different areas experiencing differential change are comparable, we can think of the group in which change has taken place as being the treatment group in an experiment and the other group as corresponding to the control group.

In the context of the decline of the ancien régime, the invasion of large parts of Europe by French armies following the French Revolution of 1789 provides a source of variation in institutions that can be used as a natural experiment. The French armies abolished central institutions of the ancien régime, including many feudal legacies, dues, and prerogatives, ending guilds, introducing equality before the law, which included freedom for Jews, and redistributing Church land. We can exploit this experience to estimate the effect of some important ancien régime institutions on economic growth. To do this we can think of the parts of Europe that were invaded and had their institutions reformed as being "treated," while those that were not invaded are the control group. Thus, as in an experiment, we can compare the economic performance of these two groups before and after the institutions of the treatment group were reformed and investigate if the reformed group begins to become relatively richer. To the extent that it does, this will provide evidence that institutional reforms contributed to the increase in relative prosperity.

Nevertheless, for inference based on natural experiments to be valid, it is important that the areas affected by the treatment (French invasion) were on a growth trajectory similar to other comparable areas before the treatment. Among other things, this requires that the French did not choose to invade places based on their future growth potential.[11] Thus, for example, if we find that the Rhineland grew relatively faster after 1815 than before 1789, to conclude that this growth was caused by the French reforms implemented there, it must not be the case that the French annexed the Rhineland because of its latent economic potential.

These considerations motivate our focus in this essay on Germany. Germany contains both invaded and noninvaded areas and is more homogeneous than all of Europe taken together.[12] By only examining the French invasion of Germany, we are considering variation in institutional reforms in an area that shares a great deal of history, culture, and institutions. It is much easier to compare Baden with Berg than Poland with Portugal. Nevertheless, the validity of our approach does not rest on different parts of Germany being completely homogeneous, as of course this was not the case. The key issue is what drove patterns of French invasion and reform.[13]

To study this natural experiment, we need some way of measuring economic development within different parts of Germany in the eighteenth and nineteenth centuries before the creation of modern national accounts and the accurate measurement of income. An attractive strategy is to look at urbanization, typically measured as the proportion of the population living in urban areas of 5,000 or more people. In the modern world, urbanization is highly correlated with income per capita, and historians, such as Paul Bairoch and Jan de Vries, argued that only areas with high agricultural productivity and a developed transportation network could support large urban populations historically.[14] Urbanization is also much used as a proxy in attempts to estimate historical levels of income.[15] We therefore constructed a database of urbanization levels in a sample of German states for the years 1750–1910.[16]

The basic finding of our essay is captured by Figure 7.1, which shows the levels of urbanization in the parts of Germany invaded

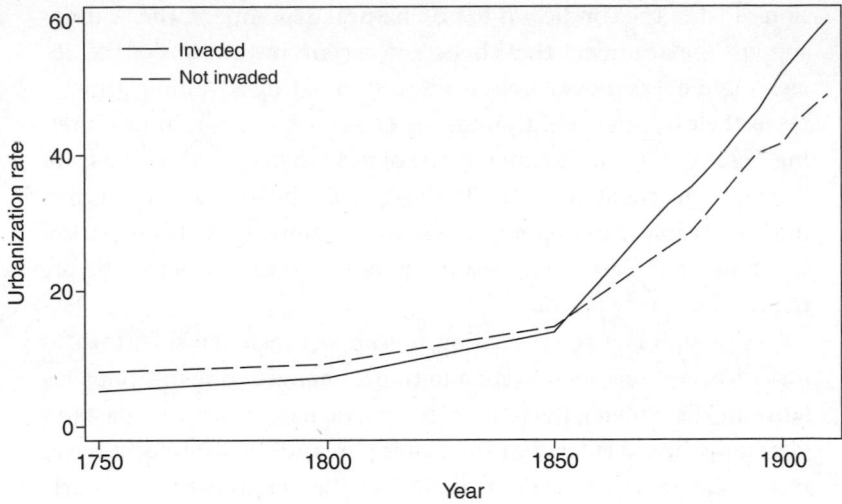

Figure 7.1   Percent of total population living in cities above 5,000 inhabitants (two groups).

and reformed by the French (the treatment group) and the level of urbanization in the other parts of Germany for which we have data.[17] The figure shows that prior to 1800, urbanization was higher in the parts of Germany that were not invaded. This fact is significant in itself because if urbanization is indeed a good proxy for development, it suggests that the French did not focus their attempts at control on the most prosperous parts of Germany. Figure 7.1 also shows that urbanization was growing in the eighteenth century but began to grow more rapidly everywhere between 1800 and 1850. Most significant, however, is the finding that the increase in the rate of growth of urbanization is most rapid in the treatment group. In particular, territories in the treatment group become more urbanized by 1850 than the parts of Germany that were not invaded. Figure 7.1 suggests that the institutional reforms implemented by the French increased urbanization and therefore economic growth relative to those places that the French did not reform.[18] If this situation satisfies the conditions to be a natural experiment, the findings support the argument that abolishing certain institutions of the ancien régime was indeed important in stimulating economic growth. Nevertheless, there are grounds for exercising caution in interpreting Figure 7.1. Even though the rate of growth of the invaded part of Germany accelerated relative to the rest, it appears that it was growing more rapidly between 1750 and 1800, implying that this part of Germany may have been on a different economic trajectory before the revolutionary period.

Although Figure 7.1 is telling, it is important to consider that for historical reasons there were additional changes in institutions related to the French Revolution. In particular, in certain parts of Germany the old rulers returned after 1815, and French reforms were reversed. Nevertheless, the Congress of Vienna granted large parts of French-invaded territory to Prussia in 1815; this was a fortunate circumstance since Prussia, having reformed itself during the Napoleonic Wars, did not reverse the institutional reforms brought by the French. These facts suggest an alternative definition of the treatment group: those parts of Germany that were controlled by the French and then given to Prussia in 1815. In Figure 7.2 we separate out this subset of Germany and compare its level of urbanization between 1750 and 1910 with that of two other regions of Germany: that part which was never invaded and that part which was invaded by the French but where the old rulers returned in 1815. A cartographic representation of these three distinct parts of Germany (within post-1815 borders) can be found in Figure 7.3. The evolution of urbanization rates shown in Figure 7.2 tells a story very similar to Figure 7.1. We see that in 1800 urbanization was highest in the non-invaded parts and lowest in the parts that were invaded but not given to Prussia. We again see that urbanization begins to grow more rapidly in the treatment group after 1800 than elsewhere in Germany, but once more there is a suggestion that urbanization was already growing more rapidly in the eighteenth century. Interestingly, the

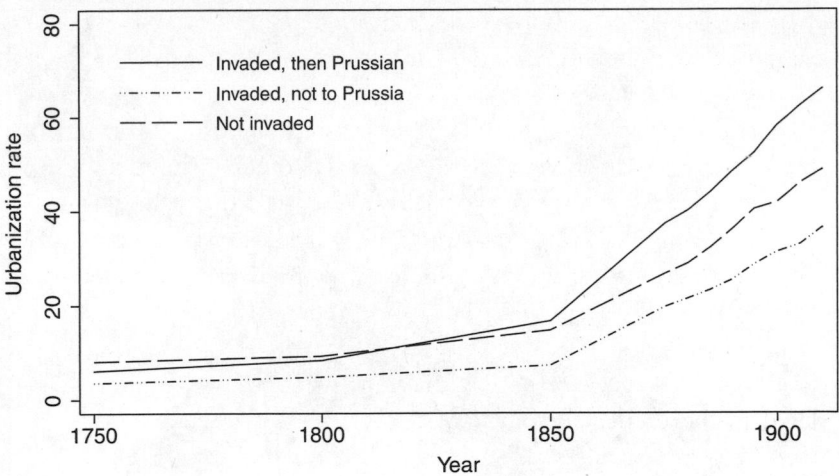

Figure 7.2 Percent of total population living in cities above 5,000 inhabitants (three groups).

figure also suggests that the worst outcomes were in the areas that were reformed but where the reforms were reversed after 1815.

This second way of defining the treatment group raises three additional concerns. First, it needs to be the case that at the Congress of Vienna different parts of Germany were not allocated to Prussia on the basis of their economic potential, but rather were determined as the outcome of a political negotiation that did not reflect the economic factors or the economic potential of places that were eventually given to Prussia. Second, it needs to be the case that the Prussians did not selectively reverse the French reforms. Finally, we should be able to exclude direct effects stemming solely from the circumstance that some parts were ruled by Prussia instead of other countries ("Prussia effects"). Fortunately for our empirical strategy, as we discuss shortly, all three of these conditions appear to be satisfied.

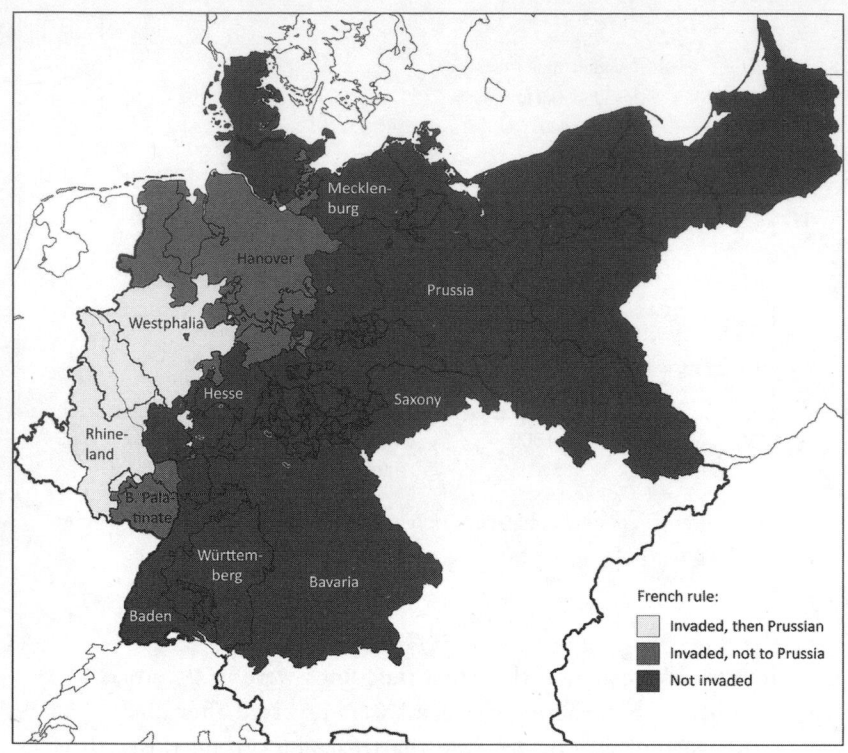

Figure 7.3   Areas of French rule in Germany. (Cartographic representation based
on IEG-MAPS: Server for digital historical maps, Mainz.)

## THE ANCIEN RÉGIME AND ECONOMIC PROGRESS

At the time of the French Revolution, much of Europe was dominated
by two kinds of oligarchies: the landed nobility in agriculture and the
urban-based oligarchy controlling commerce and various occupations. By ancien régime institutions we mean those that maintained
and benefited these groups along with unchecked royal power.[19] In
terms of economic institutions, a close relationship exists between
institutions inherited from the feudal era and those identified as be-

longing to the ancien régime. In the larger part of Europe west of the Elbe, the most extreme forms of serfdom and labor services had vanished in the period after the Black Death, but the basic order of society persisted in many parts. Though following the work of Alfred Cobban it has become controversial to talk about French society in 1789 as feudal, recent scholarship seems to have driven home the fact that feudal dues and impositions remained large in France and played an important role in the Revolution.[20] Even in urban areas, which were often a refuge from the constraints of the countryside, powerful guilds controlled the economic activities and membership of the urban community.

The most basic aspect of the ancien régime was a fundamentally hierarchical notion of society whereby some groups or social orders had privileges, social, political and economic, while others did not. These privileged groups were primarily the monarchy, the aristocracy, and the Church. These groups had different laws and rights from the general populace, and this manifested itself in many important ways. For example, the aristocracy was typically exempt from paying taxes, while the Church, which held large amounts of land, levied its own taxes, the tithe, on the agricultural output of peasants. At the bottom of this hierarchy were the peasants and urban poor whose economic and social choices were often highly circumscribed. Religious minorities such as Jews suffered the same fate, experiencing substantial discrimination. In 1789, the principle of equality before the law was quite alien in most of Europe. The political representation of groups was based on the same orders, though in the age of absolutism many medieval parliamentary institutions, most famously the Estates General in France, had mostly withered away. Prominent aspects of all these institutions were abolished in France in 1789.

The connection between this institutional nexus and economic performance is quite intuitive and consistent with basic economic theory and a great deal of evidence. Only institutions that provide secure property rights and facilitate entry and social mobility will generate economic growth.[21] The system of aristocratic privilege was a major impediment to social mobility, and in the rural sector feudal limitations on mobility and occupational choice placed restrictions on the efficient allocation of resources. The legal system, being discriminatory, arbitrary, and often somewhat chaotic, was also a major impediment to economic progress. Although revisionist interpretations of the effects of guilds have been published, it is beyond dispute that among their main functions they acted as a cartel, limited entry and competition, and improved the incomes of their members.[22] Such restrictions almost certainly retarded innovation both indirectly and directly. Joel Mokyr presents many examples of the guilds' attempts to block new innovations that would have undermined their economic and political position.[23]

## THE ANCIEN RÉGIME IN GERMANY

The ancien régime institutions characterized various parts of Germany to a greater or lesser extent. A major source of variation comes from the territorial fragmentation of the Holy Roman Empire, which was made up of around 400 different heterogeneous polities. Nevertheless, some useful generalizations can be made.

First, the notion of feudal orders and privileges was still dominant in Germany, and even though the extent of absolutism varied considerably, the general political structures of the ancien régime were in place. A telling example is Hanover, where, as Herbert Fisher notes, "The provincial estates of Hanover, despite the connexion of the Electorate with the free people of England, never supported the abolition of noble privilege or the emancipation of the peasantry."[24]

Second, although feudalism in its most rigid form was abolished in Germany west of the Elbe, with Joseph II abolishing serfdom in Austria (though not the rest of the Hapsburg Empire) in 1781, many of its remnants remained.[25] In addition, to the east of the Elbe, serfdom was still strong. In the west, serfdom had been replaced by various forms of taxes and tributes to landowners in other areas, which could nonetheless be quite onerous. For example, in the Rhineland, the first area in Germany to come under French control, a form of serfdom was still practiced. Timothy Blanning writes: "In some areas [of the Rhineland], where an attenuated version of serfdom still lingered, the peasant was also subject to restrictions on his movement."[26] According to Friedrich Lenger, "Besides the original obligations to provide services and dues to the lord the agricultural labor force was also burdened with personal servitude."[27] He continues: "In the small territory of Nassau-Usingen around 1800 there were no less than 230 different payments, dues, and services that the peasants living there had to provide to the lords. Dues included the 'blood tithe' to be paid after an animal was slaughtered, a 'bee tithe', a 'wax tithe' as well as large fees owed to the lord whenever a piece of property changed hands."[28] This plethora of taxes and the arbitrary power of local aristocracies to collect them must have created severe disincentives for investment.

As elsewhere in Europe, in Germany the legal system remained unmodernized and embodied many inequities and privileges for the aristocracy, military orders, and Church. Meanwhile, the Jews were subject to severe restrictions on choice of occupation, residence, and travel and had to pay special taxes.

Finally, urban oligarchies were perhaps even more pernicious to industrialization than the remnants of feudal institutions in the countryside and were still strong in Germany. Almost all major occupations were controlled by guilds, significantly limiting entry into those professions by others, but also indirectly restricting the adoption of new technologies. Herbert Kisch specifically argues that guilds impeded the introduction of new technology in the Rhineland, in particular in the major cities of Cologne and Aachen, where the adoption of new textile (spinning and weaving) machines were significantly delayed because of guild restrictions.[29] In addition, many cities were controlled by a few families for many generations, amassing wealth at the expense of potential new entrants with greater ability or better technologies.[30]

## THE IMPACT OF THE FRENCH REVOLUTION

Despite the fact that the French Revolution was immediately seen as threatening to Europe's elite, the War of the First Coalition did not break out until 1792. The French quickly seized the Austrian Netherlands (roughly today's Belgium) and the Netherlands. The French also gained effective control over much of modern-day Switzerland. In all three places, the French had strong control through the 1790s. Germany was initially hotly contested (with Prussia reclaiming control in 1793), but by 1795 the French had firm control over the Rhineland (the left bank of the Rhine).[31] In 1802 the Rhineland was officially incorporated into France. Following the Peace of Lunéville in 1801, the Austrians abdicated any responsibility for reorganizing the territories of the Holy Roman Empire to a deputation of imperial delegates who met with French representatives in 1802 and 1803. The result was massive reorganization: 112 independent states, 66 ecclesiastical territories, and 421 free imperial cities vanished and were made into a larger cluster of kingdoms, principalities, and duchies. The 1,500 fiefs of the imperial knights also vanished. The most noteworthy new polities were the Grand Duchy of Baden and the Kingdoms of Württemberg and Bavaria. In 1806, Napoleon brought these all together in the *Rheinbund* (Confederation of the Rhine). This move led to further reorganization and a further reduction to fewer than forty states, almost all of which joined the *Rheinbund* by 1808.[32]

During this period Napoleon also took over parts of Northern Germany. In 1803, Napoleon occupied Hanover, as a consequence of the war against Britain. The Grand Duchy of Berg was formed in March 1806, the Kingdom of Westphalia in August 1807 and the Grand Duchy of Frankfurt in February 1810. Formed out of states merged together by Napoleon, they were run by either Napoleon's relatives (Joachim Murat, Napoleon's brother-in-law, ruled over Berg, and Jérôme Bonaparte, Napoleon's youngest brother, over Westphalia) or by close allies (Karl Theodor von Dalberg, formerly archbishop of Mainz, was made grand-duke of Frankfurt).

Following the War of the Third Coalition, Napoleon imposed humiliating terms on the Austrians at the Treaty of Pressburg in December 1805. He took all Austrian lands in Italy, grabbed territory in the Balkans, and gave Tyrol to Bavaria and its upper Rhine territories to Baden and Württemberg. Prussia also expanded to compensate for the loss of territory in the Rhineland. After Prussia's defeat in Jena and the Treaty of Tilsit, however, Prussia lost all territory west of the Elbe, which became part of the Kingdom of Westphalia, and its Polish provinces became the Duchy of Warsaw. Prussia had to pay a huge indemnity to the French. Finally, in December 1810 Napoleon also annexed the Hanseatic cities of Hamburg, Lübeck, and Bremen, which became part of France.

The first important observation to be made here is that the French invaded places not so much for their economic potential or characteristics, but rather for their military or geopolitical significance. For example, Michael Rowe notes that the Kingdom of Westphalia, a satellite state created by Napoleon in Northern Germany, served as a French strategic strongpoint in Germany, and Brendan Simms makes the same argument.[33] In addition, while Napoleon was able to form alliances with the southern German states of Bavaria, Württemberg, and Baden, the northern states of Hanover (dynastically attached to Britain), Hesse-Kassel, and Brunswick remained implacably opposed to him. Thus the historical evidence does not support the idea that the parts of Germany that the French invaded were chosen on the basis of their potential for economic growth. This is the most important condition for our interpretation of Figure 7.1 to be valid.

After Napoleon's defeat and exile to St. Helena, the European powers met in Vienna to decide on the postwar settlement. Much of the outcome in Germany was determined by the status quo ante of the *Rheinbund*. Ultimately, a German Confederation of thirty-eight sovereign states emerged after 1815, and states such as Bavaria, Baden, and Württemberg, which had expanded enormously, kept their territorial gains. The territory of Prussia was one of the most hotly contested issues.[34] In February 1813 Prussia and Russia had signed the Treaty of

Kalisch under which Russia would take Poland and Prussia would get Saxony. Although Saxony's bargaining position at Vienna was much weakened by the fact that it had remained in alliance with Napoleon much longer than the other German states, Prussia's bargaining power was not strong either.[35] After the defeat of Jena, the Prussians had played a relatively minor role in the defeat of the French. Prussia's territorial demands were based on wanting to annex lands next to Prussia, hence the attraction of Saxony.

In the end, Prussia did not get what it wanted in Vienna. It was given 60% of Saxony but only 40% of its population. In addition, it received large parts of French-occupied Germany, including much of the Rhineland and of the former Kingdom of Westphalia. James Sheehan argues that the Rhenish and Westphalian lands were taken with some reluctance as compensation for Prussia's thwarted ambitions in Saxony.[36] Alan J. P. Taylor notes that the lands on the left bank of the Rhine "were not a tempting proposition: strategically exposed to French invasion . . . By a strange chance, these lands found themselves in Prussia, an outcome most undesired both by themselves and by Frederick William III . . . Prussia had imposed on her the task of defending the Rhine against the French and shouldered it most unwillingly; it was, as it were, a practical joke played by the Great Powers on the weakest of their numbers."[37] For the purpose of our second definition of the treatment group, used in Figure 7.2, the relevant factor is that there is no evidence that Prussia attempted or succeeded in obtaining parts of Germany that it saw as having greater potential for economic growth.

Finally, the Prussians, having themselves initiated extensive reforms after 1807, made few changes in the institutional regimes created by the French in Western Germany.[38] Herbert Fisher sums this up as follows:

> The agrarian reforms of the Revolution, the Consulate, and the Empire had scarcely had time to take full effect save in the Rhenish provinces . . . Indeed, save for one circumstance, in itself connected with

the career of Napoleon, there is no doubt that the French settlement would have been overthrown throughout Germany . . . That circumstance was the agrarian legislation of Stein and Hardenberg in Prussia . . . the reforms of these two statesmen were the first attack upon a system defended by one of the hardest and most stubborn aristocracies in Europe . . . but for the fact that Prussia had taken in hand the reform of her own land-system, there would have been little chance of any part of the French settlement surviving. As it was, Prussia obtained the Duchy of Posen, the Duchy of Berg, and part of the Rhenish provinces in 1815, and the Prussian administrators were strong enough to disregard the appeals of the nobility for the restoration of the feudal system. In these provinces . . . the hand of the clock was not set back.[39]

This evidence suggests that the economic characteristics of the territories did not determine which areas Prussia received at Vienna. In addition, Prussia did not selectively reverse the institutional changes brought by the French. Rather, because they had themselves engaged in broad reforms and also because they had to rule these new areas— and reversing French reforms would have implied strengthening the power of local elites—the Prussian rulers left these reforms unaltered.[40] Finally, could it be that the findings we discussed in Figures 7.1 and 7.2 represent a direct effect of being taken over by Prussia in 1815 on subsequent urbanization? The answer to this question is no, because large parts of Prussia are also in the group that was not invaded. Thus it is not Prussia that starts to do differentially well after 1815, but the parts reformed by the French. To sum up, the historical evidence does indeed suggest that the invasion and reform of institutions in Germany by the French can be regarded as a natural experiment with either of the two treatment groups we have examined.

## INSTITUTIONAL REFORMS IN GERMANY

Germany experienced two waves of institutional reforms: the first, under the Revolutionary armies, affected only the Rhineland; the second, under Napoleon, influenced much of Northern Germany through the satellite states he created.[41] As we noted earlier, these processes triggered reforms in many other parts of Germany, though some places, such as Saxony or Mecklenburg, remained almost uninfluenced. We now try to capture and measure the extent of social and economic reforms undertaken in the early nineteenth century, distinguishing between those territories that were ruled by France or by Napoleonic satellite states and then were taken over by Prussia; those that fell to minor reactionary rulers as a consequence of the Congress of Vienna; and those states that were not directly influenced by Napoleon, except through the implementation of defensive modernization.

The reform of the administrative and fiscal system, the enactment of written legal codes, the restructuring of agricultural relations, the abolition of guilds, the emancipation of Jews, and the secularization of Church lands are often cited among the beneficial reforms introduced either by the French rule in Germany or by modernizing sovereigns. Since the reorganization of administrative systems is a reform hard to define and quantify, and the secularization of Church lands could, for obvious historical reasons, take place only in Catholic territories, we focus on the other reforms. The results are summarized in Table 7.1 for twenty-nine territories of the German Confederation. Although we were only able to construct data on urbanization for a subset of eight German states/provinces (see Figures 7.1 and 7.2), we were able to measure reforms with much greater territorial detail. In many cases we had to single out parts of territories (e.g., in Prussia) according to their pre-1815 ruler, for the politics of reform were not always consistent within a territory and depended on previously implemented reforms.

The introduction of the French civil and commercial codes was one of the most long-lasting legacies of the French presence in Germany. The *Code Civil* was in force until 1900 in the territories left of the Rhine and was often cited as one of the reasons for the peculiar economic dynamism of the Rhineland.[42] Also, the introduction of the

*Table 7.1*  Extent of reforms in nineteenth-century Germany

| | Written civil code | Agrarian reforms by 1825 | Abolition of guilds | Emancipation of Jews |
|---|---|---|---|---|
| **Not invaded** | | | | |
| Anhalt | 0 | 0 | 0 | 1 |
| Baden | 1 | 1 | 0 | 1 |
| Bavaria | 0 | 0 | 0 | 0 |
| Bavaria, formerly Ansbach or Bayreuth | 1 | 0 | 0 | 0 |
| Hessen-Darmstadt | 0 | 1 | 1 | 0 |
| Holstein | 0 | 0 | 0 | 0 |
| Mecklenburg | 0 | 0 | 0 | 0 |
| Nassau | 0 | 0 | 1 | 0 |
| Prussia | 1 | 1 | 1 | 1 |
| Prussia, formerly Nassau | 0 | 1 | 1 | 0 |
| Prussia, formerly Saxony | 1 | 1 | 0 | 0 |
| Saxony | 0 | 0 | 0 | 0 |
| Schleswig | 0 | 0 | 0 | 0 |
| Thuringian states | 0 | 0 | 0 | 0 |
| Württemberg | 0 | 0 | 0 | 0 |
| Average (percent) | 29.5 | 30.2 | 15.1 | 20.9 |
| **Invaded, not to Prussia** | | | | |
| Bavaria, left of the Rhine (Bav. Palatinate) | 1 | 1 | 1 | 0 |
| Bremen | 0 | n/a | 0 | 0 |
| Brunswick | 0 | 0 | 0 | 1 |
| Frankfurt | 0 | 1 | 0 | 1 |
| Hamburg | 0 | n/a | 0 | 0 |
| Hanover | 0 | 0 | 0 | 0 |
| Hessen-Darmstadt, left of the Rhine (Rheinhessen) | 1 | 1 | 1 | 0 |
| Hessen-Kassel | 0 | 0 | 0 | 1 |
| Lübeck | 0 | n/a | 0 | 0 |
| Average (percent) | 25.6 | 30.6 | 25.6 | 33.3 |

*Table 7.1* (continued)

|  | Written civil code | Agrarian reforms by 1825 | Abolition of guilds | Emancipation of Jews |
|---|---|---|---|---|
| | **Invaded, then Prussian** | | | |
| Prussia, Erfurt | 1 | 1 | 1 | 0 |
| Prussia, formerly Berg | 1 | 1 | 1 | 0 |
| Prussia, formerly Westphalia | 1 | 1 | 1 | 0 |
| Prussia, formerly G. D. of Frankfurt | 1 | 1 | 1 | 0 |
| Prussia, left of the Rhine (Rhine Province) | 1 | 1 | 1 | 0 |
| Average (percent) | 100 | 100 | 100 | 0 |

civil and commercial codes is the reform that was most consistently pursued in all territories ruled either by France directly or in the Napoleonic satellite states. The codes were enacted in the Rhineland starting in 1802, in Westphalia starting in 1808, in the Grand Duchy of Berg starting in 1810, and starting in 1809/1810 for the territories of northern Germany corresponding to present-day Lower Saxony, as well as in the Hanseatic Cities of Bremen, Hamburg, and Lübeck.[43] At the same time, Baden, under the leadership of its liberal prime minister, Johann Niklas Friedrich Brauer, introduced the *Badisches Landrecht,* which was essentially the *Code Napoléon* with some minor additions; Bavaria, in contrast, merely revised some parts of its *Codex Maximilianeus Bavaricus Civilis* of 1756, which, however, remained a subsidiary legal source, second to customary law.[44]

After the demise of Napoleonic rule in Germany, the territories east of the Rhine were quick to reintroduce the previous legal systems and dismantle all remnants of the Napoleonic reforms. Two exceptions stand out, however. First, the lands that were taken over by Prussia obtained the *Allgemeines Landrecht* (ALR), the ambitious

Prussian civil code of 1794, a 19,000-paragraph-long codification of all legal matters. While retaining some vestiges of the feudal system such as the *Patrimonialgerichtsbarkeit*,[45] the ALR was a progressive work for its times, heavily influenced by the ideals of the Enlightenment. Similarly, the former territories of the Margraviates of Ansbach and Bayreuth, now part of Bavaria, maintained the ALR, a reminder of their former allegiance to the House of Hohenzollern.[46] The other exception is represented by the Rhineland, where both in its Prussian parts and in *Rheinhessen* (Hesse-Darmstadt) and in the Bavarian Palatinate the local bourgeoisie successfully defended the presence of the *Code Napoléon,* evidently favorable to their position.[47]

The first column in Table 7.1 reports which territories had a written legal code by 1820. The figures in this column also indicate the potential presence of both a written civil code and a system of commercial law, represented by either the French *Code de Commerce* or by book 8, chapters 7–15, in the Prussian ALR.[48] The map in Figure 7.4 shows graphically how the adoption of a written legal code differed temporally across German territories; most of the regions obtained a system of written civil law only in 1900 with the Germany-wide introduction of the *Bürgerliches Gesetzbuch* (the BGB).

The abolition of guilds is another reform intimately linked to the abolition of the remnants of the ancien régime. Although Prussia had already pushed for curtailing the powers of guilds through the *Reichszunftsordnung* of 1731,[49] strong winds of change breezed through Germany only after the invasion of the French Revolutionary armies. The development mirrors the case of the introduction of the civil code: guilds are first abolished in the territories on the left bank of the Rhine (1790–1791), then in the Napoleonic states of Westphalia (1808–1810) and Berg (1809), and finally in Northern Germany. Restoration of the status quo ante occurred just as quickly in the reactionary states of Hannover and Hesse-Kassel between 1814 and 1816. Even the Hanseatic cities reversed the reforms to which they had been subjected. Only Nassau set a countervailing trend, proclaiming freedom of commerce in 1819.[50]

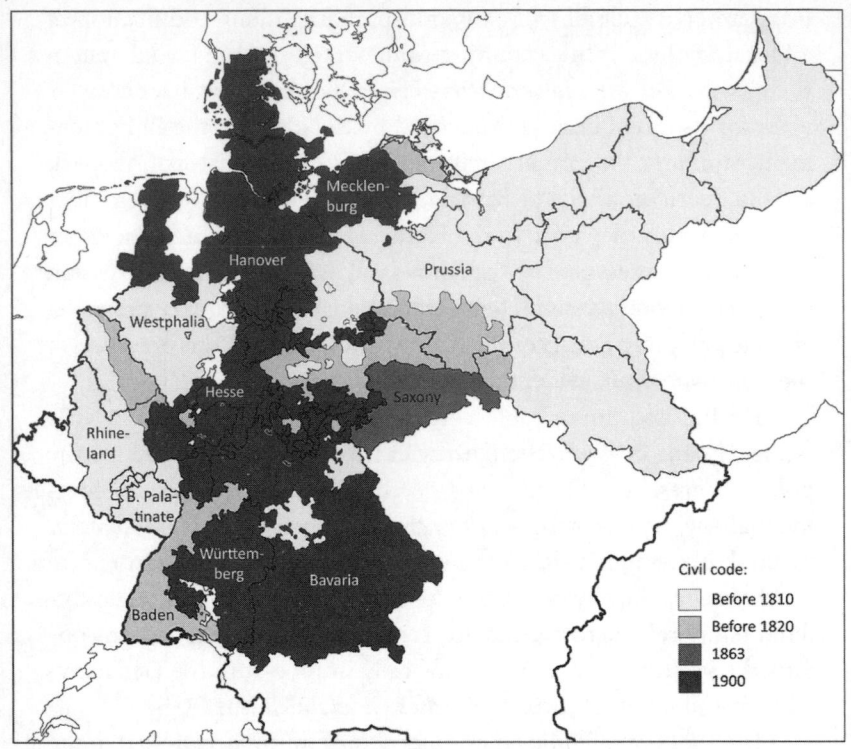

Figure 7.4    The introduction of written civil codes in Germany. (Cartographic representation based on IEG-MAPS: Server for digital historical maps, Mainz.)

The situation in the Prussian territories was varied: while the *Gewerbefreiheit* (freedom of commerce, including the abolition of guilds) was a pillar of the reforms of Stein and Hardenberg, at first it extended only to the core territories of Prussia at its minimal territorial extension after the Peace of Tilsit in 1807. Following the Congress of Vienna, the abolition of the guilds was further pursued in the Rhineland (both Prussian and non-Prussian) and in the former territories of Berg and Westphalia. However, the old structures were retained in the lands that Prussia obtained from

Saxony and Sweden, as well as in a small enclave in the district of Arnsberg.[51]

No other German state pursued the objective of freedom of commerce after 1815 as thoroughly as Prussia; Baden retained its guild structure, whereas Württemberg reorganized its guilds in larger units, allowing for a small degree of mobility within groups. Bavaria and Saxony instead moved to a concession-based system, where a state bureaucracy would determine the number of people and the prerequisites to become craftsmen.[52] A temporary backlash occurred during and after the 1848 Revolution, when there was pressure to restore guild structures in many states that had so far pursued liberal policies, and full liberalization all over Germany was eventually achieved with the new *Gewerbeordnung* (law regulating commerce) after unification in 1871. Hence the figures in column 2 of Table 7.1 reflect the status as it persisted from the 1820s until the foundation of the German Empire, disregarding the lapse around 1848. The map in Figure 7.5 shows the temporal evolution of the abolition of guilds; the laggards that followed only after the unification of Germany are displayed in the darkest shade.

Agrarian reforms are another dimension along which different approaches are discernible across German states, even when restricting one's view to the territories west of the Elbe, where feudal relations were less oppressive than in the eastern territories characterized by serfdom and the *Gutsherrschaft* form of land tenure. Again, we can see that first the French occupiers and then the Prussian "defensive modernizers" led the wave of reforms. The most radical attempt to reform succeeded only west of the Rhine, where serfdom was abolished without compensation and duties were made redeemable for fifteen times their annual value in 1798.

Reforms followed suit in Berg (1808) and Westphalia (1809), but confusion soon reigned concerning the exact terms of the redemption of feudal payments. Lawsuits clogged the tribunals, trying to extend the definition of serfdom—which was to be abolished without compensation—to other forms of land tenure. All reforms

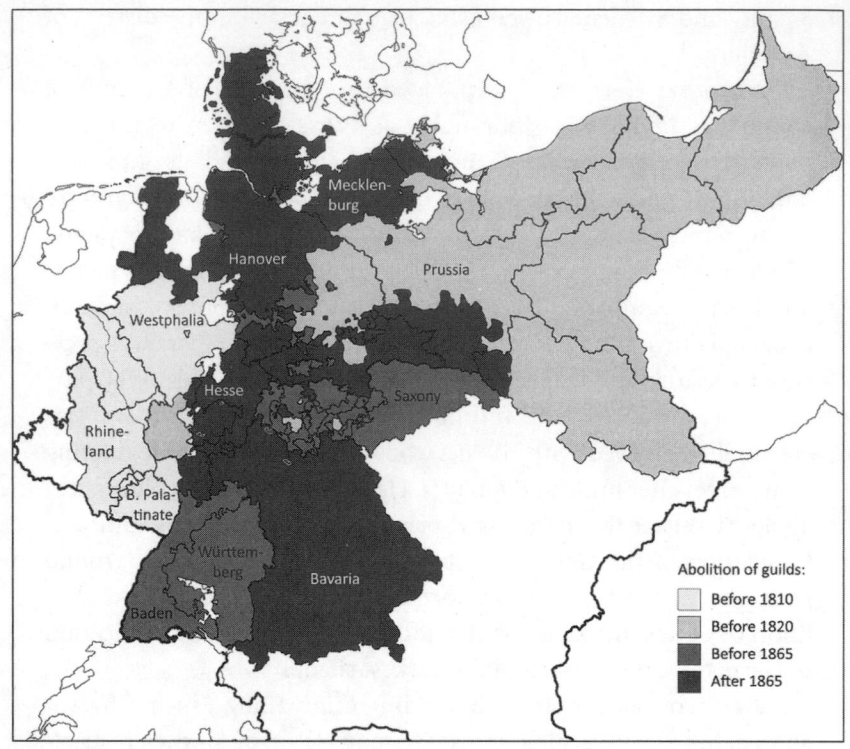

Figure 7.5   The abolition of guilds in Germany. (Cartographic representation based on IEG-MAPS: Server for digital historical maps, Mainz.)

were ultimately blocked by decree in 1812 and were not resumed until Prussian times. In fact, at the same time Prussia was already implementing agrarian reforms in parts of Prussia, starting with the edict of October 9, 1807, which in 1821 was perfected with laws regulating the exact terms of redemption of feudal duties (twenty-five times their annual value).

A law describing the exact amount needed to exit the feudal relation of the *Grundherrschaft,* bundled in some cases with the establishment of a credit institution providing peasants with the necessary amounts of money, was indeed a crucial precondition for agrarian reforms that did not remain a dead letter. Hence what the figures in column 3 of Table 7.1 report is the presence or absence of such laws, as well as the abolition of serfdom (a mere formality in most territories west of the Elbe). The values reflect the status quo as of the 1820s; in the 1840s, most other territories followed with the implementation of agrarian reforms, so that our variable is supposed to capture early modernization.[53] A more detailed description of the dates of implementation of agrarian reforms is given by the map in Figure 7.6.

The emancipation of the Jews is the one reform that was pursued less consistently across Germany. The initial steps taken in the Napoleonic states—the most liberal policy was enacted in Westphalia— were rapidly circumscribed with the *décret infâme* of 1808, which limited the occupational choice of Jews in the Rhineland through a concession-based system.[54] In a similar fashion, Prussia granted wide-ranging freedoms at first through the law of March 1812 but retreated soon afterward, when it failed to extend the freedoms to the newly acquired territories.[55] While full emancipation of the Jews, including political rights, had to wait until unification in 1871, some states granted wide-ranging freedoms to their Jewish subjects, in particular with respect to occupational choices. Baden, Brunswick, Anhalt, and the free city of Frankfurt, where the Rothschild dynasty originated, were examples in point. The figures in column 4 of Table 7.1 capture, as for the case of agrarian reforms, the state of affairs in the 1820s, indicating which states pursued a policy of modernization early on.[56]

On balance, Table 7.1 shows a clear distinction between parts of western Germany that were reformed by the French and then given to Prussia in 1815 and places that were either never invaded by the French or where the old rulers returned after French domination and reversed the reforms.[57]

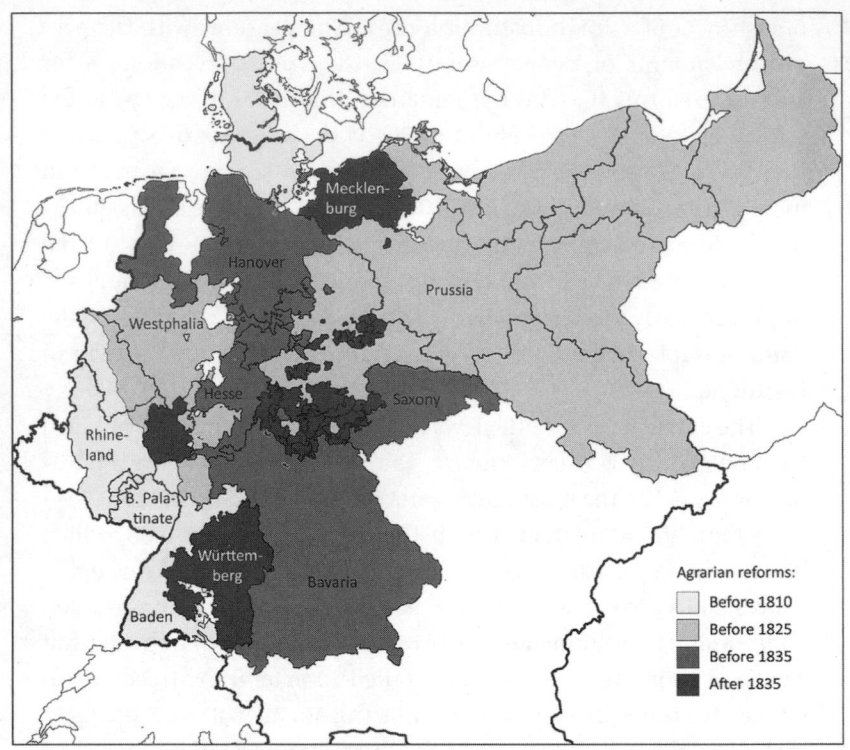

Figure 7.6   The implementation of agrarian reforms in Germany. (Cartographic representation based on IEG-MAPS: Server for digital historical maps, Mainz.)

## THE ECONOMIC IMPACT OF INSTITUTIONAL REFORMS

Modern historians have still not reached consensus on the economic legacy of French and Napoleonic reforms in Europe. A common view regarding this legacy is that of Alexander Grab, who concluded that, on a European level, the main significance of the Napoleonic rule lay in marking the transition from the ancien régime to the modern era.[58] Yet Grab himself notes that Napoleon was Janus faced—undermining his reforms by his complicity in the rule of the local oligarchs. Grab writes: "Paradoxically, Napoleon himself sometimes undermined his own reform policies. In a number of states he compromised with conservative elites, allowing them to preserve their privileges as long as they recognized his supreme position."[59]

Historians also disagree about the economic consequences of this behavior. Within France itself, seminal interpretations of the Revolution by Marxist scholars such as Georges Lefebvre and Alfred Soboul saw the Revolution as marking the transition from feudalism and capitalism and thus, at least implicitly, ushering in more rapid economic growth. The rejection of this interpretation by Cobban, George Taylor, and François Furet was interpreted by many as a denial that the Revolution had the economic implications that Marxists associated with it.[60] Yet we believe this interpretation is mistaken. First, the fact that the Revolution was not a bourgeois revolution in the traditional Marxist sense does not imply that the institutional changes induced by the Revolution did not improve economic performance. Second, France, with lower agricultural productivity and real wages, was poor in the eighteenth century compared to the Netherlands and Britain. Economic historians attribute at least part of these differences to the institutions of ancien régime France. Jean-Laurent Rosenthal has shown in the specific context of irrigation and drainage that institutional changes brought by the Revolution led to increased productivity.[61] Rondo Cameron also claims that the Revolution and the institutional changes it brought had positive economic effects.[62]

Seen in a European-wide context, economic historians have typically emphasized the negative effects of the Revolution. David Landes, for instance, views the French Revolution as a political roadblock to technological adoption for Continental countries, and concludes that as a consequence of the Revolution the gap in technique between the Continent and Britain widened, while most of the fundamental educational, economic, and social obstacles to imitation remained.[63]

The economic consequences of the French reforms in Germany are also a matter of dispute, despite Nipperdey's statement at the start of his seminal book and of this essay. Most scholars have focused on political rather than economic implications, and those researchers who have focused on the economic have often argued that the reforms had adverse effects. Timothy Blanning has prominently argued that reform was already happening and that Napoleon's effects were negligible or even negative, but Hamerow argues the opposite.[64] A literature does identify positive economic effects of reforms, but this is usually restricted to the Rhineland. For example, Herbert Kisch describes these as follows: "When the many strands of commercial legislation were subsequently consolidated in the Code Napoleon, the Rhineland (on the left bank) was not only given a most up-to-date legal framework, but also a system of government in close harmony with the needs of a buoyantly industrializing society."[65] Kisch and others argue that these changes transformed the Rhineland from an oligarchy-dominated area to one open to new business and new entrants.[66] Yet Timothy Blanning disagrees that French reforms had a positive net effect on the economy of even the Rhineland.[67]

The fact that historians have taken such contrasting positions makes a systematic statistical study of the French reforms on German economic growth an important innovation.[68] As noted earlier, for this purpose, we use data on urbanization for German states for the period between 1750 and 1910. Figures 7.1 and 7.2 present the main findings; they show that the urbanization rate with either definition of the treatment group accelerates more rapidly than in the control group and even overtakes the areas not invaded by 1850. We showed that institutional reforms were more intense in the treatment group, and this evidence supports the claim that these reforms caused more rapid urbanization and likely economic growth.[69]

In making these comparisons, we do not imply that urbanization rates were determined solely by institutional factors. In fact, considerable variation in urbanization can be found between treatment and control groups. Note, for example, that with the second definition of the treatment group, the control group includes the North Sea and Baltic ports and commercial centers, which one might expect to already have large populations prior to the period of the French Revolution and in many ways were already outside of the institutions of feudalism and the ancien régime. Notice, too, that all three series are trending up over time since this is a period of general economic and urban growth in Europe. The important result for our purposes is the relative rate of growth of these areas and the impact of institutional reforms on this rate of growth.

## CONCLUSIONS

In this essay we have used the invasion of Germany by French armies following the French Revolution to test whether or not key institutions associated with the ancien régime impeded prosperity. In the places they invaded, the French implemented ambitious programs of institutional reforms, abolishing many of the pillars of the ancien régime and the legacy of feudal economic institutions. We demonstrated that the places where these reforms were implemented seem to have had better economic performance subsequently, in terms of urbanization, than places the French did not reform. One should of course be cautious in interpreting these results. For example, though western Germany was less urbanized than eastern Germany during this period, it could be that by accident (or possibly design—though this does not seem to be supported by historical evidence), the French-invaded areas were for other reasons destined to do better economically.

Importantly, we argued that there was something special about this historical episode; it can be thought of as a natural experiment that gives us the possibility of saying something much more precise about causal factors than is typically the case in historical or social studies. Our essay shows what is involved in applying these ideas in a specific context and specifies what concerns must be addressed in order for real social phenomena to count as a natural experiment. History is full of such potential experiments; it is just that historians have not yet thought of them in these terms. We believe that exploiting these experiments in a systematic way will greatly improve our understanding of the important forces that have driven long-run processes of historical, social, political, and economic change.

We are not the first to argue that the French reforms had positive economic effects. Yet Engels's view, which we cited at the start of our essay, hardly ensures consensus in the academic literature. Our findings are consistent with Engels's interpretation, though not definitive, and suggest that more structured quantitative investigation of the institutional and economic legacies of the French Revolution is an important area for more research.

## NOTES

*Epigraphs:* Thomas Nipperdey, *Deutsche Geschichte 1800–1866: Bürgerwelt und starker Staat* (Munich, 1983), p. 1. English translation: *Germany from Napoleon to Bismarck, 1800–1866* (Dublin, 1996). Friedrich Engels quoted by Louis Bergeron, "Remarques sur les conditions du développement industriel en Europe Occidentale à l'époque napoléonienne," *Francia* 1 (1973): 537.

1. The seminal books on these topics are Douglass C. North and Robert P. Thomas, *The Rise of the Western World: A New Economic History* (New York, 1973); Eric L. Jones, *The European Miracle: Environments, Economies, and Geopolitics in the History of Europe and Asia* (New York, 1981); Kenneth Pomeranz, *The Great Divergence: China, Europe and the Making of the Modern World* (Princeton, NJ, 2000).

2. To use the phrase coined by Alfred Crosby; see Crosby, *Ecological Imperialism: The Biological Expansion of Europe, 900–1900* (New York, 1986).

3. Many different sorts of institutions made up the ancien régime. Different scholars emphasize different things. Some argue that controlling absolutism was the key. More related to our essay, however, were those institutions overthrown by the French National Assembly on the night of August 4, 1789. As we discuss later, these included aristocratic privileges and guilds.

4. Adam Smith, *An Inquiry into the Nature and Causes of the Wealth of Nations,* ed. R. H. Campbell and A. S. Skinner (New York, 1976), p. 387.

5. Jerome Blum, *The End of the Old Order in Rural Europe* (Princeton, NJ, 1978), p. 356.

6. Jan de Vries and Ad van der Woude, *The First Modern Economy: Success, Failure, and Perseverance of the Dutch Economy, 1500–1815* (New York, 1997), pp. 17, 162–163; Jonathan I. Israel, *The Dutch Republic: Its Rise, Greatness and Fall, 1477–1806* (New York, 1995).

7. On the demise of feudalism see Rodney Hilton, *The Decline of Serfdom in Medieval England*, 2nd ed. (London, 1983); on weak guilds see D. C. Coleman, *The Economy of England, 1450–1750* (Oxford, 1977), pp. 73–75; on contracting absolutism see Steven C. A. Pincus, *England's Glorious Revolution: A Brief History with Documents* (New York, 2007); and on the rule of law see Edward P. Thompson, *Whigs and Hunters: The Origin of the Black Act* (London, 1975).

8. Henri Pirenne, *Economic and Social History of Medieval Europe* (New York, 1937); Michael M. Postan, "The Rise of the Money Economy," *Economic History Review* 14 (1944): 123–134.

9. Douglass C. North and Barry R. Weingast, "Constitutions and Commitment: Evolution of Institutions Governing Public Choice in Seventeenth Century England," *Journal of Economic History* 49 (1989): 803–832.

10. Max Weber, *The Protestant Ethic and the Spirit of Capitalism* (New York, 1930), p. 11.

11. As long as this is true, then we can think of the treatment being "as if" it were randomly assigned.

12. Nearly all of Germany, including Prussia, was invaded at some point or another by the French. Nevertheless, we are interested only in those places where the French attempted to rule and reform, rather than simply transitorily occupy.

13. In a companion paper, Daron Acemoglu, Davide Cantoni, Simon Johnson, and James A. Robinson, "The Consequences of Radical Reform: The French Revolution" (National Bureau of Economic Research Working Paper no. 14831 [Cambridge, MA, 2009]), we use statistical tools to examine cross-national evidence on the relationship between institutional reforms brought by the French Revolution and subsequent economic growth, and we find results that are very comparable to those we present here.

14. Daron Acemoglu, Simon Johnson, and James A. Robinson, "Reversal of Fortune: Geography and Institutions in the Making of the Modern World Income Distribution," *Quarterly Journal of Economics* 118 (2002): 1231–1294; Paul Bairoch, *Cities and Economic Development: From the Dawn of History to the Present* (Chicago, 1988), chapter 1; Jan de Vries, *The Economy of Europe in an Age of Crisis, 1600–1750* (New York, 1976), p. 164.

15. For example, Angus Maddison, *The World Economy: A Millennial Perspective* (Paris, 2001).

16. The years included in our analysis are 1750, 1800, 1850, and all years between 1875 and 1910 in five-year intervals. The states are defined following post-1815 borders and comprise: Prussia, where we distinguish between the Rhine province (which includes the left bank of the Rhine and Berg), Westphalia, and the rest of Prussia (excluding the provinces of East and West Prussia, which lay outside of the Holy Roman Empire before, the German Confederation after), Hanover, Saxony, Baden, Bavaria, and Württemberg. For the construction of these data see the appendixes in Acemoglu et al., "The Consequences of Radical Reform."

17. Econometrically speaking, what we are examining here is a reduced form relationship between a treatment variable, invaded by the French, and a proxy for economic development, urbanization. In Acemoglu et al., "The Consequences of Radical Reform," we examine the relationship between this instrument and various indices of reforms, and then we examine the relationship between the reforms and measures of economic development.

18. One should bear in mind here that many places in the control group, such as Baden, Bavaria, and most famously Prussia under Stein and Hardenberg, reformed defensively. This fact works against finding that the areas actually invaded experienced differentially rapid urbanization in the nineteenth century.

19. William Doyle, *The Ancien Régime*, 2nd ed. (New York, 2001); Emmanuel Le Roy Ladurie, *The Ancien Régime: A History of France, 1610–1774* (Oxford, 1996).

20. Alfred Cobban, *The Social Interpretation of the French Revolution* (New York, 1964); on the importance of feudal dues see Peter Jones, *The Peasantry in the French Revolution* (New York, 1988); Gwynne Lewis, *The Advent of Modern Capitalism in France: The Case of Pierre-François Tubeuf* (New York, 1993); and Alan Forrest, *The Revolution in Provincial Aquitaine, 1789–1799* (Oxford, 1996). On the role of feudal dues in the Revolution see John Markoff, *The Abolition of Feudalism: Peasants, Lords, and Legislators in the French Revolution* (University Park, PA, 1996).

21. Daron Acemoglu, Simon Johnson, and James A. Robinson, "Institutions as the Fundamental Cause of Long-Run Economic Growth," in Philippe Aghion and Steve Durlauf, eds., *Handbook of Economic Growth* (Amsterdam, 2005), pp. 385–472. On the importance of upward social mobility in

the industrial revolutions of Britain and the United States, see François Crouzet, *The First Industrialists: The Problem of Origins* (New York, 1985) and Kenneth L. Sokoloff and B. Zorina Khan, "The Democratization of Invention during Early Industrialization: Evidence from the United States," *Journal of Economic History* 20 (1990): 363–378.

22. Sheilagh Ogilvie, "Guilds, Efficiency, and Social Capital: Evidence from German Proto-industry," *Economic History Review* 57 (2004): 286–333. For a revisionist perspective, see Steven Epstein, *Wage Labor & Guilds in Medieval Europe* (Chapel Hill, NC, 1991); Charles R. Hickson and Earl A. Thompson, "A New Theory of Guilds and European Economic Development," *Explorations in Economic History* 28 (1991): 127–168.

23. Joel Mokyr, *The Lever of Riches: Technological Creativity and Economic Progress* (New York, 1990), pp. 256–260.

24. Herbert A. L. Fisher, *Studies in Napoleonic Statesmanship: Germany* (Oxford, 1903), p. 19.

25. Jerome Blum, "The Rise of Serfdom in Eastern Europe," *American Historical Review* 62 (1957): 807–836.

26. Timothy C. W. Blanning, *The French Revolution in Germany: Occupation and Resistance in the Rhineland, 1792–1802* (New York, 1983), pp. 20–21.

27. Friedrich Lenger, "Economy and Society," in Jonathan Sperber, ed., *The Shorter Oxford History of Germany: Germany, 1800–1870* (New York, 2004), p. 92. See also the discussion in Theodore S. Hamerow, *Restoration, Revolution, Reaction: Economics and Politics in Germany, 1815–1871* (Princeton, NJ, 1958), chapter 3.

28. Ibid., p. 96.

29. Herbert Kisch, *From Domestic Manufacture to Industrial Revolution: The Case of the Rhineland Textile Districts* (New York, 1989).

30. The aggregate evidence for Germany during this period suggests that agricultural productivity lagged far behind that of the Netherlands or Britain. See Robert C. Allen, "Economic Structure and Agricultural Productivity in Europe," *European Review of Economic History* 4 (2000): 1–25. Evidence on height and life expectancy suggests that Germany was substantially poorer than these countries; see Richard H. Steckel, "Health and Nutrition in the Pre-industrial Era: Insights from a Millennium of Average Heights in Northern Europe," in Robert C. Allen, Tommy Bengtsson, and Martin Dribe, eds., *Living Standards in the Past* (Oxford, 2005), pp. 227–254.

31. Part of the broader 1795 Peace of Basle with Prussia, Spain, and Hessen-Kassel.
32. Alexander Grab, *Napoleon and the Transformation of Europe* (New York, 2003), pp. 89–90.
33. Michael Rowe, "Napoleon and State Formation in Central Europe," in Philip Dwyer, ed., *Napoleon and Europe* (London, 2001), p. 210; Brendan Simms, "Political and Diplomatic Movements, 1800–1830: Napoleon, National Uprising, Restoration," in Sperber, ed., *The Shorter Oxford History of Germany,* p. 31.
34. Enno E. Kraehe, *Metternich's German Policy* (Princeton, NJ, 1963).
35. James J. Sheehan, *German History, 1770–1866* (Oxford, 1989), p. 397.
36. Ibid., p. 402.
37. Alan J. P. Taylor, *The Course of German History: A Survey of the Development of German History since 1815* (London, 1961), pp. 42–43.
38. After the defeat at Jena in 1806, Prussia—under the leadership first of Baron von und zum Stein, and then of the Prince of Hardenberg—introduced a series of social and military reforms. Important ones ended many feudal institutions in the countryside and also abolished guilds and introduced commercial freedom. Other states outside of direct French control, such as Baden and Württemberg in Southern Germany, also reformed defensively.
39. Fisher, *Napoleonic Statesmanship,* pp. 380–381.
40. The exception to this is that the Napoleonic Civil Code was kept in place in the Rhenish provinces but replaced with the Prussian legal code in the rest of French Germany ceded to Prussia.
41. While the English-language literature on reforms in Germany is very limited, the following works provide some useful details: Owen O'Connolly, *Napoleon's Satellite Kingdoms* (New York, 1965); J. Stuart Woolf, *Napoleon's Integration of Europe* (New York, 1991); and Grab, *Napoleon.*
42. Franz Schnabel, *Deutsche Geschichte im neunzehnten Jahrhundert* (Freiburg im Breisgau, 1965), vol. 6, p. 51.
43. Werner Schubert, *Französisches Recht in Deutschland zu Beginn des 19. Jahrhunderts* (Cologne, 1977); "Das französische Recht in Deutschland zu Beginn der Restaurationszeit (1814–1820)," *Zeitschrift der Savigny-Stiftung für Rechtsgeschichte, Germanistische Abteilung* 107 (1977): 129–184.
44. Richard Schröder, *Lehrbuch der deutschen Rechtsgeschichte,* 5th ed. (Leipzig, 1907), p. 901.
45. The jurisdiction of feudal lords over their serfs.
46. Schröder, *Rechtsgeschichte,* p. 937.

47. Schubert, *Französisches Recht zu Beginn des 19. Jahrhunderts*, pp. 97–98.

48. See Helmut Coing, *Handbuch der Quellen und Literatur der neueren europäischen Privatrechtsgeschichte,* vol. 3 (Munich, 1973), pt. 3, for a summary.

49. Dirk Georges, *1810/11–1993: Handwerk und Interessenpolitik* (Frankfurt am Main, 1993), p. 345.

50. For a comprehensive description of the movement toward *Gewerbefreiheit,* see H. A. Mascher, *Das deutsche Gewerbewesen von der frühesten Zeit bis auf die Gegenwart* (Potsdam, 1866); Gustav Schmoller, *Zur Geschichte der deutschen Kleingewerbe* (Halle, 1870); Karl Friedrich Wernet, *Forschungsberichte aus dem Handwerk,* vol. 10: *Handwerksgeschichtliche Perspektiven* (Münster, 1963).

51. See Mascher, *Gewerbewesen,* p. 497, for a detailed description.

52. Ibid.

53. Friedrich Lütge, *Die mitteldeutsche Grundherrschaft und ihre Auflösung,* 2nd ed. (Stuttgart, 1957); *Geschichte der deutschen Agrarverfassung vom frühen Mittelalter bis zum 19. Jahrhundert* (Stuttgart, 1963); Christoph Dipper, *Die Bauernbefreiung in Deutschland* (Stuttgart, 1980).

54. Michael A. Meye, ed., *Deutsch-jüdische Geschichte in der Neuzeit,* vol. 2 (Munich, 1996), p. 28.

55. Jacob Toury, *Soziale und politische Geschichte der Juden in Deutschland, 1847–1871: Zwischen Revolution, Reaktion und Emanzipation* (Düsseldorf, 1977), p. 281.

56. Ludwig von Rönne and Heinrich Simon, *Die früheren und gegenwärtigen Verhältnisse der Juden in den saemmtlichen Landestheilen des Preußischen Staates* (Breslau, 1843); Toury, *Geschichte der Juden;* Meyer, *Deutschjüdische Geschichte.*

57. The average values displayed at the end of each panel (Invaded, then Prussian / Invaded, not to Prussia / Not invaded) are weighted averages of the reforms indicators, where the numbers of cities listed in Paul Bairoch, Jean Batou, and Pierre Chèvre, *La population des villes européennes* (Geneva, 1988), present in each territorial unit act as weights.

58. Grab, *Napoleon,* p. 20.

59. Ibid., p. 23.

60. Georges Lefebvre, *The Coming of the French Revolution* (New York, 1847); Albert Soboul, *Understanding the French Revolution* (London, 1988); Cobban, *The Social Interpretation of the French Revolution;* George V. Taylor, "Noncapitalist Wealth and the Origins of the French Revolution," *American*

*Historical Review* 72 (1967): 469–496; François Furet, *Interpreting the French Revolution* (New York, 1981).

61. Comparative evidence on agricultural productivity is presented in Allen, *Economic Structure,* and on real wages in Robert C. Allen, "The Great Divergence in European Wages and Prices from the Middle Ages to the First World War," *Explorations in Economic History* 38 (2001): 411–447. Jean-Laurent Rosenthal, *The Fruits of Revolution: Property, Litigation and French Agriculture, 1700–1860* (New York, 1992); Philip Hoffman, "France: Early Modern Period," in Joel Mokyr, ed., *The Oxford Encyclopedia of Economic History* (New York, 2003), argues that the current consensus among economic historians is that the institutions of ancien régime France were indeed to some extent responsible for its relative underdevelopment.

62. Rondo E. Cameron, *France and the Economic Development of Europe, 1800–1914: Conquests of Peace and Seeds of War* (Princeton, NJ, 1961).

63. David S. Landes, *The Unbound Prometheus* (New York, 1969), pp. 142–147.

64. Timothy C. W. Blanning, "The French Revolution and Modernization in Germany," *Central European History* 22 (1989): 109–129; Hamerow, *Restoration, Revolution, Reaction,* pp. 22, 44–45.

65. Kisch, *Domestic Manufacture,* p. 212.

66. Jeffry Diefendorf, *Businessmen and Politics in the Rhineland, 1789–1834* (Princeton, NJ, 1980), p. 115.

67. Blanning, *The French Revolution in Germany.*

68. The analysis we present here is a simple exposition of the basic finding of Acemoglu et al., "The Consequences of Radical Reform," where a full statistical analysis is presented of the impact of French reforms on urbanization in Germany.

69. Although Figures 7.1 and 7.2 suggest that urbanization may have been growing more rapidly in either treatment group before 1800, which suggests that these areas had started to do differentially well even before the French invasion, in Acemoglu et al., "The Consequences of Radical Reform," we show that this difference is not statistically significant and in neither cross-national nor within-Germany data is there evidence of differential economic progress prior to the French Revolutionary period.

# Afterword: Using Comparative Methods in Studies of Human History

JARED DIAMOND AND
JAMES A. ROBINSON

All natural experiments challenge scholars with certain recurrent types of methodological problems.[1] Similar challenges also present themselves, to varying degrees, in manipulative laboratory experiments and in the physical and biological sciences. For instance, no two human systems differ solely with respect to the single variable whose effects interest the scholar. Instead, there are inevitably other differences, which may also contribute to or dominate the outcome that one is measuring. No magic bullet or formula has been discovered for solving these and other challenges raised by natural experiments, just as no formula has been devised for solving the challenges involved in writing narrative history or in doing manipulative experiments. However, we can offer some suggestions. At minimum, it will help to be alert to these problems, and to learn from other scholars who have wrestled with them, as illustrated by the authors of the chapters of this book.

Let us start with a classification of natural experiments. One can think of them as involving differences either in perturbations or in initial conditions. Of course, this distinction is oversimplified, for reasons that we shall discuss below. The table on pages 258–259 lists the main differences of each type operating in the eight studies of this book.

In one type of natural experiment, different outcomes result especially from variation in the perturbation; the differences in the

The eight case studies of this book

| (1) Chapter | (2) Subject | (3) Number of cases compared | (4) Initial conditions | (5) Perturbation | (6) Outcome examined |
|---|---|---|---|---|---|
| 1 | Polynesian cultural evolution | 3 | *Islands with different physical environments* | Polynesian settlement (+ different durations of settlement) | Sociopolitical and economic complexity |
| 2 | Frontier societies | 7 | Different temperate non-European lands | Explosive frontier settlement (from different sources at different times) | Cycles of boom, bust, and export rescue |
| 3 | New World banking systems | 3 | *Different political institutions, wealth, and income distributions* | Need for banks | Form of banking system |
| 4a | Hispaniola | 2 | Two halves of the same island (different rainfalls, slopes, and soils) | *French vs. Spanish colonization* (+ different dictators) | Wealth, export economy, forest cover, and erosion |
| 4b | Pacific islands | 81 | *Islands with different physical environments* | Human settlement (+ different colonizing peoples and durations of settlement) | Deforestation |

| | | | | | Current income |
|---|---|---|---|---|---|
| 5 | Africa's slave trades | 52 | Different parts of Africa (+ different physical environments, resources, religions, precolonial development, colonizing powers, and legal systems) | *Slave trade present or absent (+ 4 different slave trades)* | |
| 6 | Public goods in India | 233 | Different parts of India (+ different pre-colonial agricultural productivity, religion, and population composition) | *3 different colonial land tenure systems* | Schools, electricity, and roads (+ literacy, electoral competition, and outcome) |
| 7 | Effects of the French Revolution | 29 | Different parts of Germany (+ different religions, prior rates of urbanization) | *3 different courses of Napoleonic invasion* | Urbanization, as a measure of economic growth |

*Note:* This table characterizes the eight case studies presented in this book. Column 3 gives the number of cases compared in each study (e.g., number of islands, countries, or districts compared). Column 6 identifies the outcome to be explained in each study. Italicized items in columns 4 and 5 identify either the different initial conditions (e.g., different island physical environments, different political institutions: Chapters 1, 3, 4b) or different perturbations or presence or absence of a perturbation (e.g., slave trade or Napoleonic conquest present or absent: Chapters 4a, 5, 6, 7) mainly responsible for those different outcomes. Items in parentheses in columns 4 and 5 are potential explanatory factors that proved not important or less important for those outcomes. See text for discussion.

initial conditions (i.e., in the place or society to which the perturbation is applied) are of less significance to the outcome. Perturbations (referred to as "treatments" in much of the literature about experiments) can in turn be either "exogenous" or "endogenous," and the experiment can consist either of comparing a perturbation with no perturbation or of comparing different types of perturbations. The comparison of a perturbation with a nonperturbation is exemplified by areas of Africa subjected to slave trading or not (Chapter 5), and areas of Germany invaded by French Napoleonic armies or not (Chapter 7). Different types of perturbation are the two halves of Hispaniola colonized by Spain or France (Chapter 4), three different systems of land tenure and revenue imposed on different parts of India by Britain (Chapter 6), institutions imposed by French conquerors on Germany being subsequently left intact or else reversed (Chapter 7), and settlement of non-European frontiers originating from four different European countries (especially salient being whether English or not) and at different times during the Industrial Revolution (Chapter 2). All of these perturbations can be considered exogenous—that is, arising from outside the studied area.

In the other type of natural experiment, the perturbation is similar across all cases, and the different outcomes instead result mainly from differences in the initial conditions. We have two examples from Pacific islands differing greatly in physical environment (especially in area, elevation, isolation, geology, and climate), all settled by a single colonizing people (Polynesians: Chapter 1) or else by Polynesians and related groups of Pacific island peoples (termed Melanesians and Micronesians: Chapter 4), with the outcome examined being either socioeconomic and political complexity (Chapter 1) or deforestation (Chapter 4). Our third example is of three New World countries differing greatly in their political institutions, as well as in their wealth and their income equality (Chapter 3). In that study, the "perturbation" can be thought of as an endogenous one: the common need for a banking system arising within countries originally lacking chartered banks, as opposed to the exogenous perturbations such as invasions and imposed revenue systems examined in our other studies.

Most of our case studies focus on explaining *differences* in outcomes related to different perturbations or to different initial conditions. Of equal interest, however, are cases in which similar outcomes emerged despite big differences in the perturbations or initial conditions. The most striking conclusion of Chapter 2, which compares the development of frontier settler societies in seven former European colonies, is the similarity in outcomes. Despite differences in the "perturbations," especially in the European sources of immigrants and institutions, and in the stage of the Industrial Revolution at which these frontiers exploded, one is struck by similarities between these frontier societies—especially in their three-stage cycles of booms, busts, and export rescues, but also in many other respects including their growth of cities, transport infrastructure, wood consumption, farms and farm animals, their shared problems of infusing capital and immigrants and imports, their conquest of distance as a prerequisite to their export booms, their impacts on indigenous peoples, and their changing attitudes toward immigrants. These shared features evidently arose from the similar internal dynamics of growth in all of those frontier societies, overriding their differences in European sources of immigrants and institutions and in their decades of explosion. At the same time, the similarities in outcome were accompanied by differences in outcomes—for example, in the percentage of the immigrants who returned to their European mother countries, and in the frequency and duration of boom/bust/rescue cycles.

Our distinction between initial conditions and perturbations is not entirely sharp. Although there is no doubt that different sizes of Pacific islands constituted differing initial conditions to Polynesian settlers, and that invading Napoleonic armies (or their absence) constituted a perturbation to German principalities, how should one characterize the different political institutions and wealth of nineteenth-century Brazil, Mexico, and the United States for purposes of understanding their banking systems? Those differences constituted initial conditions insofar as they already existed before any of those countries had chartered banks, but institutions and wealth changed during the nineteenth century, and the banking systems may have been contributing causes as well as outcomes of the differences in wealth.

We have chosen, for illustrative reasons, to focus on case studies in which different outcomes can be attributed mainly either to differences in perturbations or to differences in initial conditions. However, one can also compare cases differing simultaneously in perturbations and in initial conditions, and the importance and interest of those cases may make the comparison profitable despite the added complication of having to consider both types of differences.

A question inevitably arising in any comparative study that compares perturbed societies or sites with nonperturbed ones concerns the perturbers' "selection" of which particular sites to perturb. In a laboratory experiment comparing so-called experimental and control test tubes that are identical except for some perturbation effected by the experimenter (e.g., adding one chemical to some but not other test tubes), the selection of experimental and control tubes can indeed be made completely random with respect to the experimenter's decisions. For example, the experimental-versus-control status of each test tube can be determined by flipping a coin or by using a random-number generator. However, important historical decisions are rarely made by flipping coins: Napoleon did have his reasons for invading certain German principalities but not others (Chapter 7), just as slave traders had their own reasons for buying slaves from certain parts of Africa but not others (Chapter 5). Thus, the practical question that the comparative historian must always ask is: were the perturbed sites selected for reasons irrelevant to the outcome studied (i.e., "random" with the respect to that outcome)? Or were the perturbed sites selected on the basis of differences in initial conditions material to the outcome?

All of our case studies comparing perturbed to nonperturbed sites, or comparing sites exposed to different types of perturbations, explicitly address this question and amass evidence showing that the grounds on which human historical actors selected particular sites for particular perturbations (or for lack of perturbations) do not explain the particular types of outcome studied. For instance, the analysis of Chapter 7 shows that areas of Germany invaded by French Revolutionary armies between 1792 and 1815 became more urbanized after 1860, but that is not because Napoleon preferred to invade already urbanized areas or because he presciently invaded areas likely to become more urbanized fifty years later. Instead, he chose his targets for contemporary military or dynastic or geopolitical reasons. His targets were actually on the average less urbanized at the time of his invasions than were the German areas that he spared. Similarly, British colonial administrators variously imposed three different land revenue systems in a geographic patchwork across India, and the analysis of Chapter 6 shows that one of those three types of patches (the patches with so-called landlord tenure systems) ended up more developed today by various indices. However, the type of revenue system imposed on each patch depended on either the colonial ideology that happened to be prevailing in Britain at the time that Britain annexed that particular patch, or else on the preference of the particular colonial administrator in power at that time, rather than on the contemporary development or other features of that patch relevant to development. This concern about patch selection should never be lightly dismissed. Instead, it must always be carefully evaluated in comparative studies in which perturbation is a variable—as opposed to studies in which all patches are more or less uniformly perturbed (e.g., by Polynesian settlement) but differ in initial conditions. Indeed, Chapters 5, 6, and 7 all use statistical techniques, especially instrumental variables regression, to investigate directly whether or not the perturbation is subject to problems of selection relevant to the outcome studied.

Historians seeking causal explanations would be fortunate if effective perturbations were followed promptly by their outcomes. In actuality, the outcome may be delayed by decades or even by centuries (e.g., if the perturbation alters societal or political institutions but those altered institutions do not produce the outcome under study until other changes accumulate).

For instance, western Hispaniola (Haiti) is today far poorer than eastern Hispaniola (the Dominican Republic), largely because of consequences of their different colonial histories (Chapter 4): France's colonization of the west ending in 1804 and Spain's colonization of the east ending initially in 1821. However, those different histories resulted in ex-French Haiti being much *richer* than the ex-Spanish Dominican Republic at that time of independence, and it took a century or more for the slowly developing consequences of those different colonial histories to result in the Dominican Republic overtaking and then far outstripping Haiti economically.

Again, the new institutions established in French-conquered areas of Germany before 1814 did not by themselves make those areas more urbanized and economically developed. Instead, the new institutions were more conducive to the Industrial Revolution (which is what brought urbanization and economic development) than were the old institutions swept away in conquered areas by Napoleon, but the Industrial Revolution did not begin to pay off in Germany until several decades after 1814.

Yet another possible example comes from the long-standing debate about why Europe eventually overtook China's earlier lead in technology, economic development, living standards, and power.[2] By many indicators, Europe began to pull ahead of China only in the 1700s and especially in the 1800s. Hence some authors seek explanations in causes emerging within those centuries themselves, such as Europe's Industrial Revolution and the trans-Atlantic trade. However, other authors see the fundamental causes much earlier, in medieval Europe's institutional development and agriculture or in much older European and Chinese geographic factors, which resulted in technological and economic growth only when industrialization and trade were added many centuries later. Such phenomena—which may be represented as "A + B together cause C, but only when B arrives long after A"—are as pervasive a problem for historians seeking to understand history as they are for psychologists and biographers seeking to understand individual human lives.

A ubiquitous concern in natural experiments is whether the different outcomes observed really were due to the particular types of differences in perturbation or initial conditions noted by the "experimenter," or whether they were instead due to some other difference. This risk of misinterpretation arises even in controlled laboratory experiments. A famous example was the discovery of the Josephson Effect in physics: laboratory measurements of superconductivity initially yielded confusing results, until Brian Josephson realized that a driving independent variable was slight temperature differences, to which superconductivity proved to be far more sensitive than had been previously realized. But this risk of misinterpretation due to variables other than those initially of interest is much greater in natural experiments, where one's variables are uncontrolled.

The natural experimenter should at least attempt to minimize the effects of individual variables other than those of interest, by choosing for comparison systems that are as similar as possible in other respects. For instance, in Chapter 7 of this volume, Acemoglu et al. restrict their comparisons of areas of Europe conquered or not conquered by Napoleon to German areas, in order to reduce cultural variation extraneous to the purpose of their study. However, in other related studies not presented in this book, Acemoglu et al. relaxed that restriction, examined non-German areas as well, and reached similar conclusions about Napoleon's effects. Kirch (Chapter 1) restricts his comparisons of Pacific island sociopolitical and economic complexity to islands colonized by Polynesians. However, in Chapter 4 Diamond relaxes this constraint by comparing Pacific islands colonized by Micronesians and Melanesians as well as by Polynesians, in order to examine an outcome variable (deforestation) that is expected to be less sensitive to differences among colonizing peoples than is the outcome of sociopolitical and economic complexity studied by Kirch. Diamond compares the two halves of the Caribbean island of Hispaniola differing in colonial history, and he notes that it would be interesting to extend the comparison to the three other large Caribbean islands of Cuba, Jamaica, and Puerto Rico, at the cost of adding the complication of inter-island variation. Haber (Chapter 3) intentionally restricts his comparison of the development of banking systems after about A.D. 1800 to three New World countries (the United States, Brazil, and Mexico) and excludes European countries because all three of those New World countries began their independent existence without preexisting banks (their former colonial governments had not permitted the chartering of banks). Inclusion of European countries in the comparison would have introduced the complication of having to control for differences in bank development that already existed by 1800.

Another ubiquitous concern in natural experiments arises explicitly whenever one employs statistical tools for comparisons (though the concern is also implicit when one makes narrative comparisons without statistical tests). Does a statistical correlation by itself demonstrate a cause or a mechanism?

No, of course it doesn't: at least three further steps are required to demonstrate a cause or mechanism, and all three steps are the subjects of large methodological literatures. First, there is the problem of reverse causality: if A and B are correlated, perhaps A didn't cause B, as one assumed; perhaps, instead, B caused A. Frequently, one can approach this problem by examining time relations: in the simplest case, did A change before B, or vice versa? A statistical technique called Granger causality is often used to unravel the direction of cause and effect. More sophisticated techniques are also employed. For instance, a recent study[3] identifies which brain regions stimulate which other brain regions when humans shift from relaxed to alert, and it does so by examining how phase differences between independent and dependent variables change with the frequency of their fluctuations.

Second, one must consider what is termed the *omitted variable bias:* the perturbing variable identified by the "experiment" may actually be part of a linked package of changes, within which some variable other than the one identified by the experimenter may really have been what caused the difference in outcomes. (This is essentially the concern that natural experimenters attempt to minimize, though without the possibility of complete success, as we described three paragraphs above.) Both Banerjee and Iyer in their study of the effects of the British colonial revenue system in India (Chapter 6), and Acemoglu et al. in their study of the effects of Napoleonic conquest (Chapter 7), wrestled with this problem. Among the many techniques that statisticians use to address this problem, an often-used technique is multiple regression analysis: that is, explicitly test the effects of other possible explanatory factors, and see whether the apparent explanatory power of one's initially preferred variable drops out when these other variables are taken into account.

Third, even if one has obtained convincing evidence that A causes B, further evidence is often required to establish the mechanism by which A causes B. For instance, human colonization of ecologically fragile Pacific islands is correlated with deforestation following human arrival, and it certainly is the case that human colonization somehow caused deforestation rather than that subsequent deforestation caused earlier human colonization. However, that observation by itself doesn't identify the mechanism by which human colonization resulted in deforestation. It could have involved direct actions by humans (such as people burning forests, chopping down trees, or using wood for fuel), or various indirect effects of humans (such as rats introduced by humans eating or gnawing on seeds of trees) Additional information that can help distinguish among these mechanisms includes archaeological and paleobotanical evidence of tree stumps with axe cuts, charcoal of identifiable tree species found in hearths, and nuts with gnaw marks left by rats' teeth.

In statistical analyses just as in narrative, noncomparative, nonquantitative historical studies, one has to negotiate a middle ground between overly simplistic and overly complex explanations. On the one hand, one might be concerned that statistical analysis would lead to oversimplified explanations, if one stopped looking for further explanatory factors after identifying the first couple of explanatory factors. In fact, statisticians attempt to add more independent variables to a multiple regression analysis, and they carry out residual analyses, in order to detect even more explanatory factors than emerged during the first stage of the analysis. Conversely, one may be suspicious about unnecessarily complex explanations, as expressed in the often-cited dismissive remark, "Give me two variables, and I will draw you an elephant; give me a third variable, and I will make him wave his trunk." In fact, statisticians routinely employ tests, such as the so-called F-test, in order to ascertain whether each additional variable tested really does add significant explanatory power beyond the power that one expects just from adding any randomly selected further variable.

In general, the more numerous are the potentially relevant independent variables, the more cases must be compared to test for effects of those variables. Conversely, the more cases that one has available for analysis, the greater the number of explanatory factors that can be tested. In this book the second largest scale comparison is Rolett's and Diamond's comparison of eighty-one Pacific islands or island sites in Chapter 4, examined for the outcome of deforestation. That large database made it possible to establish the existence of statistically significant and mechanistically understandable effects of nine independent variables: island rainfall, temperature, age, wind-borne ash, wind-borne dust, makatea terrain, area, elevation, and isolation. Some of those effects were suggested to Rolett and Diamond by colleagues in the course of the study; the possible importance of these effects had not even occurred to Rolett and Diamond at the outset. With so many factors affecting deforestation, it would have been utterly impossible to evaluate them without a large database and without the use of statistics. Initially, Rolett and Diamond guessed—from their personal familiarity with two cases, the wet, warm, lightly deforested Marquesas Archipelago and the dry, cool, heavily deforested Easter Island—that rainfall and temperature would prove significant. While their full analysis did indeed confirm their hunch about the significance of rainfall and temperature, in retrospect that guess could not have been accepted based only on their initial narrative comparison of only two cases—because the Marquesas and Easter differ in other important respects as well.

But it is not true that a sufficiently large database will enable one to detect an effect of almost anything. For instance, Rolett and Diamond initially suspected that deforestation might also depend on variation in four agricultural practices: wet-field cultivation, dry-field cultivation, breadfruit arboriculture, and Tahitian chestnut and canarium arboriculture. But after expending two years of effort to tabulate the extent of each of these four practices on the eighty-one islands, Rolett and Diamond found no support for that initial hunch: none of these four agricultural practices had a statistically significant relationship to deforestation.

Social scientists have the misfortune of having to study fuzzier concepts than those studied by molecular biologists, physicists, chemists, and astronomers. The latter types of scholars aim to explain things that are easily defined, easily measured quantitatively, and often intuitively obvious—such as velocity, mass, chemical reaction rate, and luminosity. But we social scientists are interested in human happiness, motivation, success, stability, prosperity, and economic development. How does one build a meter to measure happiness? Human happiness is less neatly defined and harder to measure than molybdenum's atomic weight, but it is also more important to understand and explain.

Much of the practical difficulty in social science research resides in "operationalizing" fuzzy, hard-to-measure, but important concepts such as happiness. The scholar's task is to identify something that can be measured, and that can be shown to reflect or capture much of the essence of the ambiguous concept. For instance, historians interested in economic development today, at the touch of a computer button, can download vast, accurate databases of national incomes. But Acemoglu et al. (Chapter 7) want to understand whether Napoleon was good or bad for economic development in nineteenth-century Europe, at a time when incomes were not yet being measured and tabulated. What should they do? They resorted to "operationalizing" the fuzzy concept of economic development—that is, finding a proxy quantity which reflects economic development but a quantity for which data were already available in the early nineteenth century. A suitable proxy proves to be urbanization: specifically, the proportion of a region's population living in urban areas each containing 5,000 or more people. After searching for a proxy, economic historians have found this measure of urbanization useful because, historically, only regions with high agricultural productivity and a well-developed transport network—that is, areas fitting the fuzzy concept of "economically developed"—have been capable of supporting urban populations. Mathematicians and physical scientists who have never tried to measure something as important as urbanization or happiness often sneer at the efforts of social scientists to operationalize these concepts, and they quote examples of operationalizing pulled out of context in order to justify their scorn.[4]

What about the importance of quantitative data and measurements in historical studies?[5] In science in general, the role of quantification has been both overestimated and underestimated. As regards overestimation, quantification is so routinely essential in physics that physicists have mistakenly assumed quantification to be essential to all of science. The great physicist Lord Kelvin wrote, "When you can measure what you are speaking about, and express it in numbers, you know something about it; but when you cannot measure it, when you cannot express it in numbers, your knowledge is of a meager and unsatisfactory kind: it may be the beginning of knowledge, but you have scarcely, in your thoughts, advanced to the stage of *science*." In fact, quantification played little role in the greatest advance in biology, Darwin's book *On the Origin of Species*. But while there are still some areas of sciences such as ethology and cultural anthropology in which one often begins by qualitative description, even in those areas it has become routine to go on to count a phenomenon's frequency or to describe it numerically. Insofar as possible, it helps to express in numbers the magnitude of effects and putative causes. Not only does that then permit numerical analyses, but it also forces a scholar to gather data more rigorously, and it furnishes objective measures that other scholars can check for themselves.

However, when scholars cannot express their effects and causes in numbers, they can still do many analyses merely by crudely ranking effect or cause magnitudes as weak, medium, or strong. For instance, although Rolett and Diamond (Chapter 4) were unable to put a number on Pacific island deforestation, they could still rank it on a qualitative five-point scale as negligible, mild, serious, very serious, or complete, and that enabled them to recognize the effects of nine influences or independent variables. Scholars in many other disciplines besides human history have to deal with nonnumerical variables, and many statistical tests developed to help those scholars will be useful to historians as well.

Whether one is able to express effects and causes in numbers or can only rank them crudely from weak to strong, one should try to assess apparent relations statistically. Such an assessment can not only help to protect one against the real risk that one's impressions about the main conclusions might prove to be wrong, but can also reveal other conclusions that one had not even suspected (as when

Rolett and Diamond were surprised to discover effects of island age, volcanic ash, and wind-borne Central Asian dust on Pacific island deforestation).

Every field of scholarship, not just human history, experiences tension between narrowly focused case studies and broader syntheses or generalizations. Practitioners of the case study method tend to decry syntheses as superficial, coarse-grained, and absurdly oversimplified; practitioners of syntheses tend to decry the case studies as merely descriptive, devoid of explanatory power, and unable to illuminate anything except one particular case study. Eventually, scholars in mature fields come to realize that scholarly understanding requires both approaches. Without reliable case studies, generalists have nothing to synthesize; without sound syntheses, specialists lack a framework within which to place their case studies. Thus, comparative history poses no threat to the more familiar approach of historical case studies, but on the contrary offers a means to enrich that approach.

The tension between case studies and syntheses, or between description and theoretical explanation, has unfolded differently in different fields of scholarship. This tension is minimal in physics and chemistry, where theoreticians and experimentalists now take it for granted that each needs the other, and where it is now routine to place narrow case studies within a larger framework. Among scholarly fields that use natural experiments rather than manipulative experiments, there has been recent tension between the two approaches especially in cultural anthropology and field biology. Cultural anthropologists used to view each human culture as unique and therefore resisted generalization. But today virtually every anthropologist publishing the results of a multiyear study of some particular tribe will begin the publication with a section developing some general theoretical perspective and placing that tribe along a spectrum of cultural variation.

In the field of ecology, tension between case studies and generalization became acute in the 1960s and 1970s, with the development of many new theoretical generalizations and mathematical models. That development gave rise to nearly twenty years of bitter disputes. On the one side were the traditional field biologists who had devoted their lives to long-term studies of one animal or plant species, such as the Philippine Striped Tit-Babbler. Attempts to compare, model, theorize, and generalize were derided with labels such as "superficial," "oversimplified," and "generalizations based on caricatures without the rich detail of my study of Philippine Striped Tit-Babblers." These scholars warned other scientists that progress could come only through equally richly textured, carefully nuanced studies of other bird species. On the other side, theorizing generalists began to object, "You can't hope to understand even just the Philippine Striped Tit-Babbler, without understanding how and why it became similar to and different from other tit-babblers and other bird species."

Within ecology, today, the polar approaches of case studies and generalization coexist more comfortably.[6] Most ecologists now recognize that their discipline is developing a general framework that applies to species as diverse as bacteria, dandelions, and woodpeckers— a framework that allows an understanding of differences within the plant and animal kingdoms. It is no longer enough to describe how one bird does this, while another bird does that. One after another, the leading bird journals, although still publishing accounts of individual bird species, have come to *require* that each study be placed within a larger framework.

Setting individual explanations within a larger explanatory framework is a hallmark of science. For example, Darwin noticed that the mockingbirds of the Galapagos Islands were related to South American mockingbirds, but he also noticed that other Galapagos species as well have their closest relatives in South America. Such observations stimulated Darwin and Wallace to set those facts into a larger framework of biogeographic explanation, which combined history, dispersal, evolution, and origins or movements of land masses. Chemists studying the molybdenum atom don't explain it as a unique phenomenon but fit its properties into an explanatory framework based on the periodic table, atomic theory, and quantum mechanics.

The case studies of this book support two overall conclusions about the study of human history. First, historical comparisons, though not providing all the answers by themselves, may yield insights that cannot be extracted from a single case study alone. For instance, one cannot hope to understand late nineteenth-century France without examining why it differed from late nineteenth-century Germany or late sixteenth-century France. Second, insofar as is possible, when one proposes a conclusion, one may be able to strengthen that conclusion by gathering quantitative evidence (or at least ranking one's outcomes from big to small), and then by testing the conclusion's validity statistically.

Some specialist historians would respond with an implicit objection, which is sometimes but not always expressed openly, and which we mentioned in the prologue. An example of this objection could be phrased as follows: "I have devoted forty years of my professional life to studying the American Civil War, and I still don't fully understand it. How could I dare to discuss civil wars in general, or even just to compare the American Civil War with the Spanish Civil War, to which I have not devoted forty years of study? And, worse yet, isn't it outrageous that some scholar of the Spanish Civil War dares to trespass on my turf and to say something about the American Civil War?" Yes, if you study an event for a long time, that does give you one type of advantage. But you gain a different type of advantage by taking a fresh look at an event, and by applying to it the experience and insights that you have gained by studying other events. We hope that this book will offer useful guidelines to historians and social scientists desiring to exploit that advantage.

## NOTES

1. The books and papers cited in note 3 of the prologue will be useful for further discussion of the problems discussed in this afterword.

2. David Landes, *The Unbound Prometheus: Technological Change and Industrial Development in Western Europe from 1750 to the Present* (Cambridge, 1969); Douglass North and Robert Thomas, *The Rise of the Western World: A New Economic History* (New York, 1973); E. L. Jones, *The European Miracle: Environments, Economies, and Geopolitics in the History of Europe and Asia*, 2nd ed. (Cambridge, 1987); Graeme Lang, "State Systems and the Origins of Modern Science: A Comparison of Europe and China," *East-West Dialog* 2 (1997): 16–30; Kenneth Pomeranz, *The Great Divergence: China, Europe, and the Making of the Modern World Economy* (Princeton, NJ, 2000); Angus Maddison, *The World Economy: A Millenial Perspective* (Paris, 2001); Jack Goldstone, "Efflorescences and Economic Growth and World History: Rethinking the 'Rise of the West' and the Industrial Revolution," *Journal of World History* 13 (2002): 329–389; Joel Mokyr, *The Enlightened Economy: An Economic History of Britain, 1700–1850* (New Haven, CT, 2007); Jan Luiten van Zanden, "Die mittelalterlichen Ursprünge des 'europäischen Wunders,'" in James Robinson and Klaus Wiegandt, eds., *Die Ursprünge der Modernen Welt* (Frankfurt am Main, 2008), pp. 475–515; Michael Mitterauer, "Mittelalterliche Wurzeln des europäischen Entwicklungsvorsprungs," in James Robinson and Klaus Wiegandt, eds., *Die Ursprünge der Modernen Welt* (Frankfurt am Main, 2008), pp. 516–538.

3. G. Nolte et al., "Robustly Estimating the Flow Direction of Information in Complex Physical Systems," *Physical Review Letters* 100 (2008): 234101-1–234101-4.

4. Jared Diamond, "Soft Sciences Are Often Harder than Hard Sciences," *Discover* 8, no. 8 (1987): 34–39.

5. Some of this discussion is drawn from a chapter by Jared Diamond, "Die Naturwissenschaft, die Geschichte und Rotbrustige Saftsäuger," in Robinson and Wiegandt, eds., *Die Ursprünge der Modernen Welt*, pp. 45–70.

6. Robert May and Angela McLean, *Theoretical Ecology*, 3rd ed. (Oxford, 2007).

# Contributors

**DARON ACEMOGLU**, Department of Economics, Massachusetts Institute of Technology, Cambridge, Massachusetts

**ABHIJIT BANERJEE**, Department of Economics and Abdul Latif Jameel Poverty Action Lab, Massachusetts Institute of Technology, Cambridge, Massachusetts

**JAMES BELICH**, Stout Research Centre, Victoria University, Wellington, New Zealand

**DAVIDE CANTONI**, Department of Economics, Harvard University, Cambridge, Massachusetts

**JARED DIAMOND**, Department of Geography, University of California, Los Angeles, California

**STEPHEN HABER**, Department of Political Science and Hoover Institution, Stanford University, Palo Alto, California

**LAKSHMI IYER**, Business, Government and International Economy Unit, Harvard Business School, Boston, Massachusetts

**SIMON JOHNSON**, Sloan School of Management, Massachusetts Institute of Technology, Cambridge, Massachusetts

**PATRICK V. KIRCH**, Departments of Anthropology and Integrative Biology, University of California, Berkeley, California

**NATHAN NUNN**, Department of Economics, Harvard University, Cambridge, Massachusetts

**JAMES A. ROBINSON**, Department of Government, Harvard University, Cambridge, Massachusetts